A Teacher

A Teacher's Journal

Give a damn & figure it out

Selected Essays, Letters & Poetry
~John Fitzsimmons

Copyright

Table of Contents

Artwork by Emma Fitzsimmons

My way cool, youngest daughter

& Yes, she knit the sweater, too.

A Teachers Journal

Give a damn & figure it out

JOSHUA SAWYER

I doubt I'd ever have taken this road
had I really known how fallen it was
to disrepair—driving comically,
skirting ruts and high boulders, grimacing
at every bang on the oil pan.
I tell you it's the old road to Wendell—
that they don't make them like this anymore.

We're bound by curious obligations,
and so stop by an old family plot
walled in by piles of jumbled fieldstone,
cornered to the edge of what once was field.

The picket gateway still stands intact,
somebody propped up leaning on a stick,
an anonymous gesture of reverence.
Only nature disrespects: toppling stone,
bursting with suckers and wild raggedness.
A gravestone, schist of worn slate, leans weathered:

Joshua Sawyer Died Here 1860

Another stone, cracked, has fallen over.
I reset the stone, and scrape the caked earth
as if studying some split tortoise shell,
and have keyed in to a distant birth—
His wife Ruth died young; so I picture him
stern with his only daughter, only child—
speaking for a faith which could defy her.

There'd be no passing onto when she died—
twenty-two, more words beside her mother.
Still these stones and fields you kept in order,
long days spent forcing sharp turns on nature,
accepting the loose stone and thin topsoil.

A Wendell neighbor must have buried you

whispering a eulogy which is as lost
as your daughter, your wife, and this farm:

—Joshua Sawyer

I've never been down this road before;
I would like to speak with you of faith.

Where it begins…

DEDICATION

As a speaker is without an audience, a writer is without a reader. A writer's words are no different than sounds filling a room or echoes bouncing across a mountain valley. A writer's words cannot be stilled in silence or erased by the ravages of time. They can only be lost, forgotten, or ignored, but if they once were, they always will be.

My first dedication for this tome of essays, poems, and letters is to you—you who have the temerity to settle beside this field of words before the game begins. It is a rare bird drawn to the reading of essays, and rarer still, the daring souls who welcome an anonymous, cantankerous poet into their home. And to my students and colleagues for the past thirty years: You know me better than I know me. I have pretty much emptied my soul into your gullets. Doubtless, I also confused and confounded you as much as you have invigorated me. I have infused your collective spit and spirit into my life. You all guided me, cajoled me, argued with me, and sometimes despised me—but you always, always, always kept me laughing, kept me thinking, and kept prodded me to rethink, retool, and redo. And to all teachers giving their lives to unerringly teach.

And to my friends and extended family—near, far, or lost in time, but never lost in thought. You are the grist of my mill, the source of my remembrances, and my enveloping community of disparate souls bathed in equanimity, grace, and forbearance. And to my even children, to whom every action in my life is dedicated; who bring light to any darkness of my elusive soul; who make me wondrous and who leave me breathless; who laugh at me, for me and with me, and who are always there for me. I am beyond stunned to be the luckiest father alive. And to my wife, Denise, without whom I am a feather in the wind; who anchors me in inconceivable love, who keeps me real, and who keeps me tethered and free in the embracing tendrils of marriage.

And finally, to all who write for the sake of writing:

May all your words be known.

FOREWORD

I am not a writer by vocation or avocation. I am a teacher of middle-school boys in a small private school nestled in a suburban field of wealth and privilege. There is no coarse edge to my academic life. No monuments to courage in the face of adversity will be raised to me. The boys I teach will yet be fine without my meddling in the gifts of fate given to them. My words are more rituals torn out of succeeding days, months, and years. I am an old stonemason carving the same mantra on common slabs of granite: "Give a damn and figure it out." At some point, each of our lives turns hard. We are suddenly alone, and only words and memories stir our passions back to life and purpose. Only our words escape life un-ravaged. Only our words restore the balm of time; and only our words capture the fleeting testament of our stoic defense of life.

Words are as malleable as they are impenetrable, and so it is the wise person who apprentices the art and craft of writing well. It is a beguiling paradox, for while there is magic in words, there is no magic in writing—only tips and tricks, stuttering steps, and an indefatigable spirit to slog through the hobbling bog of an empty page. Be you a student, teacher, or writer, this book—this tome of incantations and dim-witted logic—carries the poems, essays, letters, and pleas I crafted to somehow nudge the calcitrant, affirm the inspired, and afflict the comfortable in my long and continuing life as a teacher of writing.

These essays, letters, and poetry are a mix of fruits to savor and roots too bitter to bear. There is no key to unlock my inconsistencies, but one can learn as much from a fool as from a sage.

Harvest what you will. Cast into the fire what offends you.

But if words make you curious, please, stay with me.

Fitz

THE TIDE

They are building a world
And the plastic is fading:
Margaret and Eddie's
Buckets split,
And pour out the warm Atlantic
As they race
Along the tidal flats,
Filling pools connected
By frantically dug canals.

Tommy squats naked
And screams in guttural joy
At the solitary horseshoe crab
Donated by a stranger
With a large belly
And a huge smile.

Charlie thrashes through the shallows
Chasing crabs
And impossible minnows.
Emma is happy
To let only the wind
Fill her net.

Pipo steps warily
And warns us sternly
In his broken English
To anticipate the massive toad
Lurking in the undertow.

Kaleigh stands far away
toes lapped by the edge of gravity.
She is almost a teenager.
I see her framed in a setting sun,
Stretching out her arms,
Holding back
The inevitable tide.

APOLOGIES

You are my sea

I speak the truth, not so much as I would, but as much as I dare; and I dare a little more as I grow older.
~Michel de Montaigne

I have never introduced myself to anyone as a writer, yet I have written for almost as long as I know. Writing is just a way for me to capture the nuggets and chunks of my life, polish them just a bit, and ultimately discard more than I keep, but, perhaps regrettably, writing has never been my life. My life is a recitation of what is palpable, and words are what make my life real and meaningful. My actual life is what I do and have done—what I have thought and have pondered, what I have embraced or have cast aside, cherished or scorned, built or buried...

My words are captured moments, imperfect recitations from a scouring, impatient mind—reckless, fickle, and confounding in the same breath. The seed from which my words rise are echoes of time remembered from a full and blessed life as a teacher, poet, husband, folksinger, songwriter, and father to seven children. Words reflect my solitary ruminating on the *who, what, when, where, and why* of life—or just as often simple admonitions, cajoling's, or brazen coaching to my gaggle of fourteen and fifteen-year-old boys at the private school where I teach.

Writing is like shucking corn. I don't like the labor of word-smithing as much as I appreciate how writing is the only way to get through the layers of messy husk and at the sweetest corn. Words and the act of writing are the only palpable and enduring way for me to respond to life in all its vagaries, furies, and vicissitudes. In my humble publishing house, my duties as writer, editor, and proofreader are daunting—and sometimes impossible. I fall short by most metrics, yet I stick stubbornly to the task. I push my boulder of words up a slaggy hill. More often than not, I meet the fate of Sisyphus, for the hill is high, the stone is heavy, and it soon falls back on me.

Unfazed, I simply go at it again.

I try to write well and to write honestly. I try to squeeze the prejudice, ignorance, and bigotry out of my curmudgeonly haunts and hallows. I often fail, for I am drawn to certain ephemeral thoughts and articulations as to the siren's song. In these impossible reflections, I sense an immutable perfectness. I believe these thoughts to be true—at least to me—at least in the moment given to me.

How else can a writer write?

There is recklessness in publishing a book of essays and poems. More is cast aside than scrabbled on the page. All cogency is thrown to the winds. The contradictions and mood swings are palpable. Every essay is born and borne on different days, looking towards a different horizon. The sun sets or rises. The snow, sun, sleet, misty fog, pelting rain, and fickle or raging winds are morphed in the maelstrom of my inconsistencies. But, for me at least, there is no other way. The timid in me begs and pleads to discard what is barbed, harsh, and offensive, while the warrior within barks incessantly to stand my ground and live or die on the Plains of Troy.

So, here—here is "My Teachers Journal." It is somewhat audacious and arrogant to expect or hope someone or anyone will read my garbles in the spirit I voiced and formed—and ultimately abandoned.

But this is the fickleness of a writer's fate.

The ship has gone down. I stepped up into the lifeboat. I am alone now, drifting in the pull of gravity. Aeolus has loosed my bags of wind.

I am waiting for you.

You are my sea.

GIVE A DAMN

A first lesson in writing: 2003

I never teach my pupils. I only attempt to provide the conditions in which they can learn.
~Albert Einstein

This is my first year of teaching English, and already a horizon of discontent is looming. In another place, I would probably need a bodyguard. Today, I not only assigned my eighth grade class the first five chapters—37 pages —in some pamphlet titled *A Guide to Writing Essays*, but I also told these students the same thing I told their parents—that nothing is more important than the ability to write a good essay; that essay writing is a skill that will save them time and again in this great adventure called life. I rabbled on about how educational, fun, and rewarding it would be. I teased them with tales of how they would discover huge deposits of original thought and creative speculations—rough stones crafting a wonderful creation called *The Essay*. They lived as writers, each and every one of them, and I would prove it to them. I think some of them believed me —even I believed me. I'm sure some few of them saw through my pontifications and secretly wished to be placed in another section. Their parents gazed aghast at my naivety, but they simply looked at me with stoic resignation, accepting the fate of their son to be the proving ground for an old shop teacher run amok in a "real" classroom.

But here I am now, two months into my new career, and I hate teaching essays. It's tough to admit, but I despise the core responsibility of my job—teaching this venerated form of writing. We transformed an essentially organic miracle called the mind and decided to treat it like an erector set—a series of blocks and connectors that, if put together properly, sometimes creates something resembling something. That "something" is occasionally a remarkable piece of writing.

Like once or twice a semester.

I am not alone in my fraud, although I feel somewhat lonely fessing up and questioning this sacred truth. We tell our students that the ability to write a good essay is indispensable. We warn them of the apocalyptic days ahead where the effective and formulaic writing of essays will be the final arbiter of their scholastic abilities. We extrapolate from larger-than-life stories how a single well-written essay will launch them to some semblance of Harvard, or help them find a certain job, elect their candidate, find their perfect mate, and, in some slew of words, transform society. We convince the reluctant that persuasive, narrative, critical, expository, analytical, and reflective essays can marry their intrinsic bent of genius to any situation. We proclaim the essay as the *Holy Grail of Writing*—the top-end model of the English curriculum. Our folly pulsates in every school and pushes the snarling beast of grammar and syntax into the corner where it belongs.

If poetry is not completely banished, it lives as a quaint holiday in the Berkshires—a pleasant place to spend one or two days away from the rigor of a real curriculum. Even the best of literature is splayed upon the mortician's table, awaiting the sharp, incisive, misguided probes. We are told the essay is the genius of our insight weathered into granite. Your essays will outlive you and your children—and many generations after them. If so, why have I never heard tell of a single great writer who proclaims themselves to be an essay writer?

Why? Because it is like saying you cook awesome hot dogs.

Or you've never been outside Rhode Island.

Is there something weird about me? Am I missing something? Perhaps I'm a bad teacher—or lazy or misled—but this essay writing inspires little in me. I've tried. I'm still trying. I am, in fact, writing this—whatever *this* is? I am side-by-side in the trenches with my weary students. They tense up when I simply utter the words "thesis statement." When I follow up on my tired command by preaching the virtues and efficacy of outlining headers and adding supporting facts, a bitter teaching reality settles in. Like an unwanted guest, they notice, but they don't really care.

They don't find it slightly interesting.

The majority of students drift slowly away. A few are completely shut down. The grade-grubbers exist in a purgatory hung between obligation and exasperation. The smart ones who jot down mental notes pray they will never become a teacher like me. The hibernating perk up when they hear the word "conclusion" but soon discover it is only a cruel hoax, a twist of fate compelling them to start back at the beginning. The meek surrender to the vicious cycle of introduction, body, and conclusion. The bookshelves are stacked with the detritus of years of literary massacres. Students and teachers eye each other like creatures cannibalizing their own.

Only the threat of vocabulary keeps them at their desks.

You can't be a teacher and believe in Fate. There has to be a belief in the transformative power of the moment. Jason Rude, the French teacher at our school, once told me the word essay is derived from the French verb *essaei*, which means "to try." I like this empowering affirmation of true grit and lofty spirit. There is something in *essai* that nudges awake a spirit of hope and freedom in me. It is doable. I can try, and I can try valiantly. I'll try to show you I give a damn. I'll try to show you how and why I love the sounds of words and the nuance of sentences—how I love words woven into a magician's tale; how I love every spirited gaggle of words bursts into stories; I love when my moody spirit is moved to tears by a good book, a lilting song, or an old poem.

Love! If love is not true understanding, something is terribly awry.

Here! Here are my tears! What more can you possibly need?

No, damn you and damn me. I don't need your essays—I need you to *essai*. I need you to try. I need the miracle of your mind to give itself to the miracle of language. I need you to be an unwilling heir to tradition. I need you to get rid of the erector set. I need you to get rid of the artifice standing between you and your understanding. I need you to answer whatever question I throw at you with the greatest gift of creation—words.

We know beauty when we see it. We measure the power of words by the feelings they evoke. We measure their clarity and freshness as we would a mountain stream. We are led on small and great journeys by storytellers; what writer is not a storyteller? We are carried through words to deeper wells, and from those unplumbed depths, we invoke the source of all courageous originality. We sense our common humanity.

We can learn ourselves if we *essai*—if we try.

And to try is to care.

In the end, you just have to give a damn.

THE SWALLOWS NEVER SEEM TO SOAR

They beat and drop, flapping
In waltz time—

> *Flap*
> *Drop drop;*
> *Flap*
> *Drop drop*

Until they sense
The solitary crow,
Menacing and malevolent,
Lumbering across a gray sky
Bound maybe
For some distant road-kill
Or Verrill's stubbled field.

The swallows rise in reckless folly
Pounding a grinding beat—

> *Up-flap, up-flap*
> *Up-flap, up-flap*

They meet in a crescendo
Of crashing cacophony—
Will meets stoic,
Melancholy might.

The crow curves curiously away.
The swallows swerve back,
Descending down

> *Flap flap*
> *Down*
> *Flap flap*
> *Down*
> *Flap flap*
> *Down*

A final diminution:
A determined dalliance
Did and done—

Like this…

TELL YOUR STORY

No one cares about you

We are the thoughts we choose to keep.
~A.D. Posey

Our minds shift gears when filled with imagery. We either slow down and smell the flowers, or we shift into a higher gear. Our minds burst from wombs alive with the power and rush only images and actions initiate to such great effect—ass readers, we are more alive, ready, and willing to move in new directions. The writer who does not realize this runs the risk of becoming an erudite prude at best or a self-centered mouthpiece at worst. Their words remain untethered to the real world of the reader—an audience that instinctively wants, craves, and needs to be anchored to a place powering full breath and full breadth to the senses.

Engaging the senses engages the reader. To learn the art and craft of descriptive writing is to learn how to tell a good story—and all writing is simply storytelling, good, bad, or searchingly profound. I hear the academic writers crying out in opposition: "This is such bull! We are empowered by ideas and the synthesis and explication of these concise thoughts, provoking the nuances of a brilliant mind slavishly working towards a solution to a specific and fascinating thesis."

Yeah, they got me there—but only if they got me interested in the first place—only if the tree of my life already leans in the direction of their thesis—and then only if my mind is ready and willing to plow through the muddy slough of field blithely and blindly called essays.

I am hard-headed. I need to plow the field before planting grain. I need to be reached on an intellectual level. I need real, palpable, and visceral levels completing the full cycle of being human—the blood, flesh, and bones, honing sharp the intellect keeping the blood alive, and pulsing in the iambic beats of life. Descriptive writing is the vital core that captures not just the mind but also the pumping heart and manifest soul of the reader. Even this—this paltry creation of mine—is ensconced in the sublimity of where I am, who I am, and what I aspire to be.

My mind feasts on the first full moon of the summer, splaying arcs of light through a canopy of woodland forest on this cool New Hampshire night. The dull light of my screen is more than words. It attracts more than what rests in my head. It draws a bevy of insects buzzing around or crawling across the hard glass of my screen. Yes, I have an audience already—perhaps the only audience this will ever have—yet it gives every word I eke out a greater meaning and purpose. Without a purpose for me, how can there be a purpose for you? I learned and accepted long ago that no one intrinsically cares about me or what I write. They only care about what my writing gives to them—how it feeds their heart, their mind, their soul, and their being. If they receive only a glancing blow, I will count this effort a success on the tipping scales of my life as a writer.

And if you—the completely unknown you—are still here reading with some semblance of earnestness, this is time well spent. I will reap the unmitigated joy of my words echoing deeper into my dark woods. I am no longer alone in this feral whirl of moths, mosquitoes, and junebugs. The good writer separates the wheat from the chaff. The great writer unveils the full process of winnowing—the drying and grinding of seeds into perfect flour—the rising bread and staff of our lives.

My plea is simple: if you are a writer, do not live with guppy thoughts swimming in your head. Live in the fullness of your experiences. Cast a net wide enough to strain your gears and haul in a greater catch—a catch to feed a hungry audience day in and day out—a testament to eternity, not a paean to futility.

If you are a teacher, let your students write first about what they know best, for if the seed is not in their hands, how can it be planted, tended t, and watered in a garden of joy? Our students trudge too often from the fields of our imposed labors. Their hands, heads, and hearts are deadened by defeat—proud warriors once, but no more.

Keep the passion alive. Let every essay, every writing prompt, and every scratch upon the page be a story well-told. Learn, teach, and practice how to tell good stories. Show how to use descriptive writing to perfect, enliven, and enrich those stories.

Share your stories, curate your stories, and celebrate your stories. Tell your tale and tell it well. You are yet to be defeated.

So what? It's no big deal. No one cares about you.

Make them care.

SIMPLE THINGS

We travel far to see little

It is desirable that a man live in all respects so simply and preparedly that if an enemy take the town, he can walk out the gate empty-handed and without anxiety.
~Henry David Thoreau, *Walden*

There is a heaviness in this August morning heat. I sit and sip my morning coffee. From my back porch, the half-moon hangs in a hot and hazy blue sky. The drifting sun scorches above the soft green carpet of maples, ash, sumac, and scrub-brush lining my yard. Somewhere on Marlboro Street, a trash truck beeps incessantly in reverse. The muffled traffic on 117 seems more distant than ever before. The yard is as the kids left it in June—the mower parked in front of the soccer net, Tonka trucks scattered in the sandbox, towels of every shade, mosaic, and pattern hang on the porch rail. The balls—footballs, baseballs, soccer balls, basketballs, and whiffleballs—grow like fungus scattered on our scraggly, unkempt lawn.

I am home alone. Next week, the kids and Denise will return from summer camp. In my distant ear, I already hear them screaming as they jump, leap, and tumble out of our old Bluebird bus. They disperse like a flock of startled grackles into every corner of the yard. They try to catch up on everything at once—every ball is chucked to a new home; the swings and the slide are tested; the blackberries are gorged; they chase the cats under the shed; the sprinkler bursts on, and so life as we know it is renewed. My beautiful panoply of seven kids returns home to their other Eden and once again plant themselves within this slice of paradise.

It is strange to be here alone. Denise and the kids are up at our other paradise, Windsor Mountain Summer Camp. I returned home yesterday to perform some concerts and pad our bank account. I will drive back to Windsor Mountain later today. Camp is coming to a close, and a new adventure beckons. We will load everyone on the bus and keep heading north for a weekend in Vermont with cousins and friends on Pete and Laurie's mountaintop tree farm. We will climb the mossy waterfall, fish for bass in the pond, roast marshmallows, and sing around a massive campfire. We will flip pancakes and make boasts before playing Capture the Flag; we will climb the small peak and look south and crane our necks; we will lie and brag how far we see and how distant we hear:

There, past the far mountain, I see Maynard, and I see Gramma Mary knitting on the porch—and there's Soren knocking on our door. He's yelling, "Where are you? Are you ever coming home?

In the mid-century of my life, every memory becomes a blessing—a host offered to a loving and waiting deity. In every moment, there is nothing more to be done.

We simply are what we need to be and where we need to be.

Summer is our time to live and relive every moment. These two months of summer are a tapestry we hold like a child's shawl through the rest of the year. It is the promise we repeat to ourselves when dragged back into the rituals of our tame, suburban lives. We gather our scrapbooks and laugh at the memories.

We wait in expectation of the returning dawn.

And we remember.

We go back to the cool waters—the still skin of Black Pond: Tommy paddles a surfboard and sings, "Merry Christmas, I can swim." EJ, caught in mid-air, backflips off the rope swing—his body a tattoo of bug bites, scrapes, sunburn, and young muscle. Margaret celebrates her first headfirst dive. Her wet jangles of bracelets wove during some craft's class glisten on her ankles, wrists, and neck. Emma squats at the edge of the dive tower and peers with solipsistic intensity into the waiting abyss of joy. Pipo, neck deep in the dark pond, counts out the seconds he can tread water: "One- two-threefourfive six," and then mockingly screams for help.

Kaleigh, bedraggled and smiling after two weeks of paddling and climbing rock faces and becoming a young woman, is surrounded by friends who think she's the coolest kid on the planet, and she is. Everything to Charlie is spontaneous joy— seven years old, his long, blond, dreadlocked hair soars higher and spins wildly off the rope swing as if gravity only applies to the timid. Always near, always one clutch away, Denise leads them everywhere, cheering, brokering, warning, and loving—and loving, too, every second of every summer day lived with family.

Nothing we do is grand. No place we go is uncommon, but in the steady flow of simple actions, we flow into a greater sea of ordinary joy.

Ordinary joy is all we need.

It is all anyone needs.

As a writer, father, husband, hobo, and fool, this is my cascading entropy, my food, my sustenance, my purpose, and my practice. If you are a writer, don't forget to celebrate the common and the ordinary. Don't wait for inspiration. Don't wait for something extraordinary to write about. Look around you and within you. Weave your tapestry out of the life you live. It is, no doubt, extraordinary, beautiful, baffling, and beyond compare.

If what you see gives you joy, it will give others joy to read your joy. If what you do is hard and moiling, let your writing capture the toil and torment. We will live more fully and think more deeply through your travails.

We travel too far to see too little. Let your own backyard— the life you know best—be the place where you begin.

We can only write well what we remember.

Start there.

I AM NOW THE ONE

Passing the tools to EJ
Through narrow crevices
In impossible places
To a deepened voice
Wizened by eighteen years
Of disproportionate experience
Rethinking, retooling, redoing
A hollow shell of tin—
An old bus tired of idling
In some grassy
New Hampshire field.

In EJ's reincarnation
The bus bucks and bolts
From rusted chains.
It tests and teethes
Its iron innards—
Belching diesel, fuming
Blue clouds of angry smoke,
Lurching forward,
Jolting out of the mud—
A frothy, feral beast
Awakened from dormancy
Hissing and sucking dry
Our tame suburban airs.

Married to a new destiny,
Neither EJ
Or his ponderous
1978 Bluebird Wanderlodge
Go quietly
Unto that good night.

He and his dream
Drift away untethered—
Away from the woolen swathes
Of my lonely cradle.

I wonder what he thinks
When he disassembles
Some hack repair
I muttered years ago
Was good enough?
Does he fear
My recessive genes
Are locked somewhere
Within his own?

Unfazed by Fate
He goes his way
And I mine.

I have to let him go.
There is no longer
A shared vision,
Only a fading dream
I was once attached to—

Shards of wood.
Spools of wire.
Radiator hoses and clamps,
Belts and pulleys
tightened and torqued—
Strands of memories,
My endless projects,
Shelves of memories
Buried in age—

Older days when my hands,
Bent on promise and possibility,
Young and supple, grasped,
Reached and received
This same gift
Through this same
Impossible place
Which is now
His own.

KNOW THYSELF...

The pausing point of deeper thought

*The real voyage of discovery consists not in seeking new
landscapes, but in having new eyes.*
~**Marcel Proust**

I often ask my students (and myself) to reflect on the literature
they and I read. As I have grown older—and not necessarily
wiser—I find myself seeking literature that prods me out of
my intellectual and emotional torpor, like a lizard basking in the
newfound warmth of spring. Right now I am re-reading *The
Brothers Karamazov,* a book I first read as an eighteen-year-old
literary newbie. It was the first time I didn't turn away from a
book because of a daunting length of text or a panoramic sweep
of life. Reading this iconic Russian novel so many years later is a
completely new experience, yet it still resonates with the young,
restless soul experiencing the sprawling, invigorating diorama.
My new reading permeates the fibers and sinews of my aging
and ageless self. It compels me to think, wonder, and explore
beyond my narrow experience of life into something more
enduring, relevant, and real.

I cannot read without responding. I can't sail in placid
harbors without dreaming of a deeper, darker, and wilder sea.
The reflections of my mind need an outlet. I find myself arguing,
dissenting, and assenting through long rambles in notebook
journals or with anyone who listens to me, argues with me, and
explores with me. Through the power of reflection, *The Brothers
Karamozov* remains a part of me. The more I write about what I
read, the more I know what I gained. Knowing what I know and
what I do not know, I realize that only by exploring through
reflection can I answer with an essay.

The sad reality of most of our academic writing is how
much we ask our students to write essays about subjects they

know precious little about; hence, their essays taint of soured milk—still milk, but hardly worth drinking—or remembering. We mark them down for inserting the "I" voice into their writing as if "they" do not really exist—as if there must always be proof beyond them knowing more than they know—as if the pearl of wisdom is something they can't intrinsically harbor in their souls.

A good essay reeks of what we know. It seethes, pounds, and oozes what we explore, discover, and seek to know—and it is a damn pity when a teacher robs us of any part of this triad. You are only wrong when your facts are wrong, distorted by prejudice or bigotry, or so steeped in self-indulgent arrogance that your words fail to resonate with any kind of lasting ring—like a drum without a skin or a harp without a string. You are equally wrong when you spin words into a song without music or when you pen words without meaning and without a foundation in your heart —without the essence of the real and palpable "you" speaking with clarity that guides others to see, feel, and experience "your" experience.

All reflection is introspection. We ferret through the flotsam of thought and see our warts and blemishes more clearly until those imperfections are diminished by the truth and sincerity of our search for meaning and substance, giving voice to our searching—a search extending beyond ourselves into a universal theme and a shared, inexplicable wonderment. If you wondered something, someone else wondered the same thing—and maybe even wrote about it.

Keep exploring until your inkwell is dry and your head is emptied.

And only then should you write your essay.

There is no blueprint for reflective writing that is unerringly useful for everybody. Be attentive only to yourself. Be aware of what you think and what you feel. Explore, assess, reflect, and rethink—probe yourself and ask why you are thinking what you think and why you feel how you feel. We practice this more than we realize. After any good meal, we rarely struggle to find words to express our satisfaction with the meal; likewise, if what we eat is tasteless and horrible, we readily find the words to express our dissatisfaction—sometimes impolitely.

It is not as easy with intellectual satisfaction or dissatisfaction. We are seldom clear when defining why we like or don't like a piece of literature. We fear our intelligence is on the line. We loathe to become the prey of folly. Food, however, is pretty straightforward. If you hate peppers, anything made with peppers is distasteful—and few people will judge you harshly; however, if you don't like poetry or classic literature well, you are either ignorant, bigoted, or stupid—or at least other more well-read people will smugly feel you are all of these things—even as they feign attentive politeness. If you find yourself decrying the power and majesty of an enduring classic novel, or worse yet, you can't bring yourself to admit you have not read it, you are equally damned. Your intellectual credit score won't get you so much as a Walmart credit card.

Reading is an action. You are the subject and verb who opens a new door to a new horizon. Reflection extends the journey towards more enduring wisdom. For better or worse, your thoughts palavered into words are your final testament and the way in which you remember, are remembered, and will always be remembered.

Remember the words you read.

Explore until your inkwell is dry and your head is emptied. Only then should you write your essay. But if you are honest, if you speak with the clarity of innocence, not ignorance, and if you show an open mind and an open heart, your voice will be heard—for realness is as rare to find as intellect. Aristotle called this "Ethos."

You are the singular prophet who searches for and pries open an interplay of words, ringing and singing the notes only you truly know.

There is no one else as perfect as you.

You are the inimitable you.

Just be you.

THE CONCORD TOWN DUMP

The power in community

No man is an island, entire of itself; every man is a piece of the continent, a part of the main. If a clod be washed away by the sea, Europe is the less, as well as if a promontory were, as well as if a manor of thy friend's or of thine own were: any man's death diminishes me, because I am involved in mankind, and therefore never send to know for whom the bells tolls; it tolls for thee.

~John Donne, *No Man is an Island*

When I was a kid, it was the dump. Every Saturday morning, my father and I would pile a week's worth of trash into the back of our Plymouth Fury station wagon and head to the Concord Town Dump. Back then, the dump was a graveyard of perpetual fires and massive heaps of discarded metal—bed frames, lawn mowers, refrigerators, and two centuries worth of bicycles. The town would haul the pile of metal away when it reached mammoth proportions—and what a sight for kids to behold! Some cigar-chewing man would lift the tangled webs of steel with a crane crawling off a page in "Mike Mulligan and the Steam Shovel." The crane reached with its massive paw and dangled a massive magnet on a screeching wire, and lifted the tangled webs of steel to some dizzying height. Then somehow it shut itself off and dropped the whole load with a deafening and fatalistic screeching into the bed of a monstrous truck. I could never figure out how they actually shut off the magnet, much to the chagrin of my crew-cut engineer father— some trickery of physics he explained in convoluted detail. Something to do with a solenoid; something to do with paying attention; something I could never seem to do...

But at least he tried. After the grand feast of childhood wonderment, I would sit on the bumper of our station wagon and guide him with hand signals, hoots and whistles as he backed up to the hottest fire. And then I was released to practice my boyish madness. Driven by primitive genes, I cast everything we had into the pit—as in everything, if only to see what burned or what defied the alchemy of flame. While I practiced pyrotechnics, my father sauntered off to talk with the other fathers (and rarely mothers) who gathered around talking politics, the war, cars, sports, or just handing out schedules of town meeting agendas. This assembly of Concord gossiped about everything under the sun while I searched for some classmate neighbor or feral friend to join me in heaving hair spray, spray paint, and almost empty cans of turpentine into the fire just to watch them explode. Occasionally, after a really good explosion, someone would scream at us miscreants to be more careful, but we nonchalantly hollered back, "Sorry, I didn't know it was in there." The adults would go back to their bantering, and we would go back to our heaving and blowing up of things. I sometimes wonder how anything gets resolved in Concord now that we no longer have a dump. I wonder where our townsfolk now go where they can talk on an equal footing with their neighbors.

We all need a place to meet, speak, and converse in brave and honest dialogues, no matter what the venture, time, or place —and so it is with our writing community in our class. Even if we don't know our neighbors from a hole in the wall, we need to step out of our metaphorical cars and ask, "How are you?" to our neighbors. Our class writing communities remind me of the Concord Town Dump. It is good, right, and fitting to have a place where everybody gathers, gossips, and gets the news in a common place. Our blogs are our common place—a place to dump our words and see if they explode like cans of hairspray or if our words can withstand the fiery eyes of critical readers. It is a place to sift through our jewels and junk, discard words that clutter, and keep words that capture the whims of our wit and wisdom. You may well go home with more words in your wagon than you brought to the dump. You will wave and smile at Mike

Mulligan in the massive crane and thank him for carting away what you no longer need, for you have scavenged a greater bounty of words than you tossed away.

Words matter, and in the end, it is through our words that we are remembered. We are an equal cog in a wheel of writers, and without your blog, there would be one less of each other's blogs. Our fledgling community of writers would soon devolve to an infinite degree—the degree of your potential. You will be measured and remembered by the words you leave behind. Words are remembered because they are memorable, not by virtue of being spoken or written down on a messy page. A good writer strives to craft writing memorable for their readers, and a good writer will do so in the same way a cook tries to make a meal their guests will remember fondly—a meal to goad them back again and again. We will go to that restaurant as often as we can, and we will read every book that the writer publishes—and we'll go to the best blogs in our community time and time again to see what the writer—hopefully you—produced on a given day.

Another irony bedevils the best writers—many of whom are rarely the most widely read or popular writers. Henry David Thoreau's books were scarcely read by his contemporaries in his day. He spent four or five hours every day writing in his journals and crafting his now-acknowledged masterpieces of literature. Only a handful of people ever layed eyes on his lifetime of labor. Thoreau continued to write because he believed in the value of what he was writing—and you need to believe in the value of what you are writing, not because of what anyone says about your writing but because you believe in what you write. You believe writing is important and necessary. You sense the power, majesty, and mystery of well-crafted words wrought the page.

We practice the writer's trade because doggedness is the only path up the slaggy, unforgiving slope of wordsmithing, but the journey is a lofty peak worth climbing. Although writing is a solitary vocation, sharing your writing is an echoing reminder you will never be alone—that no one should ever be alone. The world will hear what you say, see what you see, feel what you feel, and think what you think bathing in the mysterious alchemy of your words gifted to them.

You are much more than a young teenager dreaming to be a better writer. You are a connecting link in an endless lineage of writers searching for meaning, discerning truth, and keeping us inviolably human. Your words ring as a resounding affirmation that you, and I, and we are real.

Your voice is as powerful as any thunder in the universe. Shout your wobbling, yodeling words into the void.

We will hear.

We will return your cascading echo.

.

TO A TEACHER

This shift from fall to winter
Is the cruelest month:
Long days and nights
In a blather of responsibilities
Hoisted from a murky hole
I sort and sift
On a messy desk.

I pity my students who tremble
My red pen of vengeance,
Who wait with fetid thoughts
Freighted by what they did—

Or didn't do.

I hear the stern words of parents
Parse my elliptical thoughts
When all I really need to say
Is their kid gave a damn

Or didn't.

But "why?"

Why is what they
Need, want, plead,
Beg almost to know

What they already do.

REMEMBER THE TIME

A lesson in devotion

Write what you know...
~**Mark Twain**

I don't always practice what I preach, especially when it comes to the simple, unaffected, and ordinary "journal entry." My reticence towards casual journal entries is the public nature of posting our journal writing as blogs more or less open to the public. As a teacher of writing, it is hard to post what I know is trivial, mundane, and perhaps of no interest to my readers, but this is precisely what I need to do if I am to model the full spectrum of the writing process.

Keeping a journal is more than a search for lofty thoughts amidst the detritus of the day; it is a dutiful, insistent practice to keep our wits and writing skills honed for a coming feast by rambling through the meat of the day—to drift and sail to whatever port is nearest our pen. Writing is an odyssey. We need to let our minds go and journey (journal) where they will. Good words are built out of ordinary thoughts. At the very least, a journal filled with the scraps and pieces of our daily lives will outlive our own lives and serve as both beacon and reminder to future generations.

In my long-ago days as a junkman, I cleaned out an old barn in Maynard after an elderly Finnish widower I only knew as Bob passed away. While sifting through boxes of Bob's junk for anything of value, I came across a series of leather-bound journals dating back to the 1930s. A journal marked "1941" piqued my interest. I looked up the date of the Pearl Harbor attack, eager for any profound effect December 7, 1941, marked on the common person of that remarkable time. I sifted through pages of impeccable script and read how Bob and his family went to church in the morning. They sang certain hymns, and the sermon was long, yet "not without substance." They drove to Stow for dinner with his extended family and traveled home before sunset. Bob wrote about their meal, the weather, and the condition of the roads. In two brief lines at the close of his entry: "The Japs attacked Pearl Harbor today. I trust President Roosevelt will know what to do."

And that was it.

At first glance, I sensed a xenophobic, rural racist placing blind trust in an infallible ruler. I struggled to reconcile his harsh phrasing with the seemingly gentle old man I only knew in passing. I struggled to see his window into another time and another mindset. My youthful pride and arrogance failed to appreciate the elegiac beauty of Bob's day—a whole day devoted to faith, duty, and the full circle of family. It was not until years later, when I sat on the bench by the World War Two Memorial in downtown Maynard and scrolled through the scores of boys and men from this one small mill town killed in battle, that I realized the full extent of my myopia. Better had I sat in Bob's barn for days and read every word from his journals. Perhaps then I might have seen the evolution of a person through the fullness of time and the clarity of still waters.

Maybe Bob's youthful ramblings, tempered by the deaths of so many of his townsmen, somehow transformed into the pearls of laconic wisdom that old age should bring—pearls to fetch a heady price in the market of the modern mind. The greater tragedy is that we will never know. I offered the journals to his son, but he had no interest. He paid me fifty dollars for the load, which I scattered into the fires of the Concord dump. The irony of tossing away those journals some few hundred yards from the site of Thoreau's cabin on Walden Pond remained lost on me for many years, even as I dutifully trudged to the Concord library to scour through Thoreau's own journals. Bob practiced what Thoreau believed was required first of any man or woman when he admonished all would-be writers:

I, on my side, require of every writer, first or last, a simple and sincere account of his own life, and not merely what he has heard of other men's lives. [Henry David Thoreau, *Walden*]

A further ignominy is a cardboard box of my own journals, bridging my years between eighteen and twenty-five years old, was randomly tossed into the same dump by a roommate intent on purging the junk accumulating in our William's Road farmhouse.

The Concord Dump is now a series of perfectly sculptured hills slowly regaining the shape and character of the woods Thoreau tramped and stumbled through 150 years ago. It is a noble idea funded by the well-intentioned, but a nobler action would be to dig through the mold, dirt, and trash of time to truly find what the past has to offer us, buried irretrievably as it now is.

Poetry is what is left unsaid. The stolid words of brevity point us in a direction only the brave will wander, but through the daily words of an old Italian farmer, I found a new kind of poetry. Pine Tree Farm, butted against the rail line on the far side of Walden and owned by the Ammendolia's, was one of the last of the Italian family farms, and roadside stands once scattered in every corner of Concord. Tony Ammendolia was the patriarch who somehow kept the dream alive, even as farm after farm succumbed to the teeming aorta of suburbia. It was there where I worked on school breaks and on summer weekends picking corn at four in the morning before the heat of the day—followed by sweaty hours hoeing infinite rows of tomatoes, beans, pumpkins, and eggplants—long, hot afternoons where success and failure intersected in a struggle to just get by.

My goddaughters were raised there, and their parents, my good friends Deb and Jack, still kept a few acres going until the luster of farming faded. They sold the farm to Don Henley, of The Eagle fame, who was bent on preserving the woods around Walden Pond. It is now a non-profit farm, as, by default, are most of the farms in town. Tony died two years ago after defying for many years the cancer he fought with the same stubbornness he did the ups and downs of nature in the cycle of droughts, floods, and insects he faced at every turn during his long years as a farmer.

For over sixty years, Tony sat every night at his desk after dinner and wrote in his journal. Tony knew I was a writer, and he would kiddingly boast that he was also a writer, but in a good-natured poke at my transient approach to life, he was also a farmer. I visited Jack and Deb recently for dinner and asked about Tony's journals. Jack perked up as the proud inheritor of this family treasure and immediately handed me one of the many small notebooks Tony kept. I opened it and felt tears well in my eyes.

His words read like a type of poetry I had never read before.

Tony rarely meandered from the scope of his life, but his words spelled out a conviction celebrating the common fragility and majesty of life with sentences sparse and foreboding: "Potato beetles got the eggplants on Bedford Street. We will not sell eggplant this year," and further on, "Three days of rain. Lucky, as the irrigation pump needs a new valve." Each entry was a sublime excising of the profound out of the ordinary—the sky, the temperature, what was done, what had to be left undone, how much seed was needed, what was selling and what was not selling—but never a mention of the money made or not made. There is never a mention of personal angst, regret, or frustration for over sixty continuous years. Those details are best left to imagination and speculation. Some, especially myself, have to call it poetry.

Our own journals need the same attention Bob and Tony put into their daily incantations. Our journals must also chart the common unfolding of our lives. As writers and sojourners in life, it is our call of duty to map the expanse of our existence. We do not need to lay our souls bare for all to see and gossip about, but we should find a time and place to keep a daily journal. Just a few short lines each day will serve to spark your memory at a later age, and memories wizened in the vat of a thoughtful life always produce a finer wine. Journaling is a word antiquated before its time. Though fewer and fewer of us take the time to sit with pen and paper, there is still a time and a place for the spirit of journaling to continue.

Make the time to map your own quest, for the paths we trod are soon lost to memory and space, and invariably we lose our connection to the original experience. A friend asked me yesterday why I don't have a GPS in my truck, to which I replied, "First, I have to remember where I've been." I wish for more strength to follow up on those words. Bob and Tony's journals are permeated with an almost religious devotion as they chronicle the recitations of their days in rhythm with the pattern of their everyday lives.

One could argue that we use social media as a way to chronicle our days. We are literally recording and presenting our lives to the world, but there does not seem to be a sacred and solitary pattern anyone could call journaling. Our posts on social media repeat a tiresome, sycophantic obsession with random, mundane, and profligate interests and lifestyles. It is hard—and sometimes impossible—to wrest context out of the content. Nothing, except a prurient curiosity, keeps me interested—which is no road to enlightenment for either side of the equation.

Sometimes there are links to blogs and other artistic websites where a deeper and more invested side of some person comes through. For most of us, Instagram, Facebook, TikTok, and whatever else is simply an adjunct to life—a social gathering place to rest and draw water with friends and community. There is nothing wrong with this, but it should never be the destination of a true journey, and if you can't see life as a journey—an odyssey of existence—you simply can't see.

I guess the word I am looking for is "devotion." None of our lives are more complicated than the lives of Bob or Tony. The difference is how each of them created time every day to look closely at what was important in the daily unfolding of their respective lives.

Bob and Tony never looked for a response, a like, or a link.

They simply remembered.

Remember where you have been.

TEACHING THE NEW REALITY

Online Learning 1.0

Never fear quarrels, but seek hazardous adventures.
~Alexandre Dumas, *The Three Musketeers*

Damn… Our universe has shifted. We are balancing an unwieldy plank of change. We are asked on the fly to shift gears and embrace "online learning." Schools might be—and some already are—closing their doors for as yet undefined periods of time. The Luddites among us are aghast, while those geeky, trendy teachers are suddenly, and perhaps unwillingly, in vogue. Sheaves of paper need to be transformed into readily accessible online documents, and new digital platforms need to be ready—like right now—to somehow engage and empower huge numbers of students and countless schools. Teachers, administrators, students, and parents must step to the plate and deliver, but this is a fastball across the corner of the plate, and it is a small ball we have in our grip. Though I don't consider myself geeky, I have run a fair share of online classes. Hopefully, this mishmash of thoughts might be helpful as we face this collective challenge together.

Don't be intimidated. You are probably already engaged in some variant of online learning. Anytime you post an assignment online, you are taking your first step. Attach a worksheet, a link, a video, a quiz, a PowerPoint—or any other kind of digitized or multi-media resource—and you are now practically a pro. The first learning curve is to know what you can—and can't—upload to and access from your school's learning management system, aka LMS. This takes practice, discernment, and organization. Every LMS is different with different capabilities, so I can only say "embrace the beast" as well as you can. Leverage your strengths and work around the limitations of whatever platform you have in your hands. Even the most limited LMS can be augmented with other online platforms and apps. Use shared documents to write essays and assignments, explore topics of interest in discussion forums, create class blogs, watch YouTube videos, make podcasts, and utilize quiz-making software. You are only hindered by not trying or experimenting. It is a brave new world, and, reluctant or not, you are its creator.

Look to the horizon and define and limit your expectations. Online classes require a different scope of focus. You are no longer the "Sage on the Stage." You are the "Guide on the Side." This transition can be difficult for educators who are more comfortable standing in front of students—active teachers waving arms, barking orders, and shouting encouragement as they lead an energized classroom dynamic. Online teaching requires teachers to step to the side and morph into a subtle, guiding presence, yet you should not lose your commanding role as captain of your class. Create a podcast, screencast, or video introducing the unit in succinct soundbites that define the focus, guide the direction, and parse the expectations of what you hope to accomplish.

Prepare your students for battle, but don't lead the charge.

Visualize your students' experiences. You have a pretty good idea of your students' strengths and weaknesses. Your curriculum must paint broad strokes to inspire the capable students interspersed with enough precise detail to guide the more challenged students and help these students feel a sense of empowerment and defined purpose. Visualize the possibilities across the spectrum of your class. Juggle and adjust the details so "everyone" has power in their hands to engage their peculiar bent of genius in genuine ways.

Temper expectations with reality checks. Online assessments soon become a black hole of drudgery for you and a drag on the spirit of your students. Use shared documents for writing assignments and give appropriate and realistic feedback. This is where you are the guide on the side. The temptation is often to give too much feedback, which is a sure-fire path to online burnout. I use a series of text shortcuts to highlight common errors as well as common phrases and comments of praise. By and large, the kids are appreciative of short and personal comments. They need a pat on the head as much as a kick in the behind.

Finally, don't listen (or at least don't give in) to those students who argue they can't figure things out—who lament that the expectations are too complicated and too unfamiliar. At the same time, know your enemy and follow the KISS principle—keep it simple, stupid. Start with small steps and grow your online course in depth and breadth as your students become more adept as online students. You will, doubtless, soon be more comfortable in this wild and worthwhile land of online learning.

In the end, you will be amazed at what your students—and you—can do. It is what we—the grand and indefatigable—have to embrace.

It is not a choice.

It is our destiny and our Fate.

THE POET GOES TO WORK

Every morning,
Before the rush hour diaspora,
We neighbors shout to each other
Over the scratching
Of ice scrapers
Clearing icy wipers, balancing
Cups of coffee, dancing
In a steaming minuet
Of our morning rituals.

We start our wives' cars
And make monster faces
At our respective homes
To the gallery of faces
Chomping Cherrios
At the breakfast tables.

Tom pulls on his cigar
And spits aphorisms
In an unending palate
Of smoke and exhaust
And stoops and loads
His unquenchable van
With what appears to be
Aisle twelve from Home Depot.

I grab my own tools
And squeeze through
The impossible space
My wife has left me
Between our two cars.

I double-check everything:

Huck Finn.

This pen.

THE GIFT OF WORDS

Fill the void with words

The beginning of wisdom is the definition of terms.
~Socrates

If you want to learn to write well, start writing and do not stop. If you do not want to learn to write well, this will be a wasted class—empty time leading to a deeper emptiness. We are all born communicators. We feel tangible angst when our words are misunderstood, misinterpreted, and misplaced. Our lives, and the lives of those around us, are surrounded and immersed by our words. Words are the one continual reality pervading our lives, so why not create the space and the time to richen the time given to us to learn, practice, and share in the process of crafting our thoughts into words that shape our ideas, hopes, dreams, and experiences in memorable and profound ways? We are judged by our words and our actions, but it is through our words that we are remembered, especially if the power of our actions and our words is brought together to perfect our humanity and inform the directions our lives take.

I do not teach writing to help you get into a better school or get a better grade. I teach writing because I believe it lifts your life towards a more fulfilled, wiser, and more centered life—a life leading to a ripe, golden age surrounded by family, friends, and the contentedness of a life fully lived. The academic benefits of writing well are a no-brainer. You will not regret learning how to write a good essay in the crunch of pressure and deadlines, and much of this year will be spent learning to build these enduring skills; however, writing in a sustained and continual way guides you to find the words to honestly and powerfully express what is in your head and heart at any given moment—not simply in response to a boring writing prompt or assignment.

You will not grow old (or perhaps even grow up) wishing you had spent more time on your XBox or Snapchat, but you will regret the time and opportunities you let slip away from you now.

I certainly do.

My shelves are full of books I wish I had read. My mind is full of the would-haves, could-haves, and should-haves I ignored or passed off as, at the time, not worth the effort. My life is very, very good, and I am supremely happy, yet I know I have left too much refuse trashing my wake. Too many times I turned around before reaching the peak of the mountain; too many times I took the road more traveled by, and too many times I let silence fill the void my words might have filled.

If I can get you to fill your void with words, I can proudly say my job is done. If you leave this year with more love and lust for words, I will know I prepared you for the unexpected twists and turns your own lives will inevitably take and somehow hobble you as you walk your road through life. If you pick up a book or write in your journal simply because you want to, I will notch a mark on my stick of time as a great and worthy accomplishment.

I will retire as a happy teacher, satisfied I did my duty.

This is why I do what I do, but I cannot do it without you. You have to be the writer. I can bring you to the river, and I can tell you what I know about the dangers of deep water, but you are the one who needs to jump in and swim.

You won't learn on the shore.

Leap in.

Learn...

PAGE ONE

The sun is but a morning star

If one cannot enjoy reading a book over and over again,
there is no use in reading it at all.
~Oscar Wilde

I want to start reading again, which seems like a paradox for an English teacher and an author of seven published books [disclaimer: none of any renown] and one fledgling novel stuck on page fifty.

I used to read. I used to read like a banshee howling for more and more and more words in a voluptuous desert of desire. Books answered the call of my wild longings for honeyed wisdom to feed my nascent soul. I felt some strange desire to practice the bent of what I read and at least mimic the patterns of whatever book I was reading. I was transfixed by Thoreau, solaced by Dostoyevsky, invigorated by Kerouac, and inspired by Homer. I never was—or am—an intellectual of any sort. Precious few English teachers paved my literary journey, though some few did; more it was the simple serendipity of opportunity. Like Mallory climbing the highest mountain, I read the craggy books "because they were there."

And because there was nothing else to do...

I read books at every chance I had. I lived in the briny seas of endless words, trapped by the lure of twists and turns. But not so much anymore. I seem to find something else to do—some sappy Netflix series; a lingering pile of papers to grade or assignments to create; a car needing a Bondo repair and a power steering pump—or a batch of songs I have yet to learn. I am, by vocation, a teacher of literature and writing, a performing songwriter, an essay writer of screed—like this bongo of thoughts —and a deliberate poet, carving snippets of words out of quiet nights, usually late at night, most often to the small stew of friends somehow drawn to poetry. I pity the irony of being a teacher of literature and bemoaning my students to READ, READ, READ their fledgling lives through and out of the maelstrom bursting out of their childhoods—to build the foundations of purpose and power out of the impermeable stone of enduring literature. I preach what I was, not what I am. I feel hollow and distant, not real and energizing and truthful.

When I do read, I mostly re-read the books I palavered through when I was younger, as if I can once again relive the dreamy world of my youth. It is as if I can't move forward unless I start again at the beginning. But I must start again—and start anew—for nothing else instills the wonder of our fleshy universe as fully as a tattered tome of words crafted out of truth and purpose. Though I am hobbled by the commitments of time, there are still the same number of hours in my days. My life, in every sense of the word, is as blessed and rich as any man could hope for or dream to have, yet there is a lingering hole I have yet to fill—a hole I need to fill with books—the books I have yet to remember...

On the table next to our bed is Ben Shattuck's book, *Six Walks of Thoreau*. It lies beneath the TV remote—my portal to a leisurely pursuit—a baby's binky I teethed for too long, a gentle palliative and enchanting coda to a tiring day, and a head strewn with unfinished business and dutiful obligations. It is a good book, but I sense it is not an ageless book, though it still inspires me to change what I am and aspire to be—and change and aspiration are ageless skills.

But I am not so old that I cannot change. I can yet grow old with books—memorable and worthy books—or I will simply grow old, clinging and cloning to the disappearing shadows of youth. In the final words of Thoreau in *Walden*, he reminds us that now is the new beginning: "Only that day dawns to which we are awake. There is more day to dawn. The sun is but a morning star."

But it starts on page one.

Perhaps now.

FLICKS OF FLAME

I've let the fire burn
Into a small drift of coals
Piled against this cool night.
Everyone is off to bed
Or watching Netflix
Or lost in books
Or flying to the moon.

Somehow I am not convinced
This fire can die.
I kneel in the dusty ash
Clutching sticks of pine:

Tommy
Emma
Charlie
Pipo
EJ
Margaret
Kaleigh

One
Two
Three
Four
Five
Six
Seven

I blow softly
On the flicks of flame
Until I am sure
My children are safe.

MY LAST ECHO

Turn towards poetry

One day I will find the right words,
and they will be simple.
~Jack Kerouac, The Dharma Bums

Going to Canobie Lake Amusement Park with the eighth grade is the turning point of the school year for me—a primal signal that it is time to turn away from the school year and towards the future. If nothing else, I pray you gained a deeper sense of the power and importance of words. I can only trust you will tap into that power in whatever way you need or want over the course of your life. I hope I am more of a beacon than a blip. Honestly, I do care what becomes of you, so I am always around as another set of eyes for anything you write over the eight or ten more academic years ahead of you in school—and many more years of your burgeoning life pummeling towards you. Sometimes it is just good to hear from you. So put that on your to-do list, but for this year, this mincemeat of drivel is the last you will hear from me.

One final post.

A final pattering of words...

My last echo...

Life will change you, and you will change your life, so be willing to change. Nothing you are today is set in stone for tomorrow. Stay awake. Don't be limited by who you are today. Though you might only see a small stone, there is always a universe of possibilities. Be brave and cross the threshold. To avoid the pain, suffering, and struggle of life, accept that no song will be sung about you. Your songs of hardship are the ones that most need to be sung. How else can you learn? This tumult spins your heroic cycle. It is part and parcel of every life lived fully and honestly in an invigorated way.

Your life is the epic poem you are about to live, so live, damn it, live!

Don't be remembered as Pap, or the Duke and Dauphin, or Himmelstoss or Kantorek, or some nameless suitor, or even a vain and impetuous god. Be remembered as a living, breathing bolt of life who responds to the innate stirrings within yourself. Be remembered as the steady self who recognizes these stirrings as the wisdom of Mentes and who acts as if guided by the power of bright-eyed Athena. This is the power that is entwined and empowered in the actions of Jim, and Huck, and Paul, and Odysseus. Trust in your wisdom. Flesh out your thoughts. Sustain your greatness.

Above all else, be a friend. Be a friend. Be a friend.

Friendship burns as a metaphor for caring, persistence, constancy, and courage. In friendship, you never are , or ever can be, alone. Learn then what a friend should be. Be like Paul Baumer in *All Quiet on the Western Front* and risk everything for your friends. Be like the kings and swineherds of *The Odyssey* and welcome strangers as the Magi they should be, for friends will always be true and faithful, even when society is not. Be willing to carry or be carried across and through the battles of life. Don't leave these friends you have made, molded, and maddened. Don't lose touch with the varied cast of round, flat, fleeting, or forever characters who surround your life, or you will become a flat, forgettable character remembered only as a passing scene in a dull film or a footnote buried in the plot of an insipid story.

Turn towards poetry as the flower arcs towards the sun. Your life is a young poem. Your life is the soil upon which your future grows. Cultivate your mind as you would a garden you need to survive. Trust in poetry. Poetry is the greatest fruit of your being. Poetry is not just a pile of written words. It is the ability to see like Basho and feel like Sylvia Plath, or to argue with Frost and trust in Mary Oliver.

Life is never a single image. It is image upon image, powered by action—imagery that stirs our primal instincts out of our comfortable torpor. Poetry gifts life new meaning and purpose through twists and turns of thoughts brewed in curiosity. We take poetry and act upon it, and through the juxtaposition of seemingly unrelated scenes and strings of words paired together, we create meaning, purpose, wisdom, and sustenance.

Sit quietly and purposefully. Let the moon reflect off your shining skin. Nature is your greatest teacher and the only God who is always there for you—and who is always waiting. Though you can't enter the same river twice, you can always sit on the banks and be restored—but it will never happen unless you walk to the river, wherever and whatever your river happens to be.

The classroom is only the finger pointing at the moon.

Above all, remember. Remember everything. Craft carefully, and treasure the words you create.

The leaves are falling.

I have walked away.

Nothing gold can stay.

ENTER THE STREAM

Let words be what they are

Time is but the stream I go fishing in
~Henry David Thoreau, *Walden*

Writing well requires a writer to write with courage, confidence, and honesty. Your journal is your place to live fully and completely within yourself as a real and committed writer, practicing the promise and journey of a writer. Journal writing is the iteration of practice that gives form and substance to your innermost thoughts. It is a path for you to walk and be completely and inexplicably who you are—not an expectation driven by academic expectations directed and choreographed by me.

It is you. It is you. It is you—you in all of your glory and imperfections—made real and palpable just by trying.

Every trip to a blank page is an opportunity to discover, explore, and investigate your particular bent of genius. No one is peering over your shoulder as long as you are peering into yourself and extricating the stubborn stones from the mud of your inimitable life—a storied life pried out of the experiences, musings, pondering's, and proclamations uniquely your own.

Writing is not merely an academic exercise; it is a physical activity made better just by doing, practicing, and *embracing the beast* in continual and sustained ways. Writing is made better by learning and using the time-tested skills of craft in the same way you use the time-tested skills to learn and master a sport, a game, or a passion.

To get better, just do it.

Do it with equal doses of bravado and humility.

Do it because it will make you a more literate and capable human being.

Do it because you have nothing to lose and everything to gain.

All of you have just returned from a common and shared experience. You have spent the last three days side by each, mashed in small, rustic cabins, clumped in groups, tethered to swaying wires, circled around campfires, eating the same foods—living in a way to help you see, smell, embrace, discover, reflect, and rethink this special and irretrievable space of time in your life.

It is worth remembering!

The beauty in each of your experiences is common and threaded by a sameness. It is utterly and perfectly your own experience. No one can tell you what you have gained, lost, or discovered. Discovery is the work of you as a writer—a flesh-and-bones teenager skateboarding on the edge of an inimitable, distinct, dangerous, and exhilarating time in your life.

Before telling us your story, first tell yourself your story. Only then can you possibly begin the process of telling a real, true, and compelling story to others—a story boldly richening and stirring the mosaic of your life—a story to stand as a testament that will long outlive you.

Create the time to open your journal. Let the words and thoughts flow like a New Hampshire stream. Let them pool in swirling eddies and still ponds of thought. Let them just be what they are and go where they will go. Words have a way of bending around boulders, snags, and even mountains. No dam can hold back the power and persistence of unfettered thought.

In the cool gray fog of this morning, I wrote my thoughts.

It is up to you to find your own space and your own time.

It is not required by me.

It is required by life.

SUGARING IN A MILL TOWN

We do not need a conjurer
To reveal the magic
Of maple sugar—
Born from long, cold nights
And warm March days.
We drill probing holes,
Hang tin buckets
And tap gnarled trees.
We boil away the sap,
Taste the amber syrup,
Fill old bottles,
And leave another mess
To argue about
On another day.

The neighbors are happy
My kids tap their aged maples
Lining our pot-holed streets.
The gallon buckets
Hung from ten-penny nails
Seem absurdly out of place
In the close-knit quarters
Of this old mill town.

I watch Tommy and Emma
Line up behind Kaleigh,
Charlie and Margaret,
And EJ and Pipo—
Stoic draft horses
Shaking oiled harnesses,
Stamping shod hooves.
Straining and stumbling
Through soft corn-snow
Piled high before
The Ides of March.

(I remember once
while hiking through
the woods of Rumney
seeing a solitary man
with a plaid wool cap, turning
bucket after bucket
into an endless vat
and dreaming
what is never spoken.)

I fear my children
Ever being that alone.

In my myopic love
They are a roaming, uncouth gaggle—
Cocked heads in floppy knit hats
Cover single, pirate eyes—
Unlaced boots and mismatched mittens
Dance a celebratory homeward waltz,
Embracing the sloshing,
Galvanized tins
Like drunken prom dates.

The girls sing
As if they own the world:

Girls go to college
to get more knowledge;
boys go to Jupiter
to get more stupider.

The boys, of course,
Turn the cheer
To their advantage.

Held together
By the gravity of tradition,
No one is ever left behind,
Though, invariably,

Someone starts to cry.
Later, with the house full
Of steam, smoke and pungency,
We stand on tiptoes and benches
And hold the smallest ones tightly.

We jostle for space
Around the stove
And gather
As a community
And stare for hours
Into the mystery.

EDUCATION

Ride the cusp

The mind is not a vessel to be filled, but a fire to be kindled.
~Plutarch

Writing an essay is relatively simple for me. I choose some inviting path and start writing. There is not a soul in the world expecting anything out of this essay—or who even senses this anonymous screed is in the throes of a breech-birth, which will bring me comforting solace if this essay dies an early and ignominious death. I don't have a teacher pushing me in any one direction—like I push you. The writing prompt and the inspiration are already in me. I try to write well, but there are no real-life repercussions if I don't write well. My audience for this (which is you—my upper school English class) is remarkably small and polite. As much as I wish to think you are captivated by my writing, I know in reality you are a "captive" to my writing. You are a prisoner in my classroom. You are doomed and destined to read what I write, yet your actual freedom to write is hobbled by a teacher intent on extracting (by what must sometimes feel like any means possible) what you know and think about a narrow range of literature—in this case, the first chapter of *Walden*—the dense, timeless essay "Economy.

Throw your other classes into the mix, and you get a few more books, an era or two of some history, some idea of why leaves turn red, a handy way to discern volume from the breadth and width of a fruit—a smattering of Spanish words or Latin roots, a bookshelf from shop, and an abstract oil painting for your wall. Don't forget your soccer and football teams, the school play, band, and student life—and now your day is completely filled.

But is it full? Your life is filled with an exhausting range of activities designed and structured to educate, enlighten, inform, and inspire you. Your teachers are a diverse mix of characters who give a damn about you and who spend more time than you might ever imagine trying to create and perpetuate this living and breathing machine called school; however, as Thoreau writes, "We labor under a mistake." We fill our days but rarely fulfill the possibilities of each day, and until we remove the blinders keeping us on the beaten path—but we never will.

As frightening as it sounds, the lunatics must run the asylum. Students must take the reins in their tender novice hands. They must accept the command of an ornery captain and become learners and explorers, while teachers and administrators must fade into mere deckhands or die. As Thoreau writes, "New ways for the new; old ways for the old." The world really is a different place now. The "noosphere" or "omega point" predicted by Pierre Teilhard de Chardin a hundred years ago is now a reality. People can be—and are—connected in myriad ways unimaginable to the visionaries and teachers who broke the backs of tradition to create the schools we have today.

But times have changed. The desk is more a ball and chain of self-serving restraint, while the opportunities for true learning have never been greater. Something has to give. Society and its schools are slaves to assessment as much as we are creators of destiny. Measuring someone by "the content of their character" seldom makes it onto report cards; instead, we measure your progress and achievements with a reptilian calculus, defining the merits and deficiencies of your responses to specific inquiries and lessons we are convinced we taught you well. We critique what and how you write, but we rarely measure why you write. Though we seem compassionate and practice some brand of empathy, we still erect strands of razor wire that only a few of you can possibly tumble over unscathed—and those are the celebrated few—the smart, hard-working, and diligent students who somehow manage to do it all. Everyone else plays "catch me if you can."

The paradigm is set in motion. It becomes the foundation of almost every school and university in the world. The conceits of academia sculpt, shape, and polish the gifted student into a recognizable icon. Parents stumble over each other, hoping to weave their child's place on the honor roll or SAT scores. They leverage the average score of the whole town in comparison to every other school in the district and weave biases into the most casual of conversations. On the flip side of this coin, these subtle honors and noisy accolades are hardly as respected by peers and classmates. Students sense the inherent fraud and advantage of the system. Past prowess soon makes for unsavory and indelicate talk—even just mere hours after graduation.

Maybe doing well in school is not such an impressive accomplishment. It is pretty cool that we have a black president raised by a single mom—but it is only cool if we are impressed, enlightened, and humbled; otherwise, it is just starchy fluff and tasteless fodder. We use President Obama's accomplishments as praise for what educational opportunities can do, but history is full of great individuals who rose from humble beginnings. It is a recurring theme of humanity itself. It is part and parcel of what Joseph Campbell terms "The Heroic Cycle." Schools do not create greatness. Our primal need to be great creates greatness.

No one reading this essay is precluded from realizing their individual greatness and glory. We don't have to be Telemachus facing up to the rowdy suitors in his house, but all of us have challenges unmet and untested. We must meet them and test them if we want to be heroes. There is courage and strength in each of us, but not as much motivation, perhaps because the tools we use in school are not the best motivators. We instill as much fear as desire. A subtle paralysis takes hold. We are pinned to the mat by mediocrity. Only if the doors open wider and the walls fall down will we see the expanse of our opportunities— and only if you give enough of a damn to reach for the dream at hand, and then only if you see the dream. Realizing your dream is your accomplishment. Layering dream upon dream upon dream is your life.

Life doles out hardship in unequal, unjust, and unsustainable proportions. School should not be a hard slog in a mucky bog. There is no equity in who goes to what school. The schools we attend live and breathe unspoken inequity. We praise the notion of an egalitarian educational system, but we shudder at the thought of implementation. Few of my Concord friends would ship their sons and daughters to our schools in Maynard because, well, just because. Ironically, few of my Maynard friends would feel comfortable with their sons and daughters trying to mingle in the academically pressured and financially endowed milieu of Concord. And so we keep up a pleasant caste system feeding off the tension between the rich and the poor. It is like the old camp song: "Don't chuck your muck in my backyard/my backyard's full," but because of the internet, our backyards have merged; the demarcation line is blurred, and there really is a chance for every kid to play on the same field—if we let them.

It would be ironic if our schools lost the race for knowledge because we dithered at the starting gate. Julius Caesar accidentally burned down the Royal Library in Alexandria. We can't do the same with our new library of knowledge. During the first solo circumnavigation of the world, the Afrikaners in South Africa scoffed at Joshua Slocum's claims that the world was round, even as he was ninety percent of the way around the globe.

I did not start this narrative with any plans to take on our educational system. Sharper minds than mine could tear this essay apart, but only because they have had so many generations to practice. The hurricane yesterday gave me a rare gift of time today. I was just hoping to give you a few words to help you get started on your *Walden* essay. Words have this effect on me. Maybe my own rereading of *Walden* bade me to listen more closely to the drumbeat of my heart, *no matter how measured or far away*. Maybe in these political times of gloating, bitching, and belittling, I didn't want to be *one of the thousand hacking at the branches of evil*; I wanted to be *the one striking at the root*. The beauty and bane of Thoreau's words is how easily his terse words prove either side of the argument, and my mind is so scattered I could never get around to organizing all the facts; instead, I've simply scattered some seeds among the compost of my experience. Hopefully, one or two are the mustard seeds in the soil—not the pathway trod by an ignorant humanity.

If not, I will till again and plant more thoughtfully.

And see what grows.

CLOSE YOUR EYES & SEE

A mirror to your soul

The mind can go in a thousand directions,
but on this beautiful path, I walk in peace.
With each step, the wind blows.
With each step, a flower blooms.
~Thich Nhat Hanh

For some forty years, I have kept journals chronicling my wandering mind, the lifting and dissipations of my spirit, and the excesses of experience. A good part of my journals are lost, but much has survived. Lost or lasting, the written memories hang on me like a sailor clinging to a pieces of flotsam —my flagellating words prove I am real and not completely lost. My daily ramblings lend substance to ephemeral musings lost in the whims of procrastinated time. They free me from myself. In the meandering evolution of my words set to page, a lingering mark, albeit small, is etched into a marble wall of time. It is what it is, and it can never be sandblasted clean—simple reminders I am what I am.

It is frightening to know who I am because of the urgency to continually change what I am. To see clearly into myself, I must shut my eyes. Stripped bare, I am a meager and skeletal portrait of a man—a shaky scaffold of dreams and desires connected inextricably to the pulsing aorta of reality, yet I still am. I am ineffable life born of itself. It cannot be any other way.

I am doomed and emboldened to speak with a voice that barks and sings, laments and praises, and shouts and drones the inexcusable and intransigent me, whether in glorious triumph or ignominious defeat. I need reflection to define stark contrasts from blurred light. I need a barometer to sense and measure the depth of the coming storms or the balm of easy weather. I need to see the glass fall or rise. I need to know when to set anchor and when to set sail, and all I have are words to guide me and mark the pole star.

Words and love are all that are real to me, but it is only words that I question. I do not question my love for or unequivocal devotion to Denise, our children, or the eclectic diaspora of our extended family and friends. I only struggle with the constructs I create. I question my words because my words are not created for me—they are created for you. My words carry the weight of everything that preys on me, including vanity, desire, and a growing mania for a meaningful life, though this assertion is almost an anathema—a self-aggrandizing denial and an abnegation of human empathy.

Stripped of words, I can only utter and respond to what is palpably real and connected to me. I protect my own in spite of all else—viciously so. This is good and right, built into me, and unerringly bolted onto me by the hands of a creator beyond my palpable understanding. I question my reflection on any still waters transfixing my gaze. Beyond faith, beyond the constraints of circumstance—beyond anything we share, I am left with words. It simply is. I write because I know no other way. I have no illusions my stumbling path leads to a distinct and greater source. I am humbled by the misdirections I follow. I am less a guide than a foot soldier commandeered to plunge feet-first into the minefields of a dangerous field laced with weed and wildflower. Yet, I am still alive and yawp my fervor. This is my solace. Somehow I have navigated well enough to be where I am —safe, secure, and almost retired into a golden age. I covet joy like a child's inheritance of perpetual splendor. I cannot count or measure my blessings. I can only pass them on. No writer has cracked the enigma of words. We are a fledgling species at the beginning of time. We are hacks, fraudsters, and spinsters of deceit. We fool you time and time again. I am weary of the incessant battle to win any day through words. I wonder if any god or spirit can still my restlessness.

I close my eyes each night and expect an infinite dawn.

And so can you.

THE ENGLISH SOLDIER

There is a British soldier, dressed
In ancient English wool, guarding
The entrance to this old inn
Built in some colonial time.

He is lucky for this cool night
Awaiting the pomp
Of the out-of-town wedding party.
He is paid to be unmoved
By the bride's stunning beauty
Or her train of lesser escorts.

He will not notice
This granite marker
Set across the square.

His eyes do not glisten
When he hears
Two brothers fell here,
Picked out of disciplined
Lines beating
A hot and hasty retreat
Back to Boston.

He will not
Chasten his comrades
For leaving them
In foreign dust—
The dull and whistling holes
Torn into soft, homesick wool.

He betrays nothing.
Inscrutable—
He collects his check

And drives home.

LISTEN & LEARN

Keep a fire in your belly

A calm sea never a good sailor makes.
~Franklin D. Roosevelt

I hate these damned boats, yet, "aye," how well they put my life into perspective. Hating a needy pile of wood, sails, blocks, and lines is less distressing than what it teaches me about myself. Scraping and pawing the stubborn barnacles from the bottom-sides of my boat after eight months in drydock is a harsh reminder of how ten minutes of simple power-washing on Labor Day would negate the hours of my cursing and crawling on the back-stabbing scree of a New England boatyard—the labor occupying the entirety of my yesterday. Years ago, I blithely watched a friend show me how to splice a wire. Tomorrow I am paying some old salt two hundred dollars to splice the wire I need to haul my halyard. Damn me, damn today, and damn tomorrow. Why am I not the same old salt—and not some humble yuppie with a romantic notion of the sea, willing to pay twice to learn once? The list could go on, but so could my self-loathing.

In my youth, I learned a lot about sailing and boat building, but I never really went to sea on my own. My shaky skills were never reinforced by the granite memory of experience. The dream remained alive, while the lost knowledge now looms like an apparition in the distance, the ghost of an early death, haunting and enchanting in the same breath. I am relearning and re-remembering all I learned and lost. It is time to regain the footing of my nautical dreams and make a first windward tack out of a forgiving harbor.

Learning the ropes is equally true for the writer. Don't neglect the small details—the placing of commas, the quotes within quotes, the persistent run-ons, the introductory phrases, conjunctions, pronouns, colons, and semi-colons—the veritable sea-chest of tools and trinkets that enable you to construct, repair, and clarify your thoughts and embolden lofty ideas. These are the pinions of trickery binding together the sweeping power of great poetry and literature. They are the bolts, screws, frames, and planks holding our ballast of words together. They are the ratlins we climb to reach the mast hoop of our loftiest thoughts.

Everything you learned about writing is useful to the crafting of your words. It was, after all, a simple wire splice keeping me in port. If you are young, cling to what you learn and keep it close to your heart. If you are old, unearth and restore the memories you need to face the empty page with confidence and courage. Build upon what you already know. Sail to the horizon of your dreams. Don't stare melancholy from the pier.

A captain is only made at sea, not on land. I hobble my crazed, diligent, and disparate students in long preambles and digressions to my assignments. I hide details of what is due tomorrow in a muddy labyrinth of reflections, observations, and admonitions. My befuddled charges beg me to just highlight in bold what they need to do—not bore them with my incessant pedantry. I get away with it because I can. It bothers them that I assume they *want* to become better writers. They are not me, nor I them. I write because I love to write, but I, too, have a long way to go before I can call myself a captain. The few knots I know won't serve me well when the halyard is frayed and the stays are sprung. The simple act of sustained, attentive writing will make you a better writer. Connecting the act of writing with a focused study of the craft of writing will make you a great writer—a writer ready to face the open seas and sail uncharted shorelines.

Too much of education separates the bird from the wing. This is especially true in our more common ways of teaching writing. My own children spend hours of homework time circling prepositional phrases, adverbial clauses, and sneaky comma splices in dull, remarkably generic, and doltish workbooks. I appreciate that my children are learning the elemental nature and grammar of language, but, in my cynical moments, I marvel at how lucky their teachers are—as if their whole class needs work on the same mechanics. I wonder if those teachers realize how they are coddling a flock of awkward, flightless dodos dawdling around on barren dung heaps. Their skills are never tested or grasped by desperate hands in the moiling waters of angry oceans. There is nothing to show for all of their labor but some ill-suited grade and a higher MCAS score.

The skills we teach students must be useful in real-life situations. Our students need to see how these skills instill practical value in their personal odysseys as real writers. The poems, songs, stories, reflections, essays, and narratives we write take us boldly to sea, and only there—on a lonesome ocean—can we discover our greatness, our destinies, and our limitations. Without an adventurous journey, it is easy to lose the incentive to understand the entwined workings of the fleshy viscera keeping our writing alive. We are all at different places as writers, but the scourges of the sea are the same for all mariners.

See to yourself. Learn what needs learning. Stoke a fire in your belly. Let it drive you forward in your journey as a writer.

Keep listening. Keep learning. Keep wondering.

Above all else, keep sailing.

LET KIDS WRITE

Share your passions

Fill your paper with the breathings of your heart.
~William Wordsworth

There are plenty of smarter, more gifted, and more interesting writers out there than me or you, but there shouldn't be a more passionate writer. For better or worse, your blog is you—as my blog is me—and until you want a better you and I want a better me, readers will find other places to go. Few things in life are more important than a passion for something. It is an offshoot of "give damn." Without a passion for some something or somethings to experience and explore on your own is a recipe for a pitiful life.

When I was your age, I had a rock collection filling a bazillion egg crates with chips and scrapes I hammered off any interesting crop of rock I stumbled upon. I had snake and reptile aquariums filled with specimens of most any cold-blooded creature in the White Pond area of Concord. Working in the basement with my father, I built a shortwave radio cobbled out of wires, circuits, and gobs of molten solder. We stretched a huge antenna on the roof of our house to eavesdrop on scratchy, unintelligible conversations happening anywhere in the world. I had a collection of fishing poles, rods, reels, lures, and baits to somehow tease trout, bass, horned pout, kibber's, pickerel, and anything else out of the Concord River, Walden Pond, the Assabet River, Nashoba Brook, and Warner's Pond. Best of all, I repossessed a plywood sailboat my father built in our garage from plans he got in some how-to magazine, and in sailing alone in a home-built, twelve-foot biblical arc, I got my first taste of sailing on the placid shoals of White Pond—a taste as strong and heady today as it was back then.

I was a poster child for distraction, but I always read.

My bedroom was a mess of catalogs, books, and magazines. The books—The Hardy Boys, Sherlock Holmes, *Treasure Island, Tom Sawyer,* and *Ten Thousand Leagues beneath the Sea—were* neatly arranged in plywood bookcases cobbled coarsely by my grandfather. The magazines were strewn upon any and every flat space in my room—Boy's Life, Popular Mechanics, Popular Science, Field and Stream, Sears Roebuck catalogs, National Geographic's, and any other magazine, book, or pamphlet that nurtured my passions.

Most of those magazines (and, of course, the books) are still around to this day, but there is an even larger world of bloggers out there who cover everything those magazines covered—and a whole lot more. These blogs and websites are where thrill-seekers and budding sycophants go to feed their passions, knowledge, skills, and—sadly sometimes—their bigotry and bile. It is where you go and where I go, and the better the blog or the better the site, the more often we return—and the more we return, the more indelible mark a writer can pass on and abandon to the world.

And this mark says something about that person. You... Something good, I hope.

In ancient Rome, the wise bards proclaimed, *"De gustibus non est disputandum,"* otherwise known as *"There is no accounting for taste,"* which is a good thing because it keeps the world to this day interesting, diverse, and dynamic. We don't have to like what other people like or deem important, nor are there compelling reasons why we should; however, we should at least like something worth liking and be passionate about something worthy of our passion. We must buckle down and at least be knowledgeable about something. We need to be good at something and to persistently get better at something—or anything.

Think of your passions. Think of what you can do to live out your passion—or passions—and share it with the world. Ponder what you leave behind as your footprints in this life. You do not want to be like the drunk sailor Elpenor, who fell off the roof and died an anonymous death no one remembers or cares about. As Odysseus himself said, "No songs will be sung about him."

Your "digital footprint" is the song sung about you.

Twenty years ago—when I first started blogging—most people fretted about kids names being "on the internet." We built firewall on firewall behind private servers to keep you safe and removed from the real internet. In most ways, it has been great. Our blogs give you a safe place to practice living and sharing in the digital world without the danger of anyone knowing you are out there.

But times will change and are changing.

Soon you will want your name out there—and out there in a good and positive way. You won't want someone to search your name and come up with, well, nothing. I am somewhat proud to know how hard it is to study haiku writing and not stumble across my "Top Three Haiku Techniques" website. If someone searches my name, they get the best of me, not the worst of me. I want this for you. I want to keep this with me.

Don't be a drunken Elpenor. Don't dissipate your destiny. Be the kid who reads. Be the kid who explores. Be the kid who builds. Be the kid who thinks. Be the kid who writes. Be everything you are fated to be.

If the seed dies with the flower, no beauty is left behind.

There will be no you.

And you are all you got.

THE FIRE STILL SMOLDERS

Even after the heavy rain
Drenched and scoured
Clean the weathered deck,
Filled clean a silver pot
Left out from dinner,
Soaked through
The patched sweater
My sister knit for me
Some forty years ago—

I wrap myself
In yarns of sheep's wool
Reminding me of everything
Patty always seemed to do—
A perfect sister, shorn asunder
From an imperfect world.

Late into the night,
I toss junk mail
And scraps of two by four's
As perfectly as I can,
Molding a small ring of fire
Lost in empty utterance—

Quiet thoughts.
Votive complaints.
Aged memories

Etched in the pulsating embers
Of when you were here.

A TEACHER'S TERRARIUM

Where you stand depends upon where you sit

To handle yourself, use your head;
to handle others, use your heart.
~Eleanor Roosevelt

I am a small, captive gecko in a large terrarium. I live in the safe and solaced nooks and crannies created for me by others. The temperature and humidity are nigh perfect. The solar bulbs keep my circadian in a rhythm of light and darkness. I know where to scramble to find scraps of larvae and small budworms. There is always fresh water nearby. Yes, there are hard walls I bump into regularly, and every so often some gnarled hand reaches in to add some twigs or even a wet log riven with green moss and several small hollows. Less occasionally, a more reckless hand chases me around the rectangle of my life, but I am quick, wary, and blend seamlessly into the background, and the groping hand soon gives up the chase.

The wizened hand seems to know my reptilian nature and senses my satisfaction to be left alone. If and when I am clutched away, it holds me gently in a pulse of warm blood and tender skin and speaks a soothing language—words I cannot parse into meaning, yet there is a symbiosis of understanding. I am not trapped. Neither am I free. There is a small tear in the screen of my bulkhead. I could easily escape, but I don't. I am not lured by dreams of a greater destiny outside my lair, nor am I ensconced by Fate or betrayed by trust. I am where I am—safe, cared for, nurtured, and appreciated—and despite my primal leanings, I bask in stoic, lizard joy as the hand, and many other hands, answer the call of some noble human duty to keep me alive in the comforting cage of my life.

I am never trapped by the hands of my handlers, even as I grunt and lisp my forked tongue in selfish dissatisfaction at some trifling ignominy bidding me to shed and slough my barky, mottled skin before my fresh armor grows old and dated.

As John Donne wrote, "No man is an island. We are all part of the main." The main is our school, and "we" are the corpuscular cells of blood keeping the heart and soul of our school community alive in a petri dish of competing paradigms, possibilities, and purposes. No one is expendable, yet no change is immutable. We are each the cornerstone of a sturdy castle with a common destiny centered around weepy, elusive dreams, yet our walls will not crumble if any of us disappear into the vaporous ether of life.

We may well be remembered as readily as we are forgotten.

To teach is to be alive and be remembered as a carrier and purveyor of dreams and aspirations. To be an administrator, head, principle, staff, or school board is to distill the dreams and aspirations of teachers into some palatable, healing elixir, not some bitter hemlock condemning the Socrates among us. It is no easy task, and we teachers are a wily prey to subdue, yet our benefactors persist, even as they realize they may well not be remembered. They are the wiring in the walls, the plumbing in the bathrooms, and the new floor in the gym—anonymous conductors on a darkened stage in an empty auditorium.

You are the hands crafting my coddling cage, tempering my moody instincts, and bequeathing magnanimous faith. You trust that I will not gorge the students placed before me into my capacious, hinged jaws.

You are the architects.

We are the scribes droning endless scrolls of papyrus.

We are nothing without your hands nurturing the cages crafted for us, lifting us when dulled, feeding us when hungry, and abandoning us to our peculiar genius.

You are not forgotten.

You are appreciated.

You are remembered.

A NEW JOURNEY

The curse of mediocrity

And I—my head oppressed by horror—said:
"Master, what is it that I hear? Who are
those people so defeated by their pain?"
And he to me: "This miserable way
is taken by the sorry souls of those
who lived without disgrace and without praise.
They now commingle with the coward angels,
The company of those who were not rebels
nor faithful to their God, but stood apart.
The heavens, that their beauty not be lessened,
have cast them out, nor will deep Hell receive them—
even the wicked cannot glory in them.
~Dante Alighieri, *The Inferno*

Because I can imagine myself sailing in a twilight breeze across Pleasant Bay, I will put up with these days of gluing, screwing, painting, varnishing, and rigging my old wooden sailboat. Sometimes I wish I had the money to just buy a boat—a sturdy craft less demanding of my precious hours, but like anything else in life stealing my time, I must figure it is worth it— and it is. I do a lot of other things with my time, but I don't have the same clarity of purpose.

It is a rare moment of quiet in my house. The kids are off with Denise somewhere, and though the grass is absurdly high, the van desperately needs an oil change, and the gutter is hanging by a twisted coat hanger, I sit here and force a few words out of the silent emptiness. A part of me wants to show the folks in my writing communities that I practice what I preach. I face the empty page as a communal discipline. But it is not so simple. I've been doing the same thing for over forty years, seldom with any goal but the action of writing itself. I sometimes wonder if my words are worth the weight of time. I have to trust that it is worth the amount of life stolen from me. I have to trust that some elixir will distill my vat of words into some heady wine to share with neighbors and friends.

Everything I write returns to me obliquely. I've never written for a publication. I have never tried to get anything published, save for a small book of poetry and a couple of recordings of my music and songwriting. I'm a whiz when it comes to writing recommendations, and I can write a decent song or poem for any occasion, but I still can't say I write out of a labor of love or because I have some overarching goal powering my passion. I write because it gives purpose, meaning, and clarity to my life. It stills me when I need to be still. It roils me out of my ignorant slumber when I need to wake and see the light of day. Writing humbles my arrogance and guides me to open my arms and doors when I might otherwise retreat into a self-satisfied shell of complacency. It is worth a long day on the water to be there when the wind and tide beat the way to a new harbor.

But some beast gnaws upon my bones—some murky vision clouds my horizon. I remember reading a line from the journalist Herbert Stein who wrote, "That which is not sustainable cannot continue." I sense this in my writing. Maybe I have fished too long for kibber's in the mill pond. I walk past reams of books in the bookstore and wonder how many of those books were worth writing—or are worth reading. I wonder if there is something greater in me dissipating through my private ramblings and now through my semi-private blogs. Maybe I'm standing too close to the target and need to step back and string the bow Odysseus strung in the suitor's hall. I need to slay the curse of mediocrity and grab the gift of life and match it with the power of words—words swirling in the dark eddies—words bearing down from distant thunderheads and clang and crash a bellowing, dissonant, and alluring cacophony on shifting shores. I need to turn my small boat out of the safe bay, emboldened by what I know. I need to find a further shore.

It is as easy as these words.

THE OLD HUNTER

The snow changed back to freezing rain last night
Bundling itself frozen to bent field grass
Brittling and snapping with harsh pronouncement,
Startling up some young deer, tensing splayed legs
Snorting for acorns under this first snow,
More curioused by me than concerned.
They don't remember the quiet hunter
And his vestigial appendage of clutched bow.
I am an awkward heir to foolish tradition
Wedged stoically in twisted apple crotch,
Drenched in smokey scent and last night's whiskey.
I growl low—a mawkish toothless bear,
And spend my days grubbing for raw tubers;
I sing old songs stuck in my feeble head;
I spread my pungent scent with carelessness,
And pour another cup of bitter coffee
Before taking a nap on soft mosses.
I wake slowly to a low primal stir,
And for a moment, sense our manic bond—
The harsh uncertainty of decisions—
The inextricable predicament
Of dull eyes drawn in each direction;
Until I regain my brute, dumb arrogance,
The smugness of knowing I am not prey.
I only know the whispering woodsman
Who plods these woods with an ineptitude,
Defrocking all of the false dignities—
No longer becoming anything.
I have come so far to know so little—
Satisfied the old buck is still out there.

LIFE IN THE TIME OF COVID

Making do and making better

Sua Sponte—*It is in your hands…*

This…is…just… weird… and me, who never seems at a loss for words, stutters for normality in an unnatural time, but it is only through words, graced by magnanimous and selfless actions, that we can use to carve new paths through uncharted woods. No lesson plan, no "Week in Review," no enlightened curriculum, and no "how-to-video" are readily at hand—only an indefatigable spirit, suffused with stubborn persistence (and an almost intolerable patience), will keep the axe in our hands and keep our lives flailing forward. In time, the path —our unique paths—will open before us and lead us to where we need to go.

As I sit here writing in my journal, I hope you might be doing the same. I imagine ourselves cheek-to-jowl around the big table in our classroom. Some of you are falling off your stools. Some of you are pretending to listen. A rare few of you have finished your work. Your shirttails are out, your shoes are untied, and your hair (and mine) looks like you stuck your tongue in an electrical socket.

But none of this matters.

Right now, I would give the world for some reason to find something wrong in what you have done—you didn't put a comma after the conjunctive adverb; your essay lacks a unifying theme; it is obvious you didn't read "Chapter Six" in *The Call of the Wild*, nor can you name the one-eyed monster in *The Odyssey*. You can't comprehend my overuse of semicolons, and heck, you don't even know what the word "obfuscate" means.

Our old reality is now a blessing. Our new reality seems a curse cast upon us by a malevolent beast. At this cusp of time, you are supposed to be on some warm beach with your family, or falling knee deep in powdered snow, or hanging out at the playground with your friends, or simply chilling at home on your much-deserved spring break—and what a break it is—a break from what is normal and a time to start something new with wisdom and fortitude—with as much humor and faith as you can muster, kindled with more kindness than you ever dreamed possible. I can't say to go to the malls, streets, and corridors or to get out and roam and do something with your friends, but I can say, *go within and find your inner strengths*.

Nurture time with your family. Reach out to anyone and everyone who needs company. Our hardships pale beside the hardships of others. I never thought I'd say this, but pick up your phone and text grandma; download Zoom or Twitch and invite your brother to chat with your friends; clean the house without being asked. Learn what the buttons on the dishwasher do.

Open the dryer door and fold your own clothes.

Don't ask. Do. Be understanding.

Richen yourself. Read a classic book. Read a junky novel. Create a podcast. Write. Write some more. Maybe even edit what you write. (What an enlightening concept!) Post to your blog, comment on your classmates' blogs, and engage the community we have. If little else, we are stuck with the gift of time—an unfolding serendipity to write in our journals, flesh out some poems, and finally complete my stupid writing exercises. Really, just do what you always do as classmates, soulmates, and comrades. When you are done, go into your yard, turn some soil over, and prepare a garden—literally and figuratively. If you have no yard, fill a bucket with moldy soil and plant a perfect seed.

Know that in every nanosecond of time, you are loved...

Don't wait to live a fuller life. Live your life in every way possible. We are not imprisoned. We are not condemned to dank cells. We are home and engaged in an untimely battle against Fate, and we are simply doing what needs to be done. Live within. Stay home. Follow the curve of your genius—and yes, again, give a damn and figure it out.

Cut your new path today.

We may be out of class, but we will never be outclassed.

Every moment is a quiz. Every day is a test. Your grade is the degree to which you live. Your diploma is the life you live. Your destiny forms itself. Mark Twain once wrote, "Don't let school get in the way of your education," so seize this weird day—this weird time of COVID—and learn stuff, make stuff, create stuff, and do stuff you never dreamed possible, and trust me, if you don't, I plan to bother the hell out of you all spring (which I plan to do anyway).

After break, of course.

Now is for you.

GEORGE WRITES HIS ESSAY

Just do it

So long as you write what you wish to write,
it is all that matters...
~Virginia Woolf

Why am I the poor smuck saddled with a teacher who insists we find meaning and metaphor in everything we read? Like *The Odyssey*: I mean, the book is full of random everything's; like just when Odysseus starts to figure something out (and I have a half a clue what is going on), he breaks off into some wild story with a hundred new characters.

"Oh," says my teacher, "this is an empowering literary technique that builds the scope and sweep of the poem. It is the hallmark of an epic literary work." If so, then I have a crazy old uncle—a guy who never knows when to stop talking—who is probably a direct descendant of Homer. Yeah, from now on, I'll call him "Uncle Epic." The only reason I half like the book is because I actually believe I'm supposed to like it—or at least appreciate it.

I can't imagine every fuddy-duddy English teacher for the last three thousand years or so being wrong. Maybe they've all been hypnotized by the Siren's song of conformity.

I liked that part of the book: Odysseus getting his crew to lash him to the mast so he could hear the Siren's song, but still not doing something stupid like getting lured away by the Siren herself. "Stairway to Heaven" probably had the same effect in the 1970s when it first came out.

Jeez, I'm as bad as Homer. Listen to me getting off track. And I shouldn't get off track because this foolish essay is only one of six assignments over the weekend.

SIX!

Oh-my-god... There was that six-headed monster in the book, too. So life does imitate art. I'll keep repeating to myself, "It's only an epic; it's only an epic..." And if I don't do my homework, then I'll probably have to work in the yard. Oh no! That's simply a metaphor for the whirlpool sucking in Odysseus' ship.

How does a kid find his way in life? Monsters on the right, whirlpools on the left, and so many vain gods plotting to make my day miserable...

My teachers think they are gods sometimes. Oh, for one bright-eyed Athena of a teacher to understand...

Dear Gods, I fear I will probably fail this essay because I'm using the "I" in my "voice!" Not to worry. I'll just rant and rage and think and write, then I'll go back and change everything to the third person—you know, the guy we never really get to meet.

Really, it's like going on a date with a mannequin.

Somewhere in here is my thesis statement. I hope my teacher finds it. I hope I find it. I wonder if I just write what I know he wants to hear, he'll go easy on me.

It works, you know; I tried it once.

Actually, I just looked, and I couldn't find my thesis statement. But if he has read this far and has not flunked me, then maybe he'll read some more. That would be kind of fun. Write something that looks like it is leading him somewhere wicked profound, and then say, "April Fools" at the end.

I wonder if my teacher would find meaning and metaphor in that?

I love these short paragraphs. I'm already well over the minimum of five paragraphs. I really wonder who the first teacher was who ever coined the term "Five Paragraph Essay." There's probably a statue somewhere. Ha, and the statue holds a copy of *The Odyssey* in one hand and a gradebook in the other. LOL :)

Okay. Here goes:

The Odyssey survives not because of what it is, but because of who it is.

Figure that out for yourself, my dear teacher—my nautically inclined teacher who, at this very moment, is leaving to visit the New Bedford Whaling Museum for a day of much-needed rest and relaxation while we slave like oarsmen in a tempest over his stupid assignment.

I'm done now, I think.

P.S. Please don't grade this.

I HAVE BEEN HERE BEFORE

Trying to pull the day
Back into the night, executing
Some stay of time,
Some way to wrap
The soft fabric of Summer
Around the balky,
Frame of Fall, sloughing
My skin, unable to stop
This reptilian ecdysis—
This hideous morphing
Into respectability.
My students,
Tame as lab mice,
Won't understand
My unblinking eyes,
The hissing of my speech,
The expansive hinge of my jaw
Or my insatiable appetite `
Until I swallow them whole, swelling
My elongating belly, feasting
On their impeccable,
Transient joy.

I AM YOU, AND YOU ARE ME...

Give a damn & figure it out

In the end you just have to give a god-damn. Just get out on the mat and show us you care. It is all that matters.
~Christian Bilodeau, *CCHS Wrestling Coach*

Right now, I feel like one of my students. It is the night before my big presentation at the all-school meeting, and I still do not know what I am going to talk about. I just know I am supposed to talk about me.

It's pretty scary because, well, I'm me. At any given time, I know myself too well, and at other times, I'm like, "Who is this guy?"

I'm the guy whose socks probably don't match, and one of my socks is inside-out. I'm the guy whose engine warning light in my van was probably on the whole way to school—and I never noticed. I'm the guy who forgot to post an assignment online, and his students are plotting a revolution and mass protest.

I'm the guy who tries to be a teacher, and so he is.

So, how does one start something like this?

I am John Fitzsimmons.... Let me tell you about me.

No... Too vain and presumptuous.

Hi, I'm Fitz, and I may be old, but I'm slow.
No... You are not here to hear the truth.

Hi, I am Mr. Fitzsimmons, your new teacher. I just flew in from Chicago, and boy, my arms are tired.
(Nope... That was only funny forty years ago.

Hi... I am so glad to be here. Last night I went to a fight, and a hockey game broke out.

But if you know me, you have heard this all before.

I'm the kid who got grounded if I ever got a B for a grade—because my mother would think I cheated...

I'm the kid who went to Peabody, Sanborn, and CCHS and who warns all of you going to CCHS next year to wear thick-soled boots to school, so you don't cut your feet on the broken hearts I left behind. Not really, because I'm really the shy kid who spent an entire summer after 8th grade trying to find the courage to hold Megan Tassini's hand—and I never did.

I'm the kid who spent entire dances lurking in the corner of the Hunt Gym, fearing "Stairway to Heaven" would start and a whole night would go by—and I didn't ask a anyone to dance.

I'm the kid whose father spray painted his sister's figure skates black and told me everyone would think they were hockey skates, and then after the miserable, frozen game, I'd walk home in the dark from Greenes Pond, down Plainfield Road, to 38 Longfellow Road, still wearing my black figure skates. I mean hockey skates

I lived in and on and through Greene's Pond, White's Pond, Walden Pond, Warner's Pond—the Concord River, the Assabet River, and the Sudbury River. I was fish and fisherman, sailor and yachtsman, landmark and explorer—all within this beautiful, precious, magnificent expanse of earth called Concord.

I was an ADD wonder child whose eyes could dart in a thousand directions in a single glance, whose head was built out of dreams, and who made sunburned skin a living, breathing whirl and endless dance of motion and adventure. I was you, and you are me, and our lives are inextricably linked in this adventure called life. We know nothing gold can stay, so we breathe in the best of each day and never let it out.

I was a wrestler and am now a wrestling coach. The coach whose only wise words to a wrestler heading out on the mat against a Goliath of a monster—a skinny kid from Fenn facing certain annihilation—to whom I shrug and say, "Do one good thing. Do one good thing and accept defeat with a smile, for you don't learn much from winning, but you learn a lot by trying."

I was a reluctant, timid student, and now I am a teacher.

Go figure...

Maybe this is why I drive you crazy with answers that are not really answers. I respond to simple questions with things like, "Get through it; get over it." "Give a damn and figure it out." "It is your essay, not mine." "Make it as long as it should be and as short as it can be." "Give me a pebble, and I'll show you the universe; show me the universe, and I'll give you a pebble." "It is not where you go; it is how you go." "Good writers don't always make good poets—but good poets always make for great writers," and ad-nauseous, "Don't mistake the finger pointing at the moon for the moon itself." My list goes on and on because a juicy response is better than a dry answer. I ask myself the same question every day: "*Who am I, and what should I try to be?*"

This is how my life is shaped and formed, sculpted and forged out of the fire of my mind—a fire as bright and intense as when I was you—you who are probably dreaming and scheming of what is possible as soon as the old guy finishes his presentation and you can go off to recess.

After sixty-five years on this planet, I return to the same question: "What then am I?" In short, I am a poet—everything else is tentacles on the octopus of my life. So I am also a folksinger, a songwriter, a tinkerer, and a maker of meatballs. I'm a father to seven wild and unadorned children and a husband to a beautiful and forbearing wife. I am everything I ever hoped I could be, and far short of where I still can be—and could be.

I am you, and you are me.

I love teaching, but I equally love the coming summer as much as any of you, for summer—blessed summer, nectar of every teacher and every student—gives me the time to live in the woods of a rustic summer camp in New Hampshire—to swim, fish, sail, and hike; to write in my beloved journal; and to sing at campfires with piles of weathered, mosquito-bitten kids bunched like starfish on a beach, singing their heads off—even though technically starfish don't have heads.

But you do. So use it.

Build it from scratch if you have to.

If you still have a head...

APPROACHING POETRY

The admonitions of a poet

*Publishing a volume of verse is like dropping
a rose-petal down the Grand Canyon
and waiting for the echo.*
~Don Marquis

In my perfect dream I want to be called a poet, for poetry is the most elevated art, and apart from my love for Denise and our children, it is the closest I come to touching the hand of the truest and most present God. Perhaps to a person unmarked by any sort of poetic ardor my statement reeks of intellectual arrogance and conceit, but to me it is as simple as real love.

It is what it is. It can never be a point of discussion.

Those of us who aspire to be poets will always be left on the sidelines. My tragic flaw is to recognize true greatness in poetry. I am astute enough to see with some depth of vision through the swath of mediocrity academics and effete sophists pass off as poetry, but I still cannot compose verse reaching the grandeur of what I know to be true poetry. Even now, over forty years into my journey as an aspiring poet, I feel like a kid swapping shots with Larry Bird at the free-throw line. All I can offer him is a a rattling rim, an elusive hoop and my smothering, child-like passion for the game.

Poetry is beguiling and bewildering—not here and not there, and so it is vexing and futile to pin poetry on the mat of parchment, except to say, "I know it when I see it." When I was first out of high school and wandering the back roads and railways of the country, I was convinced poetry could only be the unfettered, unedited expression of who and what I was at any given point in time. I practiced a rambling, unexpurgated style of poetry—a style mimicking the freedom I embraced for the first time in my predictable life. I filled notebook after notebook with long-winded rants and rambles. I was convinced my every word was too precious to alter or edit in any way. I hitchhiked through every state in the west. I wrote in the back of pickup trucks, along the sides of back roads and interstates. I sat by lonely flames of sterno cans in makeshift camps and hasty bivouacs. I may not have created remarkable poetry—but I payed my tithe to the archaic muse.

I carried more books than luggage. I read with a passion I never thought possible. I wrote constantly. I emptied my heart and soul and being as if it was my last gift to humanity. In my first dawdling steps, I was too timid to share my poetry with anybody. I couldn't let go of my old self completely. I couldn't reconcile the simple Concord townie barely scraping through high school with the searching vagabond now weeping with Odysseus by his ancient campfires. Odysseus had an Ithaca he longed for and fought to restore. My kingdom was yet to be made, much less found.

My panoply of Gods were the poets who lived, breathed, wrote, and spoke before me—poets who tormented me, mentored me, castigated me and inspired my convoluted odyssey towards a greater kingdom—a castled, sprawling garden where poetry lives and breathes in an endless reign of jostling provocateurs.

Aside from intuition, I had no idea where or how to start writing poetry. I was not even sure why I wanted to write poetry. It was as if I picked up a rough gem from the side of the road and recognized the stone was not an ordinary stone—and so my first poems were rough, reactive and rambling. I was both hunter and prey searching for and escaping from my wily, elusive self. Constantly transforming, I shifted between stout brevity and rambling anthems. I thrashed like a drowning man entangled in an entangling web of porous net—panicked and gasping for rarified air—yet still manic and joyful for life. I cursed my teachers for not preparing me for this maelstrom, and I thanked them for leaving me untainted.

My new syllabus became the open road and whatever books were handed to me by fellow travelers and lost saints who picked me up off the side-roads and interstate on-ramps. These itinerant scholars bequeathed to me the best of what they had, and I gave them back a naivety resembling genuineness. They sensed I did not want to just read. I wanted to be transfixed, enlightened and resurrected.

These wandering pilgrims filled my backpack with the giants of the beat generation—Kerouac, Miller, Proust, Ginsberg, Snyder, Brautigan, and Ferlinghetti. Older couples gave me Shelley, Wordsworth, Dickinson, Whitman, and Yeats. In my nostalgia for my hometown of Concord, I picked up a copy of *"Walden"* and some selected essays of Emerson. Whatever writer I was reading, I imitated in my writing. I was not as interested in *what* they wrote, but in *how* they wrote. It didn't matter I was not a great poet. I was happy to live like a poet—a lesson that never escaped from my grasp.

Time and experience are relative. I grew like weeds in the night. I learned to trust myself. I learned to be myself and accept myself. I eschewed Fate and charted a new destiny—an unwavering tack sailing to a richer shore. My past became my now. My present begot tomorrow, and my future sailed to a distant horizon. I realized poetry has to be real and spring from an examined life. I accepted that poetry must recognize the beauty and majesty of the most common of images and actions, and it must be crafted and constructed in endless rhythm and cadence—not cast like wild seed, sometimes laboriously. Labor is the life of a poet, for the poet and the hunter, a bird in the hand is worth two in the bush, but only the poet captures the bird just to set it free. Only the poet smiles as the bird soars from the hand. Only a true poet smiles at anonymity.

The words have to be enough.

Out of the hundreds of thousands of words in our language only a few can make it on to the page, and fewer still can rightly be called a poem. Every moment is an opportunity lost or gained. The person who does not recognize this urgency is not a poet.

This sea of sand is your starting point.

If you want to be a poet, live like one.

TONIGHT THE PANOPLY OF STARS

Mirror into the water of Black Pond.
My old canoe drifts slowly.
I cross galaxies in bold sweeps.
Somewhere in the swirl
Of a long, slow stroke
Andromeda is caught
Drifting in galactic passion
To mesh and mate
With our pebbled Milky Way.

"It is not as hard as you think," I say,
"To reach the polestar trapped near the boulder
On the south side of Blueberry Island;
If we have the time—and I'm sure we do—
Orion's Belt is just under the pines
Not far from the Herman's mossy, old lean-to."

Denise, in silent beatitude,
Is not in the mood
For my florid words
Dallying in mystic speculation.
Whatever bardic
Inspiration left behind
Is bored to death
By yesterdays poem
About an old stone wall
And an orange salamander
Caught resting
In soft moss.

Silence is the only tool
Left to cleave meaning
And parse the palpable
From the night sky.
Her world is a borrowed plank
drifting slowly into the universe—
A wondrous point

Balanced between two worlds—
A strange juncture
Where reality and perception,
Earth and water, air and sky enmesh.

Visceral. Palpable. Ethereal.

On this dark, glistening skin
We are immeasurably alone—
Old swans in a long, enduring marriage
Inextricably bound in Fate, Faith & Fortitude.

She weaves a wake into the lee
South of Wadiko Island
And traces the arc
Of a shooting star
Burning to the west.

She turns quietly towards the Pleiades.

I watch her lift into the night sky
And cup my hands
Into the cold water
To assure myself
This is illusion—

Not real.
Not real.
Not real.

I thrash the dark water
Into a frothy, manic sea.
I rip apart the silence—

I…
You..
Love…

To see if she returns.

NO ONE CARES ABOUT YOU

It is in your hands

Freedom (n.): To ask nothing. To expect nothing.
To depend on nothing."
~Ayn Rand, *The Fountainhead*

Really. One more time: You are a writer, and no one cares about you. OK, your parents care; your grandparents care, and probably a few friends; and maybe a teacher or two, or a coach if you are freakishly good at some sport; but as a percentage of the world population, you are in a pretty lonely spot.

It is you against, like, six billion or so.

The dilemma of a writer is how to get a chunk of that six billion—the 750 million speakers of the English language—to want to read what you have written. Luckily, it is easier than you think. When everything else is stripped away, we are pretty much the same as each of those 750 million and equally so with the rest of the six billion. We cry when we are hurt. We laugh when amused. We seethe when maddened and smile when gladdened. We search for the perfect mate, friend, or mentor; we live for each other, and we die for each other. We recognize greatness in large actions and small gestures. We seek and nurture love in an infinite variety of ways; in short, our flesh and blood and heart and soul are our communal bond, and if you can tap into a shared communal bond, the hardest part of your journey as a writer is over. The next challenge is to tell your story—and tell it well. Do not tap out of the match just because it is hard to write well. It is hard to do a lot of things well.

But unless we are fools, we still try.

If you want to be a writer, your writing must battle against the reality of being a writer.

All a writer needs to succeed is to somehow convince a reader to want to read the next line..., and the next... until that final moment—that final word shuttering the page with a sacred appreciation of the moment. If you succeed in even some paltry way, you can ignore just about everything I have ever preached to you about writing. Heck, I will learn from you, for no writer worth their salt reads without wondering how or why a piece of writing works or doesn't work. No writer with a vested interest in creating good writing reads without some part of their psyche focused on the craftsmanship involved in a piece of writing.

Writers are builders walking into a way-cool building. Writers notice more than the beauty of the architecture—they peruse and parse the strength of the foundation. They study the intricacies of construction and define the balance of purpose and effect. They examine the form and structure and ask if the building fulfills the promise of the architect and if it will meet the expectations of the buyer. The builder then proceeds to weave what they learned into a new building attractive to a buyer, a reader, and maybe even a follower—or 750 million followers.

Engaging a reader is pretty much what writing is all about—to witness and reflect—to write, read, learn, practice, and figure out how to become a better writer. Figure out how to play the common chords and scales of life in a new and vital way, and draw a curious ear to the song you sing. The ironic journey of a writer is to create in solitude what is reflected in solitude, yet gifted and regifted to a larger community of readers seeking to improve their own lives—or even just a given space of time in their lives—but not necessarily your life.

So, yeah, no one really cares about you, especially as a writer. But you have to care about your readers. And that's the rub—to fully know our readers, we have to fully know ourselves. Writer's block is just emotional and intellectual avoidance of ourselves. Like, "Whoa, I really do not want to go there." But if you give a damn, you do go there. If you do it well, readers will beat a path to the door of your page—and they might even come back to your page again to bask and linger in your words.

And that's pretty cool.

It would be for me, anyway.

Right now, I should be grading the essays you wrote over the weekend, but honestly, you should be the ones grading your own essays. What I want from your writing should pale beside what you want from your writing. It is the grade only you can give—and should give. A reader craves a burning desire to read more of your splay of words. When or if they want more, there is money to be made, or, as in many artistic ventures, when there is no money to be made, you will at least be appreciated as a craftsman who practices the chops of writing.

Though I am no great shakes as an artist, I do appreciate being your teacher, but as Buddha says (and I repeat too often), "Don't mistake the finger pointing at the moon for the moon itself." You can learn from me, but I can't help you grow a greater prowess. Your stammering growth and potential are up to you. Writing is a tough wrestling match between the reader and the writer. Sense your imperfection and probe for perfection. Give a damn and perfect your craft.

It is you against them. Losers never win.

Tap in to your reader.

Don't tap out.

JOHN ADAMS & ME

The detritus and the bounty

To be good, and to do good, is all we have to do.
~John Adams

From the deck of my sister Mary Ellen's house in Manzanita on the Oregon coast, I watch breakers lumbering under and through a heavy morning fog slowly burning away. In true west-coast style, I brew a coffee strong and pungent enough to guide me through my own morning fog. Until late last night, I read David McCullough's book, *John Adams*. John Adams is an intriguing character with whom I feel a marked affinity at every turn in the book—a book with way too many turns. Maybe it is my distance from New England that creates this affinity. Maybe some new crevice in my brain unlocked a dormant self. I am certainly not a political person, but I relate to Adam's need for and dedication to his family, his love of walking the countryside, and his practical working of the earth closest to him—an earth replete with stone walls, fields, orchards, rivers, wood splitting, and escapes to the sea—but, more importantly, his escape to "quill and paper" to better expose his vanities and define his commonality. Adams found a pathway to express his speculative and probing thinking. Though he often lived low, he always aimed high.

I wrestle the same demon and angel every day.

With summer almost over, there is as much undone as done. I am a fickle waterbug, skittering across a great expanse of time and water without ever breaking the surface to exploit the riches below. There is no new batch of songs, no folio of poetry, and precious few chapters in *Hallows Lake*, my own—and only—labored attempt at fiction. I console myself with ten or twelve decent essays and narratives written in support of the writing communities I oversee during the summer months, but not much creative work, which, ironically, is the strongest suit in my deck of writing cards. Writing is still time stolen from the day and not the purpose of the day itself. My own purposes and instinctual priorities, like Adams, are the myriad responsibilities of the lifestyle I lead, but Adams took his life further, wider, and deeper.

As a public figure, Adams was prodded and coerced by the dictates of a needy public and the enormity of the political upheavals of his time. I am inspired by a vague sense of my potential and a mysterious dream to put words to the narrow confines of my experiences and my sense of the world closest to me. At this juncture in my life, I wonder if this is enough. I wonder if I need to put myself on a larger stage and summon the courage to place my life in front of a larger audience and let the chips fall where they may.

A week from today, I will be back in the classroom in front of sixty fourteen-year-old boys—boys I must somehow inspire to give a damn about everything I ask them to do. My looming monologues must be reinforced by a model of hope and action. Too often we teach what we do not undertake ourselves; too often we only build a scale model of our true greatness out of brittle plastic and weak glue, weakening and cracking over time; and too often we shun the clarion incantations of our singular callings. We sit smug and satisfied within the diluted reality of our lives, lolling and wallowing in stilted predictability.

What we think is only made real through what we say, write and do. The waves rolling onto the shore in front of me are barely perceptible to the trawlers fishing out of Nehalem Bay. The power of the water is only evident where it breaks and crashes onto the beach. No one in Manzanita is content to look beyond the horizon. We are here because the sea meets the land in a continual, foaming expectation of wind-worn beauty and awe-inspiring power. We walk the beaches in search of the detritus and bounty of the sea. If the roiling sea gives us nothing —if we are not convinced there is not more to be had here than from the confines of our own yards—we better had stayed at home and gathered the glory of our own paltry gardens.

I must set to sea and trawl the infinite stew of what I carry within me. I have to take myself to where words cusp and curl onto a more public shore. I need to take my garden to the sea, spread my wares upon the waves, and let the beachcombers gather what they wish to keep.

It is not the history of John Adams that I am after.

It is his bold, unflinching spirit.

GAMBLING WITH MAJO

Are these bobbling heads
Just gnarled stumps
Floating on brackish water
In Baggerdoff's swamp
On this cool August morning?

Or are they lazy sapos—
Toads resting in swirls
Of morning mist,
Sipping swampy air
Waiting to slurp
Some wayward fly
With a sticky tongue?

Yesterday we stared
With perplexed uncertainty—

Stick-ends? Maybe toads?
Or grumpy Rana toros—bullfrogs
Waiting for some fat,
Warty mate to froth up
The dark, steeped
Swamp-water?

"Sapos," you mulled
In your perfect
Columbian Spanish.

So sapos they are.

Today we are old hands
And cobble a new ritual—
A jackpot guessing game
To notch our time
During morning hikes
Down the rutted road
Of Campbells Gore.

Savvy seers and and shamans
We peer thoughtfully
Counting the sapos
Floating idly
Among lily pads.

You say, "Seise."
I say, "Ocho."

I steady myself
On a mossy ledge.
And summon a gambler's prayer.

I tap the water gently
With my walking stick.
The sapos leap, dart and dive
In a splay of circles.

"Damn! Only seven!"
"Siete!" you laugh.

We are an odd pair—
An old New England Yankee
Farmer of words, hobbling
Behind a young, spry and wise
South American woman.

We walk on down the trail
With silent, disparate thoughts—

I wonder how
I could be so wrong
In a game I should win?

You simply ask, "Where
Do the Sapos sleep?"

YOUR PARENTS ARE PETRIFIED

A lingering distrust

I'm at my most hypocritical when telling my kids
they've had enough screen time.
~@thedad

Yes, your parents are petrified. Your iPad and phone screens are the constant and continual portal through which you live your lives. It is not like the old days when we looked in our backyards and saw with clear eyes exactly what our kids were doing. When our kids were in the house, we saw what they watched. When they answered the phone, we knew who they were talking with and what plans were being hatched. We knew what book they were reading, what game they connived to play with seedy friends, and the trajectory of their messy inclinations.

It was, simply put, easier to know what our kids did with their lives.

But to you—my cunning class of 8th grade boys cutting the edges of a new age—everything—as in everything—is based on trust in the unknowing uncertainty of murky technology. I live it every day with my own kids, and as much as I trust them, I am also petrified at what is going on behind the screen for so many hours of the day and night. I am also increasingly wary of my own role as a teacher in a paperless classroom, a careless, unwitting Frankenstein creating a petri dish of demonic possibilities with every assignment.

I give you the same amazing tool I am hammering on right now. I trust you have the wisdom and discretion to use this tool efficiently and productively to complete my endless assignments. At the same time, I enable you to flip between the worlds of WeChat, YouTube, Instagram, iMessage, and any one of a million different games, chat rooms, and websites that live and breathe and entice you away from the heart and soul of my intent and what you should be doing.

Sometimes I feel like an ignorant Samaritan pawning hard liquor on an incorrigible drunk.

My plea is simple: Do not drink the wine of distraction in some dark corner of your room. Don't build a virtual wall between you and your family. Don't take a tool and turn it into a toy. And don't get all pissy when someone questions why you are spending every hour from dinner to bedtime pecking away on a piece of glass.

I get it. You are sullen students saddled with an enormous crush of homework; you can multi-task with the best of them, and, you probably say with exasperation, you are just doing what everyone else is doing.

And you get done everything you are asked to do.

So what's the big deal?

The big deal is not what you are doing; it is what you are not doing. Thoreau once wrote, "You can't kill time without wounding eternity." Hours upon hours on a screen are hours and hours of time wounding the greater eternity and arc of your life. It is time subtracted from the greater possibilities of a real, vibrant, and active existence during a magical and mythical time in your fledgling lives. You are not engaged with those closest to you and who love you with every fiber and sinew of their being. You don't look up when someone shouts, "Dinner is ready." You are not outside on the brightest and best of days. You are not hanging out with friends on beaches, hillsides, and riverbanks.

You are a flaccid lump of visceral fat on a soft couch.

You are immersed in an entropy of your own undoing. You listen to music instead of learning to play music. You read posts on your wall instead of reading good books. Your bike rusts in the rain, and your brain rusts in its shell. You do not get lost in the woods or grapple frogs in the streams. Your skin is uncut, and your hands are continually soft. A bird in the sky is just a bird in the sky. A tree is just a tree. You cannot call any of them out by name. You hide from the natural world of flesh and blood and spontaneous, joyous play and unfettered exploration.

Your iPad wakes you, and your iPad lulls you to sleep.

You are, in fact, asleep.

It is from this torpor that you must wake up and begin to live life like a man, or at least as a boy. Don't go gentle into that good night. Your parents should be petrified if your tree fort is too high, you are riding your bike too fast, the waves are too massive, or the axe is too sharp. Make them wish they raised a quiet and sedate son who is a bit of a homebody. Make them wish you hadn't come home when the streetlights went on. Make them regret not knowing what mountain you chose to climb. Make them a son who fixes things and figures things out. Make them a son who lives life with passion, daring, and uncommon wisdom. Make them a son who will look back on his childhood and have his breath taken away by the reckless energy and utter audacity of his youth.

Put down your iPad after your work is done.

Do something real.

Give a damn about your life.

It is the only one you got.

THE UNMOVED MOVER

A lesson in gravity

Reason is in fact the path to faith, and faith takes over when reason can say no more.
~Thomas Merton

I am not done with God, nor is God done with me. I remain obsessed with the notion of an unmoved mover—the whatever or whomever set the pattern of creation into its initial motion. I stubbornly trace my existence back to some infinite beginning—so much so that I loathe the deficiencies and inconsistencies of my intellect, which, in the end, I always cast aside, for I can't help but fall into a wondrous rapture before the miracle of life and the turnings and meanderings of my heart, soul, mind, and being.

We are trapped in time and limited by its confines, and so my search for Faith or Fate is hobbled by the simple handicap of being alive, and though I struggle with Faith and disregard Fate, I am in awe of any true search for explanation amidst the inexplicable. I know my God is embraced, denied, manufactured, and packaged in the fickle streams of my thoughts, which is why and how I distrust the leanings of my head—for as the tree leans, the tree falls. All I can do is dig among the inexorable to discern what is effable and real amidst visions and imaginings construed from undeniable fact.

As I write this, a monstrous nor'easter is screaming over Cape Cod. Swirling snow and howling winds tear at the fabric of trees, beaches, waters, and the very air itself with a persistent and insistent voice calling attention to itself—and to me—to live within the storm and within the cloud of unknowing. There is nothing to know, nothing to parse with words, and nothing to gain from argument or sophistry. God can only be the truth without truth, the reality without substance, the nameless name before the gaping maw of the universe.

I trust God moves within our noblest actions and equally within the baseness of our greatest transgressions. Out of this stew—this holy mixing with the unholy—grace is distilled, a grace that feeds, guides, and sustains us through the daunting, heroic odyssey of our lives. We need to be persistent and stubborn and remove ourselves from ourselves. We must consciously and deliberately extricate our tangled limbs from the muddy morass binding us to ignorance, defeat, and despair. We need to move forward into the blinding miracle of life—even as we are strapped and clasped to its binding chains.

We are born to live. Death does not set us free. Life sets us free, so we can die free with some semblance of palpable holiness clinging to our bones in spite of whatever vagaries beset our lives.

Faith is the proverbial beggar's banquet—the promise of a feast never making it to the table. Still, I wait, brood, celebrate, and live on in this wild arc of existence within an endless prayer.

Gravity tells me I am not in heaven.

But I am damn close.

Amen.

AFTER EIGHTEEN YEARS

I hear the cuckoo clock chiming midnight
From its perch in a cluttered kitchen
Locked in cadence with the tower bell

Gonging this old mill-town at midnight
To a deeper sleep
In a votive call to vespers

Reminding me this new day
Starting in the dark of a hallowed night
Is more than just an ordinary day

Stirring in palpable realness
Your soft breathing beside me
Mixing with crickets and peepers

Calling out into the darkness
Searching for a dream
Fit to be called a true marriage

Our gift constantly opening
Reveal a mystery and majesty
Larger than the box itself

Stunning in the simplicity
Of renewed remembered
Resplendent love.

WRITING A SONG

Nothing Ventured. Nothing Gained.

The song and the drumming were like this: Behold, a sacred voice is calling you; All over the sky a sacred voice is calling.
~Black Elk, *Black Elk Speaks*

Writing a song is not just an exercise in seeking some kind of future fame. It is an exercise in making your indelible mark upon the world—a setting in stone of a harp-string before eternity—patterns of rhythms, notes, and chords capturing an infinitely unique sound, sense, and sensibility —a hardened imprint against the ravages of time of who and what you are and what you aspire to leave behind. Songwriting is not rocket science. It is a craft to take you farther down the wending streams of being a writer and further into the realms of possibilities of wordcrafting and creation. Writing song stands alongside poetry and prayer as the nearest thing to perfection in words. Writing a song is a hammering and shaping of the malleable into an uncrushable icon of our being. Though created by us, a song is born and released into the greater world as a gift parceled from our fleeting time on this planet.

The interplay of words and music is a ringing magic that leaves us astonished—sometimes for reasons beyond our understanding. Few people are unmoved by music, and it is a sad and cynical teacher of writing who does not lay bare the underpinnings of song and set free the genius of their students by providing the time and place to create what is undeniably the most universal of our needs because we—the great "we" of humanity—need, want, and crave music. We always have and always will, but what makes a band of notes into a memorable riff or an ineffable tune we whistle in our idle moments during redundant labors or in long aimless wanderings? What gives to make what survives and what stubbornly lives on within us?

What makes one song survive and the other song die?

Music is, if anything else, an alluring mystery within a stubborn conundrum.

I am no scholar of music, yet my life is a university of song. On nearly every wall in every room in our house hangs an instrument begging to be played—guitars in different tunings, banjos in different shapes and sizes, two or three mandolins, and a smattering of ukuleles—and an old upright piano with ivory keys darkened and swabbed by decades of pounding and tinkling under my children's more deft fingers. Each instrument, at some point or another, proffers a promise of celebration, solace, or experimentation.

As Plato said in an ancient time:

> *Every heart sings a song, incomplete, until another heart whispers back. Those who wish to sing will always find a song.*

Sometimes songs elevate words into the sublime. Sometimes songs need no words—and perhaps suffer more greatly with words. Sometimes songs tap out an inexorable repetitive rhythm, beating out the heartbeats of an inner life and an alluring primordial yearning. Despite the source, every song lives because the music endures. Every song endures because music fills the void of silence with an inimitable passion that lifts our souls above the passage of time.

There is no music greater than any other music. There is only music cleaving and molding itself to our dispositions, inclinations, and aspirations. Music echoes what our hearts desire. My old folk songs are no better or worse than Beethoven's Ninth Symphony. The chants of a Gregorian choir might pale beside my friend Maroghini tapping his goatskin drum deep in a Jamaican forest, gently hammering 'bah-boom, bah boom'— chanting "Do good. Do good" over and over until goodness transforms into the actions and purpose of his life.

And then he will turn to me with a wry smile and say, "Sing me a Willie Nelson song."

Love what you love, and you will learn the patterns of your destiny. Gang and gong the spirit of what is you, but do not be a slave to your inbred prejudices. Tune your heart to what seems despicable and find the beauty within the cultural discord. What is cacophony to one is the unbound universe singing to another.

Only then can you say you love music.

No day is darkened by music. No mean and miserable life is cheapened by composing songs. No bird is silenced in the breaking dawn.

Set aside these words.

Whistle your tune.

THE PHOENIX

But every five-hundred years, when it grows weak,
It returns and builds a nest with fragrant herbs.
It sings to the sun again and is surrounded by flames.
And each time it rises from its ashes young and strong...
~Ancient Greek Myth

Rising from the ashes is one of the most enduring metaphors of humanity. The hope of transformation gives us the strength to crawl in the mud and squalor, melding with a moiled and diminished life. The animal shivers in her den in expectation of spring, but only we are empowered to create a new spring within ourselves, and only we can share in the miracle of creation through a simple act of will. This is the magic of our lives—we do and undo all we've wrought on ourselves and others.

We pledge ourselves to each other simply by saying, "I do." We change course with astounding ease, but only if we break the shackles binding us to beaten ground and only if we stop pushing unwieldy stones before us, all the while dragging a cumbersome sack of regret behind us.

We never fully open our eyes.

We are content to live vicariously in a half-light—a purgatory lulled between sleep and wakefulness. In this groggy hades, we chew on the bones of the day.

Half-starved, we look upward and bleakly remember the story of the Phoenix.

We remember the Phoenix, not for everything it did, but for the *one thing* it did.

Do that one thing.

THANKSGIVING

I am surprised sometimes
By the suddenness of November:
Beauty abruptly shed
To a common nakedness—
Grasses deadened
By hoarfrost,
Persistent memories
Of people I've lost.

It is left to those of us
Dressed in the hard
Barky skin of experience
To insist on a decorum
Rising to the greatness
Of a true Thanksgiving.

This is not a game,
Against a badly scheduled team,
An uneven match on an uneven pitch.

This is Life.
This is Life.
This is Life.

Not politely mumbled phrases,
Murmured with practiced,
Meticulous earnestness.

Thanksgiving was born a breech-birth,
A screaming appreciation for being alive—
For not being one of the many
Who didn't make it—
Who couldn't moil through
Another hardscrabble year
On tubers and scarce fowl.

Thanksgiving is for being you.

There are no thanks without you.

You are the power of hopeful promise;
You are the balky soil turning upon itself;
You are bursting forth in your experience.

You are not the person next to you—
Not an image or an expectation.
You are the infinite and eternal you—
Blessed, loved and consoled
By the utter commonness
And community of our souls.

We cry and we're held.
We love and we hold.

We are the harvest of God,
Constantly renewed,
Constantly awakened
To a new Thanksgiving.

THE FARMER, THE WEAVER & THE SPACE TRAVELER

Sing your song. Tell your story

No, no! The adventures first,
explanations take such a dreadful time.
~Lewis Carroll,
Alice's Adventures in Wonderland

Words matter. Words crafted carefully and artfully expressed matter more. There is a compelling nuance in a well-timed turn of phrase, arresting images juxtaposed upon arresting images, and broad ideas distilled into lucid and singular thought. Every writer is empowered, but not every writer is empowering. Weak writers share stale thoughts and shallow opinions. Their readers are left to scrounge enough crumbs of dry bread and somehow make a meal. Powerful writers trust their words engage and effect change; they alter perceptions and shift mindsets. They articulate what needs to be writ in a wall of words sturdy enough to stand the test of time and speak powerfully to the present generation—and inspire succeeding generations.

Words... These damn words clabbered together—they are our gift to eternity. If you want to be a writer, hell be damned, live the life of a writer. Learn how to weave and cobble words together. Learn the craft, and the art will follow. Let the engine pull the train. Avoid dead-ends. Don't push a loaded cart up a slaggy hill. Don't fear the echo of your voice, and don't be a drunk stumbling down a dark road, howling inanities in the night.

But even ludicrous howling is better than no howling at all.

Howling is the birth before the epiphany. After the primal howling in the dark, after the grimacing at fate, create the time and the space to till, sow, and reap a more perfect garden with the seeds of your original howling. Nurture this garden as a farmer of words, and bring your fruit to the market. It may well be your basket comes home more full than sold, but you are now the farmer of your mind, soul, heart, and being, not the hungry pauper stuffing a crumbling sack, scrounging for cheap seconds before the shutters of commerce are drawn.

"A stitch in time saves nine," or so the old adage goes, because a writer is also a weaver of tapestries. Everything we write is a new mosaic of woven cloth—an original expression of who, what, when, where, and why we are at any given point in our fleeting attempts at existence. We are not born weavers, but we all possess some rudimentary concept of a needle pulling thread. We understand the process, if not the practice. Every time we speak, we stitch a mosaic together. We weave words into phrases and struggle to hold together a wretched pattern of thoughts worthy of a coherent conversation. Our opinions, however, fray too soon, are soon too tattered to wear, and are equally too soon forgotten.

But not so for the committed writer.

The unflappable writer returns to those tattered, convoluted, and ultimately forgettable conversations—interplays of words sown with strong seed on thin topsoil where even the heartiest of intent withers on a dry vine. Any writer worth their salt does not give up on possibility; they go back and rebuild those same words and thoughts into a more perfect and palpable tapestry—a living, breathing garden of succulent fruits worth bringing to market. What starts as a pensive rambling in an innocuous journal entry evolves into something somehow resembling clarity and ultimately something worth sharing. It does not just happen. It happens because we want it to happen. It does not happen because we make it happen. It happens because we learn to weave and stitch, and we learn to till, plant, and cull the good from the bad in every endeavor.

The recipe for success is as old as time—learn, practice, and persist. As a teacher of writing and as a writer, I am one of many droning pedants pointing a twitching finger at the blackboard of Fate. Your journey is uniquely your own, and you may well not follow the stealthy plotting of my design. If you are not thirsty, every well is the same. But if you are thirsty, go to the deepest, purest cistern and drink deeply until you are filled or have sucked dry the finite well. Living the life of a writer is to live with an unquenchable thirst for the purity of thought etched upon a page of time. Your journey is an ellipse towards a distant nebula winding into the unknown, but everything you scribble in myopic fervor serves as waypoints to map your journey—those linear, pinpricked dots across a darkened empty space arcing across the universe prove you have escaped the lure of gravity and the wet and wildish confines of our small, muddy orb circling a common burning star.

This journey proves you are a writer. You have not chosen the easy path with words, but the path of the explorer, the weaver, and the farmer...

Genesis

If you are still with me and even slightly agree, get off this page and tend to your own genius. Time is short, and life is never as sure as the dream. Go your way and show me what you find. But if there is lingering hesitancy as to your place in the panoply of writers, stay with me for a short while longer. We can't begin without a beginning—without exploring what an essay actually is.

For many of you, an essay is simply a synonym for an assignment, a heroic duty on the warring plains of education. You are neck-deep in the Big Muddy, facing an equally menacing shoreline. You believe the teacher who fails you as readily as you believe the teacher who praises you, but do you ever listen unerringly to yourself? Do you believe in the power and promise of your writing? If you say "no," I implore you to say "yes!" You are never too young to shape your own destiny.

For those of you whose diplomas hang in musty hallways, your essays are distant memories, relics left behind in a manic fervor to be done and finished. Those essays, rat-trappy as they may be, are your heritage. They are your scrolls scribed on faded parchment, as valuable as any painted urn or etchings on a silver goblet. The edges are frayed and the ink is smudged and dry, but the words remain, and it is a wily explorer who realizes the treasure scattered in some moldy grave, for these words are your beginning—your raw and nascent self unearthed before the ravages of time and Fate stole it from you—but you, too, are not so old to shape a new destiny. You can yet leave this world the harvest of your genius—some testament befitting the life you led, the life you still lead, and the life you hope yet to live.

I am not here to teach you how to write essays. The world is awash in scribes more apt than me. I am here to remind you that if you have the gall to call yourself a writer, you need to look with clear eyes on the field you play upon and ask yourself if you really know the rules of the game, if your body can contort itself and make it to the bitter end of the desperate fight, or if you have mastered the skills to match your dreams or even the point of your beloved pastime. If you are too timid and weak to give a damn or too weary to sense the magnitude of your potential, put down this drivel of words and tend to the artifices of a diminished life. There are other less challenging games to play.

Writing is a series of failures, and unless you focus on a very small audience—such as your mother and a crazy aunt—it is also a continual, ringing reminder that nobody cares about you, and they care even less if it is the third or thirtieth draft—for there really is no such thing as a rough draft, but only the best you have yet created. Few artists unveil their work before the paint is dry and a crowd is milling in the gallery; likewise, a writer unerringly knows when their work is done, as a wise captain knows when to abandon ship and step up into the lifeboat. Experience admonishes sailors to never give up on the foundering ship of genius unless and until all else is lost. Everything is your final draft, your best effort, and, at that precise moment in time, your top-shelf item. Who puts a square block on a table and brags that it will one day be a wheel? Readers do not care how it is made. Finish your work. Clean up your shop, and then bring out the wheel. If it rolls in the right direction, it will be of some use to someone.

Essays are Everywhere

The emphasis placed on writing essays is one of the great ironies of education—as if life without writing essays is unworthy, unthinkable, and untenable. And it always will be if we continue to live in a world of thinkers intent on ferreting out the dark matter of our souls upon some tattered page. On the other hand, reading essays is seldom in the playbook of the classroom. And that is a travesty. Reading a good essay is like drinking the purest water and breathing the most rarified air, yet we rarely assign "essay reading" to our students; instead, we force great poetry, great short stories, and great books down their gorged, swollen gullets—the good stuff that just might nurture a life-long love and passion for great literature.

But reading essays? No way. No can do. Too boring. Too opinionated. Too... whatever. Show me a good essay that some disenchanted teenagers enjoy, and I'll show you a very rare student. So for a guy like me who actually writes essays, who believes in them, and who even publishes whole books of his essays, it can be disheartening. Being a writer of essays could well be my punishment for some heinous transgressions in my previous lifetime. Some sultry, vengeful angel called me out of the line of the worthy and laid bare my litanies of sins and transgressions: "You have been banished to a new lifetime of writing essays. You will work slavishly, yet your work will never be read by a single soul. Very sorry. Deal with it!" I deal with it the only way I know how—by writing yet another essay. I am a cat at dinnertime, swatted to the floor every time I jump onto the counter. Still, I keep jumping, and I keep getting swatted because I want, need, and cherish my food. Getting tossed from the counter is central to my survival, and if I don't suffer in some palpable way, I will never lure a reader into my wordy mesh. Or enjoy my can of oily fish.

I am not alone as an essay writer. Our lives are awash in essays. We just don't call them essays. We call them things like tweets, newspaper articles, emails, TikToks, Facebook posts, iMessages, dumb assignments, boring NPR dronings, right- and left-wing rants, teenage disses, and predictably pointless adult pontifications. Every time we put thoughts into words, we literally create an essay. We just don't treat them as essays. We treat our words—our precious utterances—as if they live and die in the moment like some hatch of mayflies on the Assabet River or a half-empty bag of Doritos cast overboard into an ebb tide; hence, our ephemeral words live, die, float, sink, and are carried away into the placid ocean of common ignorance and perpetual anonymity. To change this tide, change yourself. Treat your strings of words as they should be treated—as generous thoughts explored on a page, cud-like rumination's cobbled together and gifted to humanity—all at the cost of a simple click. Do not measure yourself to Shakespeare or let Shakespeare measure you. Measure yourself to the scope of your imagination and the breadth of your experience. Your life is as rich as any other life.

A coin is worthless if one side is empty, so good writers read and good writers write. A writer's life is a codependent ecosystem where thought, words, experience, and creation mix and flow like batter in a bowl. Study and learn what makes for good reading, and you will unerringly discern good writing—or at least decent writing. It is not a vexing task. Read essays that actually make you think, ponder, and wonder—and sometimes just laugh.

Search for essays that speak to some corner of your life—ramblings out of nooks and crannies that bring clarity to your thoughts and make sense of the scope of your experiences. When you finish reading an essay, open your journal and write. Good things happen when you make the leap to live the life of a writer. You are no different than a football player studying a playbook, a cook learning a new recipe, a sailor tying a befuddling knot, or an engineer testing an engine. Learn by learning to know. Practice what works, figure it out, and be a writer. Mimic what amazes you. You already have a voice. Use your warble and whistle now, and learn as you go. Make what you write, say, and preach mean something. Maybe what you say, write, or preach will be meaningful. And memorable. And remembered. But only if you do it—and even more so if you share it. So sing your song.

Tell your story.

WHAT WOULD THOREAU DO?

Facing the Empty Page

I, on my side, require of every writer, first or last, a simple and sincere account of his own life, and not merely what he has heard of other men's lives...
~Henry David Thoreau, *Walden*

I open and stare into this empty page and sift my thoughts for wisdom and possibility. I imagine Thoreau did the same—probably for the same reasons. This page, barely edged by any wall of words, is a field yet tilled. I do not yet know who I am, for at any given time I am also a teacher, a poet, a songwriter, or a folk singer. By less equal turns, I am also an essayist, a woodcarver, a sailor, a tinkerer, and a fledgling philosopher. It is a rare day that dawns for me without something worth doing or begging to be done. Do what needs to be done. Each thing to its time. Each time it is due.

Today I am an essayist looking at this blank screen—an empty page stirred into cud-like thoughts mixed with an unsettled sense of duty. The emptiness is the core of who I am—an unkempt time-filler pillaging for meaning. I am here doing the same thing I asked my freshman English class to do for weekend homework: "Go to a spot in nature and think—and then write. Write from your heart and soul and mind and being, and yes, it is what Thoreau would do."

To practice what I preach, I do my assignment. My spot—my slice of nature—is a wet hillside field overlooking Cedar Lake in central Massachusetts. While it feels secluded, I hear the distant drone of the I-90 Mass Pike somewhere to the south. I am surrounded by songbirds—innumerable wrens and sparrows, a pair of cardinals, a nuthatch carrying a string of blue yarn, a solitary, extremely agitated bluejay, and some red-headed somethings I do not recognize—finches maybe, but I don't think so.

I used to know them all—birds, at least—but not so much anymore. It is hard to carry everything into an older age. The flimsy canvas rucksacks of youth might have been better spent on building heavy sea-chests—a bigger hold to store my burgeoning memories and fleeting trinkets of experience—hard, palpable mementos I can hold in my hand in a beleaguered night.

What exactly does an empty page represent for you? In short, it is what is written within you. The words are already there. You only need to tap the tree and pour the virgin sap onto an empty page. Let time distill your words into a sweeter syrup. Do not be discouraged. To search for sense is to baffle yourself. The first words are, by necessity, a scramble for meaning, an unclear image upon a distant horizon—a hand trying to grasp smoke from the flame. Out of this scrambling screed exudes some elusive broth of truth. The more difficult task is to make sense of your sound and make the ephemeral real and palpable. Reality is the craft of a writer. Plank on plank. Nail beside nail. Art follows craft in any endeavor. And we are not yet artists.

Mine is a willful search, and, as always, I am hampered by my limitations, trapped as I am in the sarcophagus of a corporeal body.. I have yet to push the limits of what I know into the murky world of unknowing. I trust some nugget of wisdom lies within. When I am at a total loss, I turn to my journal, poetry, and prayer. When I am searching, I turn to the essay. When I am perplexed by the moment, I sit and think.

Then I walk.

Every essay begins with a walk. This, too, I learned from Thoreau. Nothing is lost in pondering, but everything is lost in giving up the search. But you are the malleable you—you are teenagers living on the cusp of a new life—a life shaped impossibly into perfect form by you. The decisions you make now inform your actions, and these ponderous steps change the evolution of your destiny. Only a fool puts off the inevitable, for, at some point in your life, only you can judge yourself.

What can Thoreau possibly tell us today? The answer is simple. Reading Thoreau's writing is an exercise and exploration that just might literally change your life, if in any way shape or form your life wants or needs changing. The truth is that if we do not change, we do not grow. We consign our lives to a desperate search for meaning trapped within the confines of a common life—an "unexamined life," which Thoreau argues is not worth living.

Thoreau found, shaped, and nurtured wisdom out of the natural world around him—but so have, and so do, many other slavish writers and pondering poets. I am not amazed by Thoreau's thinking, nor am I enamored or jealous of his life. I am amazed how he crafted, out of tomes of journal writing, crystalline gems of words, phrases, sentences, and passages— strings of stubborn words bellowing prophecies that continue to ring in the modern mind with unnerving clarity and persistence.

Thoreau is most remembered for a few of his essays, a few extended travelogues, and his one enduring masterpiece, *Walden*. I would argue he should be most remembered for his insistence on living the life of a writer, naturalist, and philosopher. Within the confines of Concord, Thoreau measured and catalogued the natural world around him. He read broadly and deeply. Every day, he dutifully captured the physical world around him and the metaphysical world within him in a voluminous series of daily journal entries where he distilled the essence of his utterly common life into the uncommon beauty of his remembered words.

It is a greatness worth imitating.

As my students, perhaps you see no need to change. You may feel no compulsion to grow beyond who you are and what you aspire to be. You accept the present paradigm and the bleak lessons of your elders—the teachers, parents, guardians, and arbiters of your future. We fill you with heady expectations and pierced admonitions. We rob you of childhood and strangle your adulthood. We coddle you and call it caring; we implore you to act and be a certain way. We are convinced we know a better path for you; we implore you to accept our wisdom and grow fruits in line with our expectations. More often than not, we are wrong.

You know it.

And I know it.

Only you can do anything about it.

You are the inimitable you. There is nothing and no one else in the universe exactly like you. Every word you place on the page in an honest and sincere search for truth is as real as an acorn dropping from the towering oak of your life. Cover your husky seed with moldy soil. The pithy promise is inevitably you.

Nurture your life and become who you really, really are.

This is what Thoreau would do.

This is what he did.

Will you?

POETS & POLITICIANS

Inside of every poet there is some craziness—
Like a magnet attracting
And repulsing
The same breath.

Taylor Mali could probably write a really cool poem
About the snowblower sitting in my driveway
On this warm spring day,
But I bet he wouldn't know
How to start the damn thing—
He'd think it was a rototiller or something,
And I would have to shout,
"No, no! Taylor,
Out of my strawberries!"
And in the blue smoke of the ensuing chaos

Mary Oliver returns
From her long walk
Past old cloth mills,
Carrying trinkets
Of broken glass—
Shards of memory
And distant longing.

She will be surprised to find Seamus Heaney
Drinking beer with Billy Bulger,
Quoting Homer,
And lamenting the exodus
Of the Irish from Boston.

The shadow of Emily Dickinson
Moves slowly away from a broken pane
In the eave of her attic room,
Weaving wild and wisping
Strings of words in waves
Of whispered lace.

Robert Frost squints disdainfully,
And tells me to just slow down,
Take a breath,
And throw this all away.
(He is already annoyed
By my kids chalking
Murals on our driveway
And Walt Whitman's incessant celebrating
With some guy in a bucket truck
Bending and reeving splices of wire,
Spitting chew and coarse words
Into a styrofoam cup.)

For some strange reason,
A sad and petulant Allen Ginsberg
Cries on my back step
While Gary Snyder sets up a pup tent
Beside my garden.

Jack Kerouac shoots hoops and wonders
What his mother is cooking for dinner.

Shakespeare's friends are plastering
Posters on telephone poles,
While Shelley swims across
The Assabet River
And holds a painted turtle
Over a cold, dark eddy.

Billy Collin's dances to a scratchy jazz record
And thinks he should write a poem about it.
Wendell Berry helps Taylor
Blow the snow from my strawberries;
Wordsworth walks away
Through a crack in the fence—

And Basho just laughs
And laughs
And laughs.

DON'T DO IT

Unfettered and audacious freedom

*There is no greater agony
than bearing an untold story inside you.*
~Maya Angelou

I was eighteen and studying to be a shop teacher at Fitchburg State College—the only college I could afford and probably the only place that would have me. My first project was to design a production line for making stepladders. I remember thinking, 'Man, this ain't no life for me.' I barely possessed a working idea of what *life* meant, but I was pretty sure it didn't mean to start a journey without meaning or purpose—and I certainly didn't want to spend my life designing a better stepladder.

But what did I want to do? What morphing of my life was even possible? Did I have the courage to even make a change in my life? If I had read *The Odyssey*, I might have known what to do. I might have known I was on a heroic journey and my call to adventure was the churning confusion in my gut—and that no quest is real until we realize we cannot go it alone. If I had, I might have known to look for a helper to get me over the threshold. I might have known my pen was my amulet.

I might have known my first helper was my freshman English professor. I can't even recall her real name, but she was old and sweet, and so we undistinguished public college scholars called her Aunt Bee. And she was sweet—sweet enough to ask me to stay after class to meet with her one day early in the fall. I thought she might be plotting to expel me for charging five dollars to any kid in my dorm to write their English papers for them.

Instead, she held a paper in her hand—a paper where I actually cared about what I wrote. The day before, she gave us an assignment to walk alone through the streets of Fitchburg, Massachusetts, and when finished, to write about the walk. Most of my boisterous classmates stayed in the dorm, played beer pong and laughed about the naivety of Aunt Bee. They wrote some insipid scrawls they assumed would qualify as an essay—or they tried to get me to write an essay for them for less than five dollars.

But I took the walk. I wandered through the poorest streets in Fitchburg. I sat on the front steps with little kids and old men. I talked with drunks and dreamers and wondered...

I wondered if my walk was actually real or if I was even real. I wrote some convoluted story about a kid who couldn't tell if he was awake or dreaming—or even which state of mind he wanted to live in. Aunt Bee shook this paper in my face and said bluntly, "You shouldn't be an industrial arts major. *This* [shaking the paper ever closer to my face] is your *gift!*"

No one ever told me I had a gift of any sort, except perhaps for whittling birds out of scraps of soft pine. I didn't think Aunt Bee knew how ready I was for a change—any change. I seemed to take her off guard when I responded, "Okay. So what do I do?"

"Leave this place," she answered.

So I left.

Never had a decision been so easy and so hard at the same time. It was easy, as I knew in my heart Aunt Bee was right, but hard because my parents thought I was throwing my life away—and I was. I threw my old life in a convenient bin and charted a new course into a world of words and literature—a world I knew little about.

My impetuous decision in the fall of 1976 is the reason I am writing this today. My odyssey proved to be the proverbial long and winding road, but I have never been let down by a book or hobbled by anything I wrote—although much of what I have written is pretty dumb and forgettable—and often lamentable.

There was little academia on my new journey. I learned to write by writing. I learned to write better by listening to what people thought and felt about my writing. I joined some writing workshops. Each week, each person brought in some poem or story to share with a circle of other would-be writers. I learned what worked in my writing, and I marveled at what didn't work —at least in the small universe of my writer's circle. I never thought I was a good writer, so I was never really bothered by what people said. I just thought, 'Cool. I guess I should change this or that.'

Even after a few workshops, I did not perceive myself as a writer by any definition of the word until my old friend Lana introduced me to one of his friends by proclaiming, "This is Fitz. He's a writer." I protested that I was not a writer, and Lana just said, "Then what the hell else are you?"

"I don't know, an apple picker, I guess," for at the time I was picking apples with a crew of Jamaicans in an orchard in New Hampshire, eponymously named "High Altitude Apples." Lana responded, "At any rate, Fitz is a better writer than he is an apple picker. That much, I'm sure."

His words sealed the deal and sealed my fate—a fate that, by and large, has been good to me.

But be careful, for you, too, might become a writer, and once you become a writer, you can't turn back; you can only turn away. Such is the power and allure of writing. If schools really knew what happens when a kid becomes a writer, they would ban the teaching of writing. It is like giving a ten-year-old the keys to a bad-ass car. It is like pointing across a canyon and screaming, "Jump!" It is like opening a window and pointing in every direction and shouting, "This is all you need to know, everything you will ever try to know, and all you will never know."

Writing is unfettered and audacious freedom.

Don't do it.

REDEMPTION

Be bored by the easy and mundane

Be small. Be simple. Be wise. Be happy.
But above all, be ready
~Fitz

Finally, the tall green pines standing sentinel beside this cold and black New Hampshire pond are framed in a sky of blue. After a month of steady rains, foggy nights, and misty days, I am reborn into a newly created world—a world finally answering my prayers. No more searching for the elusive spot under the camper awning not drenched in leaking rivulets of warm rain. No more running across the wet field dragging Tommy bouncing and laughing like a half-inflated beach toy towards a smokey campfire—no more endless scrabble, monopoly, shallow books, and card games. This fresh, blue morning barks out the possibilities of the day: "Here is my rope swing. Here are my trails. Therein lie my waters."

The window is small, and the day is large. I shouldn't even be here, teasing words from an empty page. I should embrace the possibilities of today, for as Thoreau wrote, "My life is the poem I should have writ/ But, I could not both live and utter it." The ignorant and lazy part of us might want to rally around Thoreau's sentiment and say, "Amen to Thoreau," but we would miss the irony and wistfulness of our collective predicament. Like kids balancing on a plank set on a log, we scramble back and forth to find the sweet spot on the plank, a point of perfect balance between the forces of light and darkness—but when we find the balancing point, we only allow ourselves a few moments of self-indulgent awe before searching for a more elusive and demanding prey.

To live fully, we must be bored by mediocrity. We must set a larger plank across a larger log. There is no legal limit to how many balls a juggler can have in the air. We are only captive to gravity and the ticking sun dropping to the horizon.

I need this blue sky to illuminate the horizon and define the infinite juxtapositions between the earth and heaven. I need to remind my stubborn will that my page will always be empty if I refuse to embrace the day rising before me. I need to rush headlong from the dark night of my soul and into the blinding light of a true day. I need to fall and rise time and time again with a contagious and courageous rhythm. I need to remember to spend my day and not simply save it—as if I could redeem it tomorrow.

My life and my words are my final redemption, rushed and woven imperfectly into the rags I wear.

See me.

Feel me.

Free me.

Hear my words.

IT IS STRANGE GAME I PLAY

With this skunk in the night,
Who tears into a bag of chips
I left beside the Adirondack chair.
I throw pencils
And wads of paper at him,
But he seems
Barely annoyed
And not so amused as me.
If there was not
A language barrier between us
He would probably ask,
"Where the hell is your old, pea-brained sheepdog?
The one who chases me below the shed;
Who I must have sprayed a hundred times—
My God, that dog never learned a damn thing."

I decide to play his game.
"She is gone now, buried out by the fence,
Near Joe, our cat, and Guinness our husky.
(I can't even mention the name Guinness
Without my wife telling another story
Of the perfect dog in our perfect home.)

The kids at least have come to accept death—
The backyard littered with crosses and gravestones
For salamanders, goldfish, gerbils and voles,
Two beloved dogs, two feral cats and several chickens.
There have been other deaths, too—people deaths,
But we don't really about talk about them much.

You go do your thing; tear the bag apart.
I will sweep it all up in the morning,
But we will have to keep this 'thing' between us...

I know you know what I mean.
It's just really hard to explain
These conversations with a skunk."

THE GRADING REALITY

A slice out of life

Don't let school interfere with your education...
~Mark Twain

Grading is that hefty slice of a teacher's life that should bring some sense of satisfaction to our work as educators —but it rarely does. Doling out reams of grades day to day and weeks to months is an uncelebrated chore, if only for the sheer time it takes to grade well, grade fairly, and assess in ways that help our students in wise and equitable ways. After a long round of assessment, I am less dispirited than many of my colleagues, yet I wonder if I am more reptilian calculator than warm-blooded human on a mission to inspire, cajole, and enlighten a willing and eager gaggle of students. Teachers juggle the competing demands of reality with an objective mission to further a subjective aim—coaxing the best out of a myriad of living, thinking, and feeling students who bring a mosaic of disparate lives onto the platter and splatter of our heady curriculums. Amidst the competing demands of a common day, doing what is best for the student seldom coincides with what is best for the teacher.

After thirty years of teaching, I should have mastered the hacksaws and chisels of the grading toolbox, yet I sense I have much to learn, do, and practice before I head off to my retirement with some smug satisfaction befitting a master of his trade—yet I am cursed by burdens of reflection. I miss out on the path to enlightenment, and I do what others do simply because it is what is being done or has been done for generations before me. I wonder if I have the strength or wisdom to rally academia towards a wiser, more just, and more doable solution.

I wonder about a lot of things, and grading homework is prime among my wearied thoughts. I wonder how much of a grade should be based on homework. Most of us have no clue what "home" means to our students, yet we continually assign "home" work. Too often, this work is graded as daily take-home tests. We are masters of building pressure, but we have no clue which way to adjust the valve of relief. Useless homework adds several more hours of pressure to what is already an overburdened day. Homework should never be a test, a gift that only rewards the gifted, whether a grace of intellect, a stable and nurturing home free from distraction, or the munificence of having the financial resources to tutor, guide, and direct a student through their paces. Teachers should teach in class and not expect a student to learn what has not yet been taught. Homework is for practice, not perfection.

Parents and administrators are masters of expectations, while teachers are merely the limbs and heads of some monstrous and manipulated marionette. For the good of our students and our school systems, teachers are tasked with doing the bidding of forces we barely know or recognize. We are forced to bend in the opposite directions of the winds of wisdom. Common core is rarely common. It suggests there is actually some common iteration of a student devoid of idiosyncrasies who can possibly model the expectations we are fated to meet. This is not a battle between public school versus private school Private schools, free from the constraints of common core, have the equally insidious monster that expects those well-heeled extra dollars and extra attention will lift their gifted children further up the ladder of privilege—a privilege that will poise their progeny squarely on the next higher rung towards admittance to an even more prestigious school. It is a fools errand to make sense of nonsense. There is little sanity in insanity, so why search for it? We are removing the wing from the bird and asking it to fly. But we have to try. To be a democracy, we need be democratic. It is a sacred right to be taught and a sacred duty to teach the communal breadth of society—rich, poor, or indifferent.

If anything should be common, it should be common sense. Parents deserve to know what their children are studying and why. Administrators deserve to know if a teacher is teaching what they have been hired to teach. Teachers need to teach what they know best, and if they do not know it, to learn it well or beg to be excused from fakery—but don't fake it. Don't let myopic, budget-constrained business sense overrule common sense and don't make a fisherman rule over a farm.

I consider myself fairly well-rounded and open-minded enough (arguably, I am sure), but every professional day takes me further away from the core of my passion. I am being asked to teach grit and resilience. I am tasked with developing the moral character of my students. I am tasked with instilling honesty, empathy, respect, and courage. I am tasked to eliminate prejudice, and define marginalization, and smother bigotry; in short, I am burdened with shaping the form of a perfect society out of the hard-scrabbled flesh and bones of imperfect youth—noble, maybe, but I would rather show all this than demand it. I bow and bend to these winds of pedagogical change like a dory anchored outside of the harbor, but I don't really go anywhere.

Can I grade a kid on the substance of their grit? Is there a way to assess courage, parse lack of prejudice, or judge the moral leanings of any given student? Should schools define and be the arbiters of social change, policies, and correctness? Will this noble gesture be codified and ruined to the point where it can, should, and must be graded? If so, there is money to be made somewhere by some professional presenter to tell us how to do it —and soon it will edge and creep into another form of another demand in the life of a teacher.

And I will have to sit through it.

But we all must live through it.

TOM & MARTHA

Playing the game of names

Then love knew it was called love.
And when I lifted my eyes to your name,
suddenly your heart showed me my way
~Pablo Neruda

I avoid cracks in sidewalks and never walk under a ladder, but I am not Superstitious unless a black cat crosses the road in front of me, a mirror breaks on my wall, or that third bit of bad luck appears. Serendipity—the lucky twin of Superstitious—is another ball game. Just hearing Serendipity" reopens the box of childhood in me, not the dark, cultish paranoia of the Superstitious. Until a few years ago, there was a funky coffee shop and cafe in downtown Maynard named The Serendipity Cafe & Coffeeshop. It was a funky, forward-thinking place owned by Johnny and Laura, transplanted Vermonters carving out a dream in an old mill town just outside of Boston. Sadly, it is now a shuttered storefront, but the memories persist.

Several of our kids worked there as waiters, and they ran the teen open mics for years. Denise and I stopped in most every weekend morning for coffee, tea, simple fare, and the lure of watching our kids in action. Some floret of Serendipity flowered on any given morning, some bloom of the unexpected to add a lilt of grace to our lives—usually friends, sometimes our own family waiters—Emma, Margaret, or Charlie—but often total strangers to share and mold casual banter into a profound art form. The fine food, drink, and conversations lingered as brushstrokes painting a living portrait that captured the unfolding new day. The name "Serendipity" became more than a moniker for an eponymous, small-town cafe as it transmogrified into a magical beast of wondrous purpose and clarity, and it set me to wondering how the power, or lack of power, the game of naming plays out in our lives.

I'll admit that my thesis here is fairly shallow, but it is the bent my roaming genius often travels; hence, my wondering and wandering begins...

If I walk into Aubuchon Hardware, I rarely wonder about the original Mr. or Mrs. Aubuchon, yet when I walk into True Value Hardware, I do wonder what is meant by "True Value" and where to find it. Most things I value are not sold there as merchandise or commodities. I can never find the aisle for True Friendship. I can never find the bin of Kind Actions, and I can never find the vaunted Universal Key—the fob that opens every door and unlocks even the most stubborn heart. Job Lot does not sell jobs, nor does Tractor Supply sell anything heftier than a Cub Cadet lawnmower. The Apple Store only sells Macintosh— no Granny Smiths, Braeburns or anything remotely resembling a Delicious. Harbor Freight, though often near some ocean, is never on a harbor of any kind—and neither is Lands End ever at the end of some spit on a rocky outcropping of a peninsula.

I appreciate names like Burger King, The Fudge Factory, and The Cheese Shop; but as dull as their names may be, there is no fraud. They are what they aspire to be, claim to be and are— places to find burgers, fudge and cheese. Other stores with names like Wendy's, Wegmans and Woolworth's must fight the tide of Indifference and Curiosity. They fret in corporate offices and must prove their names are worthy in the sea of reputation and branding. To discover what wares these stores peddle, customers must make a leap of faith to walk through the door. Over time, we associate these disparate "names" into the fabric of our lives —and over a longer stretch of time, we assign value to these names—and hence judgment: good/bad, worthy/unworthy, dull/exciting... and so on and so on... The sheer volume of these names is astounding and reveals the stunning array of opinions and misconceptions stored amongst the greasy gears turning in the oily goo of our fat, barnacled heads.

It is a pity we are named at birth. It would be better if our names were bequeathed at some later age and stage of our lives

—a more wizened time when our pedigree of humanity—or lack of humanity—is more clearly established. Perhaps then we could choose our friends and mates with a greater degree of certainty. We could surround ourselves with characters named Magnanimous, Earnest, Daring, Gentle, Thoughtful, Beguiling, and Faithful. If we were named Lucky, no doubt we would become great friends with Wily, Willing, Wealthy, and Cunning. We could avoid Petty, Spiteful, False, Yackety, and Entropy. Messy could avoid Tidy, and Tidy could easily find Orderly and, if really lucky, marry a spouse named Anal.

Our current paradigm of random naming forces us to mix Good with Evil, Spite with Graciousness, and Depravity with Humanity. Our cobbled communities are not as communal as we might hope. Our precious cul-de-sacs devolve into battlefields; our homes become citadels to save ourselves from cannibalizing neighbors. The self-aggrandizing signs and xenophobic flags in our yards proclaim our proclivities and pronounce our self-affirming hypocrisies and loathings. It is, at best, an inefficient system to find a tolerable and knighted neighbor with whom to share a neighborhood.

If only our names bore the unmistakeable reflection of our actual selves, all this could be avoided. Our molding and parceling of townships, counties, and statehoods would no longer be draped in the gloom and doom of predictable and opposing Blue and Red leanings. A more inclusive panoply of colors painted in a mosaic of swatches, brushstrokes, and drippings would fill the landscape of our Community. Elections would be Passé, Needless, Caput. Politicians would be Obsolete, left to jostle in breadlines ruled by Anonymity and—the most common and despised name of all—Mediocrity. We would laugh uproariously at reruns of The Dating Game. The final Survivor would be a pre-ordained litany of fate. Dating apps would prove fruitless. Tinder would go under. Resumes would read like tawdry fiction, and Children, untainted by Mystery and Fear, would be set free in a Paradise of Possibilities. Innocent of the original Sin and the Burden of names, their lives could be an unending game of Hide and Seek, looking beneath and behind the Obstacles of life to find the name they are meant to be and destined to be. Parents, too, would be freed—freed from the Angst and Burden of raising their flocks of feral Miscreants in petri dishes of erring society, schools, and playgrounds. These universal Parents could then watch Joyful and Wondrous from afar. They could place bets, scratch quick-win tickets, and draw lotteries on who of their precious cherubs will first find the title worthy of His or Hers or Them's or They's intrinsic inclinations. and dispositions—their unique and ineffable self cobbled out of a braided spectrum that places every human being on a specific and singular point of orientation and trajectory.

But we do not have and cannot have this dreamy Illusion. It is just not possible or practical, except in the vacuous Diaspora of my Dystopian mind.

It is up to us as Discerning and Erudite consumers to define the value of infinitely recurring names. All John's, Betty's, Sue's, and Alisha's are never the same, except by chance or, occasionally, through some foolish bigotry bred into an entangled DNA of Prejudice, inculcated, nurtured, and manipulated from a young age, or hung by the heels over some evil brainwash within a bath of Hate. I wish every Tom lived with the magnanimity of my brother Tom, or with the Sincerity and Kindness of my own Tommy, or with the Indefatigable energy of Tom, my incessantly busy neighbor, or Tom, my friend who fixes anything and everything with just a call, or with the can-do spirit of my student Tom, or with the "Yes, I'm here for you" availability of Tom, my dentist.

With the exception of friends and family with names akin to Maroghini, Sheenia, Livingstone, Musala, Hatrack, and Pipo, I could iterate through this plethora of possibilities with almost any common, ascribed name. It is somewhat easier when we can pair names together in poetic couplets crafted out of deliberate pairings of names. For me, slowly drifting into my golden age, it is usually marriages, but often simple matches of friendships based on kindred ships of like-minded souls—each pairing of names evoking some pure, distilled elixir of thought steeped in reflective Wonderment.

I hear or think of Sally & Catherine, and my mind settles on the Steadfastness, Enthusiasm and Audacious approach to life they practice in their lives. I hear just a whisper of Tooey & Laura, and I am fortified that wisdom and sincerity can somehow cobble meaning from crushing bereavement. My brother Tom becomes Tom & Karen and their marriage that bloomed and blossomed from two teenagers falling irretrievably in love. Karen died some fifteen years ago, and Tom & Karen are now Tom & Ginny, and the regeneration of Love doubles itself many times over. No Love and no Thing is ever irretrievably Lost.

My own Family sprawls out in front of me in pairs—Charlie & Emma, Tommy & Pipo, EJ & Jude, Kaleigh & Kyle, Margaret & Aiden, and, most blessedly, Me & Denise, but also Mom & Dad, Eileen & Dan, Patty & Don, Mary Ellen & Paul, and Annie & Jeff. I could play this game forever—Tracy & Ted, Nan & Mike, Wally & Jen, Steve & Shubra, Alexandra & Paul, Paula & Geoff, Joy (aptly named) & Dave, and Jack & Linda... I could stand over some echoing abyss for hours on end and never repeat the pairing of hearts and souls that seed my world.

But it is not a game. It is a Celebration. My head bursts, my Soul sings, and my Heart throbs with every incantation. I cannot stop. I need to remind myself why I am here—why I even started this slavering of disparate thoughts? It started and ends with this —*Tom & Martha.*

Tom & Martha "is" the thought that birthed this Convoluted essay. It is somewhat Sad to think it started as a simple text message to a pairing of close friends—a couplet of Magnanimous & Love. I had not seen them in a long time. I simply wanted to let them know I was "thinking of them," but somehow tapping "Tom & Martha" on an iPhone screen unleashed this Monstrosity of Unfettered, Unencumbered Love, Respect, Admiration & Awe. Tom was once another Tom in my life—a good and charming friend and a wise Citizen of Humanity. Martha was once another "mother of a student"— Sweet, Kind, Accepting, and Generous beyond compare. At a late age in life, Serendipity blessed Tom and blessed Martha, and they found each other. They must have sensed that Tom and Martha would be better as Tom & Martha.

I bragged to Denise that I sensed it first, saw it first, and I had dibs on discovery as they sat Goggle-Eyed at a corner table while I sang some Insipid folk song in the Village Forge, a small tavern recessed in The Colonial Inn, an Ageless pub I've sung in for many, many years. Denise simply rolled her eyes with a "Duh, you just noticed this?" I fell humbly into line alongside a streaming queue of savants who also realize Tom & Martha "is" more an inspirational quote than a name—a sum greater than the parts where two lives become one. We became good friends, then close friends, then Unforgettable, Forever friends.

Tom & Martha married in a simple ceremony in their backyard, presided over by Tooey, of Tooey & Laura fame. A hawk soared overhead. "Luke," said Tooey, pointing upward, his only child and only son come from beyond to Consecrate the moment—Serendipity, not chance. Enlightenment, not Knowing. Grace, not Will—Glistening eyes blurred in Infinite time.

It is as close to The Unmoved Mover as I will ever get. Martha and Tom or *Tom & Martha*...

Search for the Cafe of Serendipity in your life. Taste the Fare & Fortune. Give it a fitting name. Become the finest name you will yourself to be.

Figure it out.

Let the world remember the Ineffable you.

Your name will echo in the halls of the universe.

PASCAL'S WAGER

In the dark of an early morning
I fumble the beads awkwardly,
reaching to the nearest and most familiar God,
never sure of the sequence of prayers,
and only obliquely in consequence.
I think more of the old man
I bought these rosaries from,
his staring in contempt at the party officials
politely wishing me good morning
outside the church door.

My roommate, Ren Qi Wei, laughs
when I leave each morning,
and speaks the few words of English he knows:
"Fie Xi Meng, the bed bugs have bite you."
I laugh too. I'd tell him it's only a sacrament
that underlies an inner grace —
but I have no idea how to say it.

I always want to continue the 'Our Father':

...and deliver us O' Lord from every evil,
and grant us peace in our days,
and in your mercy keep us free from sin
and protect us from all anxiety...

I still picture John Tortorella—
the unrepentant and unlikely altar-boy
sticking his finger in the chalice
And licking the blood of God
while Father King held up the bread
Thrilled to a pounding heart to know him:

.

For thine is the kingdom
and the power
and the glory...

I look for God in the night sky.
There's a nervousness I feel
staring towards Orion,
like I'm young and staring at a welder—
"You'll go blind, you'll go blind."

Then you find you don't.

Before sunrise Linda stops by
and we ride our bikes
down the wide flat streets,
in the heavy smell of sulphur —
the daily stoking of small coal stoves.
A song about Mao Ze Dong broadcasts
from tinny speakers, strung
like paper cups throughout the city,
tentacled into every dirt
and clay hot alleyway, stenched
by cabbage and nightsoil.

We stop in a park and buy
a bowl of warm bean whey, richened
with sugar and a doughstick.
I tell her I love the grease
of fried dough. She smiles. I know
she will soon break into talk
I'm not in the mood for.
I kick a soccer ball back to some kids.
They stare awhile and laugh, reciting,
"Thank you, thank you,"
and then charge back
behind each other.

I try my own words,
but they only steam
into the cold morning air.

A horde of women
appear suddenly,

sweeping packed dirt—
students bang at each other
playing ping-pong
on concrete tables
over bricks laid end to end.

The 'Lao Ren', the 'Old Ones',
wrapped in heavy quilted blue
slap thighs and chests,
hold their arms open,
And breath deeply,
slowly...

Little kids squat off the sidewalks.
My voice, trapped in viscera,
is guttural and chokened—

There is no now and forever.
I am a fraud in a foreign land
and haven't the faintest idea
what grace really is.

~Beijing,
December, 1981

WHAT WRITERS DO

A lesson within a storm

You must stay drunk on writing so reality cannot destroy you.
~Ray Bradbury

This is perhaps the biggest thunderstorm I have seen but not felt. To the west of the camp, lightning is flashing and bolting in massive arcs to the ground. Thunder is booming in every direction—though at least some five miles away. Here, there is no wind or rain. The sky is bright directly overhead, but the tall pines on the far side of the field are backdropped in roiling, dark clouds—then, strangely, there is a shift in the clouds. They surge towards me, attacking from the northeast. In the passing of a few minutes, the storm shifts again and renews its course to the west, bound for the rocky shorelines of Maine. I am equally perplexed and curious. What gives rise to this baffling twist of meteorology?

Writers often do the same thing with their writing. They build up a storm of unimagined intensity. They create a looming confrontation between the opposing forces long at battle in the storyline. Readers sense the impending conflict, and the richly thickened plot seethes and swirls. The wind whips, lightning flashes, thunder crashes, and suddenly, in some freakish twist of nature, the storm blows all hell and fury in another direction before resuming its insidious and relentless march to the sea.

To the all-knowing writer, all seems well, but their reader is no longer in the path of their storm. They are stranded like desperate mariners on a lonely shore, watching the clouds boil away over the horizon. The writer, caught up in their storm, assumes the reader is still with them, anticipating the gloried climax.

But their reader is no longer with them.

The once wondrous patron of their art sits bewildered, unconnected, and disillusioned and wonders how and why the storm took such an irrational, discombobulating jog to the southeast.

The rational response to any mystery is to ask why. Why throw this twist into an otherwise interesting story? Why ruin good soup with a bulky stone? Why twist a stick into the spokes of a moving wheel? Why throw sand into the gears of a literary machine?

Why let good writing turn bad?

There is no compelling reason, aside from perhaps a teacher's admonitions, that requires us to wade through the muck of tortured writing. The covenant between a writer and a reader is a tenuous relationship. Good readers are oft-jilted lovers wary of another disappointing affair. They know when to put a book aside and find another book—a tale that will not let them down. Readers appreciate the rewards of a well-written story, an inspiring essay, a pithy poem, or some compelling narrative. Readers love writers who consistently reward them. They return to those writers over and again with their time, attention, and money. A good writer lives and breathes in the life and breath of their reader. A good writer recognizes, respects, and remembers the reality of their living, breathing, and thinking audience.

No writer should be in love with their own writing. A writer should be in love with the process of writing well for a specific audience. *Curious George and the Man with the Yellow Hat* is no *Tale of Two Cities*, but each is a wondrous masterpiece of literature for whom it is intended. Even as I write this, I see, hear, and feel the presence of my audience. I do what I hope will work in a class of 8th-grade boys scrabbling away in a short story unit—and perhaps to other teachers sailing this same folly in the leaky barge of education.

So goes my fame and fortune. Luckily, my purse is full of greater trinkets than coins. For each reader, there is a writer to spark their imagination and set their mind afire. As much as I ply the sea of ponderous classics upon my students, I am equally enamored to read a book as a simple and relaxing respite from harried existence. Much of what I waste time reading is stupid and shortsighted, but the bent of my leisurely reading lets me drift away into my dreamy fantasies of some other life, all the while ensconced in a shady hammock strung between two birches on a warm summer's day. This time is never wasted. It is restoration and renewal.

I will read and re-read Patrick O'Brien's endless repertoire of naval sea novels, not because O'Brien's novels are masterpieces of literature, but because he consistently provides a rewarding reading experience for "me" as someone who loves stories of naval battles and distant shores. O'Brien found his niche, and he found his audience. We are the audience he respected and worked tirelessly to please before passing away (sadly for his devoted audience eager for more novels) at a ripe old age. Though O'Brien will never be placed among the pantheon of great writers, what he aspired to do, he did well—and certainly well enough for me.

Thoreau once wrote, "Measure a man, not by what he is, but by what he aspires to be." My readers are, by and large, writers who aspire to be better writers. In the grand scheme of things, I can only give my readers small bits and pieces cobbled out of my limited insights, experiences and aspirations.

I am only a lowly mate in an impossibly high mast hoop, shouting, "Thar' she blows."

That call is for us to scrabble down the ratlines and slide down the stays. Your dory is waiting for you.

But the whale you seek lurks in another sea.

Find it.

.

LIFE OUTSIDE THE CURRICULUM

My teachers could have written with Jesse James
for all time they stole from us
~Richard Brautigan, "Trout Fishing in America

My classroom is often a bit of a mess—a mass of sprawled bodies scattered around like casualties of battle—scarred warriors ensconced in various states of sloth-like repose on and over the armchairs, couches, and often each other. My students may resemble sloths, but the kids—8th grade and freshman boys—are engaged and productive in whatever dreary task I ply upon them.

Until someone brings up some aspect of school injustice, and soon the conversation shifts, spins, and rises into collective rants against the travesties cast by us teachers upon them. For the most part, it is myopic and self-serving commentary, but there is always some kernel of truth in the sincerity of their complaints, for, no doubt, we expect a lot of them. We steal their time in all varieties of thoughtful ways, artfully designed and full of earnest intent to better them in some way, shape, or form and mold them into some configuration of a student who makes us proud to be their educators; hence, we teachers get pissy when things do not go as artfully as the plan.

Somewhere, there is a disconnect. Somehow, our expectations are not in line with those of our students. They are frustrated. And we are frustrated. Something is wrong with the system. We are incarnations of Jesse James stealing their time—their most precious and fleeting commodity. To quote Henry David Thoreau, "We are "trying to solve the problem with a formula more complicated than the problem itself." Our schools have become labor camps with an incredible assortment of add-ons: committees they should join, service learning they must do, philanthropy they must engage in, speakers they must hear, and outside projects they must dutifully complete.

And all of it is outside the demands of a rigorous (or so we believe) curriculum—outside the demands of homework, sports, musical performances, outside tutoring, and beyond the expectations, rife with pressure, from family obligations. We celebrate them as individuals, yet expect obedient, acquiescent students. Therein lies the crux of the problem—we are robbing their last gasps at childhood. There is little time or room for them to grow like the weeds they are. We raise them and teach them to be crops brought to market and sold to future schools. Is this the generation we want to create? Is there another way? A better way? Is there a healthy balance between weed and fruit?

Yes, there is—and to quote Thoreau again: "Simplicity. Simplicity. Simplicity." Put all things needed in the basket of curriculum. Prune away what is not needed, and let the fruit suckle their mother root and grow in fresh air and warm sun. My students are willing—and they have proved themselves dutiful— to do whatever is asked of them within the confines of the curriculum, but they smolder with rancor when they smell the deceit of artifice. They intuitively sniff and ferret out the sweet from the odorous. If something is worth doing, it is worth being taught within the borders and the expanse of our classes, not as one more obligatory dish added to the feast of the day. There is little day left before the shade of night. The thief of time lurks in the snares of shadows.

As teachers, we may be willing to sway and even bend, but we seldom break out of our habits; we rarely agree to cut back on what and why we teach, and we rarely admit less is more. We teach the hell out of our packs of students and preach there is yet more needing to be done; there are more notches to notch on your achievement stick; there are more ways to bolster your fledgling resume, so come early to school; learn to be a philanthropist; stay late and prove you embrace service; give up your lunch and learn and respect and embrace diversity; skip recess; go to the Makerspace and embrace design thinking; wow your class with a better presentation—and then go home and do the real work—forty minutes, at least, for each class. After all, we only have you here in school nine hours out of your day. And the homework is due tomorrow. No excuses. Be sure to do some outside reading, too. Everyone should love reading.

No wonder there is grumbling. No wonder our students feel marginalized. No wonder the totality of expectations seems—and is—oppressive. It is no wonder they cling to the draining minutes and the dwindling vestiges of time to simply be the kids they are—irrepressible, irreverent, and incredible.

At the same time, our students need guidance. They need structure. They need to see the blueprint before they build. They are still kids who need to be held to high standards of conduct and respect. They need to do the work they are asked to do, and they need to figure out what needs figuring out without some pricey tutor prodding them out of a state of torpor.

As teachers and administrators, we need to look at the days we design for our students and create curriculums to enlighten without deadening the spirit and clogging the drainpipe of time. We need to accept and acknowledge that we are not the totality of their education. Everything does not need to flow solely from us. School should be a more simple affair. Demanding moral conduct based on enlightened and progressive values is a given, but we should not presume to be the totality of their ethical lives. We should be more wise and assume moral values are taught, practiced and embodied by parents, guardians, friends, and strangers. It is almost an anathema to say, but even in our most earnest efforts, we hobble our students with chaffing constraints more than we unshackle them from our insistent drudgery.

What we teach, what we practice, and what we cultivate must grow from a thoughtful, embracing, and invigorating curriculum taught by teachers who give a damn and know what they teach, but above all, who know their students and who appreciate and respect how we—the proverbial we—cannot do it all. And neither can our cast of young scholars, but some things we can do incredibly well, and whatever the bent of genius of an individual teacher, I say, "Set them free!" In the long run, those freed slaves are the life-changers and authors of lasting and effective pedagogy. It is those teachers who are remembered and revered for giving truth and caring to the lives of their students.

Oh, but the game of freedom is fun, easy, and invigorating to pen to this page. I am a curmudgeon at heart and sense the bad as early as the good. Freedom is a fickle beast, and I have an instinctive aversion to progress for the sake of progress, especially if it strays from teaching enduring and proven basic skills. My school is an incredible school and has freed me to follow my chaotic genius, which, for better or worse, reveres the old as likely as the new. Like any teacher, I am convinced that what I teach is what my students should, can, and need to learn.

And they learn.

Or so I convince myself...

My students are raised by caregivers who are insistent on raising well-educated children. They are willing (and sometimes barely able) to pay the price for their child's education. Their children are coddled and cajoled to be good students and good persons. By and large, they meet with uncommon success in their future lives. However, I can't help but think that we inculcate and perpetuate a feudal caste system, a subtle tool manipulating the few; hence, their education is necessarily incomplete and rife with inequality. We have an increasingly diverse community, but not real diversity—a diversity that mimics the reality of the real world. We embrace diversity as an ideal more than we reflect diversity as a messy mix of disparate realities.

I have seven well-educated children. My four boys had a mixture of elite private schools (because I work at an elite private school) and public schools, where my three girls spent all their school lives in small schools in the gritty mill town of Maynard— a small town that is not the envy of the wealthy surrounding towns of Concord or Sudbury or Acton squeezing Maynard's small borders into conformity. Yet, even as a teacher of some thirty-five years, I would say, "Come to Maynard. Here is a true community. Here is unabashed natural diversity. Here are basic skills taught well, though you might not know that listening to the flopping of disgruntled tongues." Here are parents who embrace the reality of small paychecks, multiple jobs, and tough daily choices. Kids learn grit because their lives are a gritty mix of unsifted life, not because grit is taught as a value to learn, but because they are allowed to fail as readily as they are encouraged to flourish.

Still, the odds are always stacked against our townie kids. It is tough to say to our children (my children included), "Yes, this school offered you a good scholarship, but we still cannot pay for a more entrancing school unless you want to hobble your future with a debt taking years of your best years to repay." So, all of my kids (so far, six of them) enrolled in some UMass or another. I followed the words of my practical father before me, spouting, "U-Mass or you pay." But lo and behold, despite limited options, they still harbor some slice of the American dream. Their intellects are yet intact, and their future is yet bright, and they truly did it on their own.

My apologies: I am a wordy and rambling writer. My own students will admonish my lack of a unified theme, my intrusions of personal bias, and, no doubt, my lazy adherence to a dull singular topic—not to mention my lack of rhetorical techniques. I actually began this essay as a brief plea to simplify education, to think outside of the proverbial box—to find ways to give time back to those restive students who have huge reservoirs of energy, intent, and excitement to explore their own potential, their own passions, and their own perspectives.

I am a traditionalist at heart. I want schools to get back to teaching time-tested skills that build lasting foundations to shore up the dreams students will build their futures upon. If I am radical in any way, it is to thresh the wheat from the chaff and to see with clear eyes the purpose of our pasture. The values and morals we wish to instill should be modeled on the actions and ethos of a vibrant school community and the local community, not as a series of moral scriptures and political dogmas inserted into another long day. Schools need to create possibilities, not conformities. Schools need to be launching pads, not factories of conventional thinking. Schools need to trust the wisdom of parents and recognize the parameters of what can and should be accomplished on any given school day. Above all, we will not survive as a country unless we give students what they need to mold and manufacture a more enlightened and just society.

The paradox of education is that the more you offer, the less you accomplish. We can't assume breadth will ever equal depth. There is no compelling reason schools should sharpen and hone every tool in the shed. More labor, spread broadly across the table, brings diminishing returns; instead, choose the most useful tools and focus pride and effort on mastering what those tools can do—and whatever time is left outside the curriculum should be given back to what most interests our students. We must figure out ways to help our students become really, really, really good at something. Helping students become adept in some passion also means we need to give them time and freedom. It means potentially missing out on all the add-ons that fill an increasing bulk of every day.

It might mean they miss the walk for hunger. It might mean they miss this or that speaker or the workshop on sustainability, conflict resolution, or white privilege. Or it might mean they lead the walk for hunger, or they are the speaker telling their story of discovering racial inequity. Or it might mean they are part of a radical movement to unmask white privilege and show us—me—what white privilege really is. Or how we are screwing up the planet. Or how sexual identity is not a choice. It might mean they become incredibly good at soccer, archery, or chess. It might mean they grow a YouTube channel with a million hits. It might mean they rip out every Led Zeppelin riff with blazing speed. It might mean, god forbid, they become world-ranked gamers, fishermen, meme-makers, or avatar aficionados.

It will give annoying, overbearing, hovering (and generally wealthy) parents even more time to mold and morph their offspring into some perfected version of child genius—some kid with perfect SAT scores, impeccable musical virtuosity, a portfolio of essays ripe and ready for the admissions process, a history of philanthropy and good deed doing, and athletic prowess in some obscure sport. It will, however, be a huge pain in the ass for working-class parents shuddering at the thought of their feral, unkempt children furloughed too early from school— freed to roam the streets, freed to smoke legal weed, freed to have sex, freed to Snap or Bing-chat for even more hours of the day. For these busy and frazzled trustees of childhood, it is critical that their workday more or less mirrors the school day—and a teacher, god forbid, they need to work a full day for an honest day's work.

So, damn, this is a conundrum.

It is great sport for parents to criticize schools, teachers, and administrators; nonetheless, it is high treason to question any aspect of how any invested parent or guardian raises their child or children. Trust has to start somewhere; trust has to be embodied and embraced in some way, shape, or form somewhere. Trust has to begin with giving it to our kids. Some will certainly fail. But they will probably fail anyway. Some will be slow to adapt to opportunity. But their sluggishness is on them. If they squander opportunities now, they may well learn much from their adolescent sloth in their looming future—a heady lesson to remember and guide them in their newly invigorated lives.

But some many will soar beyond their wildest dreams. They will realize unimagined majesty from their efforts. They will learn about choice, priorities, perseverance, and vision.

They will not become street punks. They will not become anarchists. They will not squander the magi's gift. They will become our future.

We need to hand the reins of that future to them and give them a better future now.

Blemished, broken, and bankrupt as it now seems.

CAN A POEM HAPPEN

Out of something as tedious
As a flooded basement,
Strewn with sogged socks, books,
Tools, dryer lint and throw rugs?
Is there any intrinsic beauty
In an old shop vac
Pulsating and slurping
The slopping mucky mess
Lugged up the stairs
And poured into
The already wet garden?
Did I need this reminder
To purge the dross and flotsam
Of my overburdened life?

The trashman came
On this fortuitous day,
And I helped him heave
The heavy bags and tilt
The awkward barrels
Into the hopper.

We shared cold lemonade
And stories of common miseries
As my morning's labor
(our mutual dependence)
Squeezed, oozed and morphed
Into a perfect, oblong carcass
Carted away
In the blast of an air horn
And a waving hand.

Back here
In this glistening basement
I convince myself
Whatever remains
Is what should be.

GRANDMA'S WORDS

Be old before you are new

In the beginning was the word...
~Genesis

We do not live in Grandma's world of words, and neither did Grandma live in her grandma's world of words, and so on and so on in a downward devolution through untold millennia. From primal grunts, whistles, and gestures, language—words—were born, evolved, and morphed in the churning's of an ancient time. We are now blessed, and burdened, by a burgeoning mosaic of linguistic and expressive possibilities. Few feelings, thoughts, emotions, and wonderings are locked away from expression or driven into some illiterate corner. Each new generation slurps from a lexicon continually expanding and emboldening in breadth and scope to capture and freeze the fleeting fury of transient life.

Words make real what is palpably sensed, and no doubt our first spoken words were once a mere coupling of sounds— surprised mutual understandings, practical, primeval grunts, and whistling's structured towards survival in a clannish, harsh, and unforgiving landscape. These sounds evolved into words to remember histories, to strengthen traditions, to weave parables from experience, and to give meaning, direction, and substance to the purpose inherent in the mysterious perplexion of life—the viscera of flesh and innards coiled within a skeletal frame wrapped in tender skin.

After thousands of years, our first written words were scratched on walls and papyrus. These words gave expediency to memory, and ever since the longer veil of ignorance lifts slowly and inexorably—new light shines in dark places, recurring epiphanies too precious to lose are retained, the ravages of time and misfortune placated by remembrances, and the power of reflection ruminates in the fire of insatiable bellies.

Humanity and words coevolved in a steady march forward—words meshed and melded in a swirling symbiosis of needs, yearnings, and aspirations. We are distinct in our utterances. Our thoughts are made palpable and immortal by a procreative stringing together of sound married to sense. The collective memories told and perpetuated by bards, prophets, and seers transformed into individual exhortations, laments, songs, and stories open to anyone brave enough to look beyond and within, using sounds wedded to sense, cadenced, and formed from the rhythm of breath into the rhythms of life.

Rudimentary technology cleaved pages plied to pages in steady iterations of progress—reams of stories and poems, screeds of drivel, letters and journals and diaries, discoveries and dissertations, insults and insinuations, politics and propaganda—all that could be put to a page found a home, an audience, a stage, a platform, and a purpose. We now live so fully in words that it is unthinkable to live mute and deaf amidst this stunning cacophony birthed on this muddy orb spinning its transitory ellipsis around a warm and common star. Words equalize the pauper with the king and kindle genius in every child. The strength of words is passed to the weak. The balm of solace is laced into the tea of aging. Life becomes more of an odyssey of meaning than a reptilian adventure of bitter, arduous survival.

Folksy phrases capture our unfolding dilemma: *All good things come to pass; familiarity breeds contempt,* and *every empire disintegrates through its excesses.* Our words, increasingly common, dull, and predictable, are more a babble of inanity than a heroic addiction to truth. It is a miner's labor in a hard-rock mine to ferret the gem out of the slurry of slag. The greater irony is that in our present sea of words—a sea imbued with inexplicable variety—we have lost our bearings and drifted away from the distant polestar. We are more addicted to a junkie high of email, texts, fake news, real news, and viral blogs than we are drawn to real words wrought and crafted in a primitive forge of deliberate attentiveness. We wake and post to Instagram. We check our Facebook feed and turn out the light. We love words without seeing, grasping, and feeding on the intrinsic power of words. We are factory workers hammering out salvaged parts. We live and die like mayflies in a day. Little left is lasting—a ripple on still waters, a shimmering gleam in a fading light. We are more prey than predator. We hide in a tangled scrub, content to merely survive.

This power eroding us is also the power strengthening us, but only if we exercise our wills. It is a new paradigm. It is neither good nor evil. It just is. Words—great words and worthy words—are simply a click, clack, and download away, and any ignorance of our own is a willful decision—a conscious abnegation of a magnanimous gift. Some part of our lives and our days need a devotion to this bounty, to what is buried in the ground before us before we escape to the lesser pursuits of the day.

We have a duty to literature, to what has stood and tested the erosions of time and place. Equally so, we have a duty to find and celebrate the enlightened creators of today. But even more so, we have a duty to ourselves to lay a cornerstone of literacy in our own lives—not to just write with words, but to think with words, to reflect with words, and to create with words. No pickaxe is stronger than the pen to find the intrinsic beauty, poignancy, and urgency of our own lives. We have stories to tell and wisdom to utter. Our headstone in a quiet graveyard should be a finger wagging towards a distant nebula—a testament to our unique eternity—not a dirge to futility.

This is not a call to make bookworms and poets of us all. It is a call to appreciate how words have changed—the mediums carrying words and creating words have changed in the same breaths we are changing, and we do not and cannot know the future. Our visions seldom bend over the horizon. All clairvoyance is sham and delusion. It is sacrilege to even whisper, but I can foresee a world without books. Not some *Fahrenheit 451* dystopia, but some new and mystic way to experience, appreciate, and work with words. We have not reached our omega point. We are merely arcing towards it.

Reading is not some timeless tradition. It is a relatively recent evolution—a cart of sorts to convey piles of words with some semblance of cogency. It has always been (short of conversation and oratory) the most efficient and expedient way to carry words to our minds and to other minds, but a good podcast, documentary, Netflix series, or movie can well do the same thing. *Doctor Zhivago* stills my heart, whether I read it or watch it. *Nature's First Green Is Gold*, recited from memory, is as precious as the pithy words on a brittle page. In the end, it is the effect and memory of words, not the conveyance, that seize the day. I can learn any given point in history just as quickly—and in a way just as edifying as reading—by watching some Ken Burns series. I can experience the sublime in the cinema as deeply as in a classic novel. Words wed to form, but words are not married to any particular structure. We should not be shamed by our choices or pushed from the path while our genius moves inexorably within the gravity of inertia.

As Thoreau writes in *Walden*: "Old ways for the old and new ways for the new," and so it is with how we learn to use, create, and craft words. By and large, English teachers give a damn about how and why they teach, and most are pretty damn good readers—great readers and avid readers—gifted men and women who embrace, experience, and desperately try to pass on the transformative power of reading. Hell, I am one of them! Good-hearted, gracious, gifted, dedicated, and wise teachers— they absolutely and fully believe reading is the cat's meow and holy grail of any school's curriculum, for how else can or will anyone succeed in any future endeavor without reading?

The irony is that almost anything we read must first be written, and, no offense intended, most English teachers are no great shakes as writers, at least not in any real way. In most English classes, time spent reading dwarfs time spent writing. These teachers, however, are damn good graders and critics of writing. Regrettably, they are more quick and ready to slash and burn most any piece of a painstakingly novice effort passing through their clumsy, twitching hands and under their squinting, critical eyes, as they are effusive in their praise for a noble, but ultimately insufficient, response to a writing prompt.

They cannibalize the young like frogs gorging on tadpoles. They are quick to condemn, but unwilling to be condemned. It is a weird thing, for I doubt a school would hire a trumpet teacher who can't play the trumpet or a shop teacher who is unsure how to build a table. I wonder if more teachers wrote—even just as much as they ask their students to write—a new breed of mutual respect for the power of words would take root in the classrooms and in the assignments. The boat of reading and the boat of writing, and its molding and shaping of words, would rise with the flood of a newly enlightened tide, for it is a rare writer who is not also an active and astute reader.

The idea, promise, and potential of a certain pedagogy often supersede common sense, and we are seldom as smart as we think we are. We weave new meanings into old words and phrases. We believe we are creating new paradigms, when in reality we are simply reworking the old—gifting new and catchy words to time-worn traditions. My school just spent a sizable sum of money building a new makerspace—a new word for *shop*. No one will dare say it, but the unbreathed insinuation is that our design-thinking exercise is simply a shop—a shop for smart kids —engineery kids, kids destined to shape and mold our technological future—but not for the greasy kids classrooms never served, the kids who gravitated to old-style metal shops, wood shops, and auto shops, if only because these havens offered the only places they actually learned and the only places rewarding their oily bent of erudition.

My school also built a new woodshop along with our new Makerspace, so I am happy to be where traditional working with hands is at least marginally celebrated. I shudder to think of the schools dismantling traditional shops for some flotsam dream of the future. To be fair, much of the blame falls on shop teachers, noble teachers, but often teachers who are not comfortable or fluent in creating new words for new times—words that might possibly capture the hearts, minds, and imaginations of school boards and administration's desperate to be on the cutting edge of education. Or at least better than the towns around them.

Our new lab is a marvel of engineering and purpose, designed thoughtfully, if a bit impetuously. It is meant to spark creativity, ingenuity, and experimentation. It will be full of nifty gadgets—3D printers spinning out gears and trinkets; solenoids and batteries tethered to spider-like robots; reams of duct tape, cardboard, and wires cobbling together dreams and visions into unlikely inventions. Teachers are tasked with joining in the circus and bowing and bending our curriculums to a vague, new covenant of an age-old process.

I actually like the word *makerspace*. It has a nice ring to it, and it is easy to coil my imagination around its intent. I'm happy we are latching onto this vision of learning and creating for a new breed of kids, but I would take the makerspace vision one step further, for there is no place in our new makerspace to work solely with words, no makerspace to push new boundaries of expression with the greatest tool and gift we have—words! Every classroom should be a design thinking lab—a true makerspace, equipped as a makerspace, and experienced as a makerspace, for if we cannot form something from what we have learned, we will have lost the palpable touch to the words teaching us in the first place.

It takes no genius of the mind to create an orchard from a fallow field. Fortunately, my school is prescient and forgiving enough to let me follow the bent of my madness. I don't have desks in my room. I don't allow backpacks trundled in to litter my floor, and I remind my students of the baggage of every other academic demand they carry through the rest of the day. I don't allow notebooks, pens, or loose sheets of paper to doodle and dawdle upon. They can only bring themselves, a willing spirit, and an iPad, which to my mind is simply a tool—an incredible tool serving and purposed as their library, workbench, and portal into the world of words. There, within the confines of a small space, a greater universe can be experienced, toyed with, reflected upon, and re-birthed in a panoply of forms, all built upon the vision of making things with words, appreciating things with words, sharing things with words—and sharing ourselves with words.

I do not deny the power of the printed page. In my classroom, I have a huge library of tattered books cornered with a pair of musty couches. At any given time, my room, littered with sprawled, unkempt bodies, resembles more of a mob hit than a meticulously furrowed alignment of dreariness. The two large closets are now home to video and recording studios. When students struggle, I tell them to "give a damn and figure it out"—which, in the end, is the only thing they really need to know. When we stop to share, we sit on stools around a massive wooden table crafted by my good friend Tom Cummings, a gifted and iconoclastic local cabinet maker. Around this table, we gather every day. We laugh at our pathetic mistakes, and we are equally wowed by uncommon perfection. I don't carry home any sheaves of papers. I don't sigh and bemoan the drudgery of grading. I come home and sit on the back porch, energized and eager to immerse myself and taste the fruits of their weary efforts. I grade myself more harshly than I grade my students. I stumble and fall, but I also try to lean forward into something resembling progress. I try to live what I ask them to do—love words and what words can do.

Damn… I ramble on. I am, as often as not, a parody of what I preach—I am the unmoved mover. I am life without conclusion. Points without centers. A diaspora of wandering words sucking manna in a desert, but, like anyone, I am convinced of something wild and ultimately inexplicable—possibilities camouflaged in full view of the world—and, yet, there is no word for it. I spill the cart of my head with willful abandon. I collect the trinkets spilled on the page because I can't foresee or imagine a world without words carrying more heft than their weight. I am a gong in the night from a distant bell tower, reminding myself that words are part of our ancestral lineage and future promise. I am my Grandma's words and the words of my youth. I cling stubbornly to the notion that sculpted and crafted words are our only way to move forward and beyond what we ever were, are, or will be.

We are blessed by a cursed Fate. We live in the infinite, recurring now. We are horses led to perfect water.

So drink today before tomorrow—before the rosy fingers of dawn shine once more.

And the Word was made flesh, and dwelt among us…full of grace and truth… [John I: 14]

BENEATH THE HIERARCHY

The cat and the mouse

On the highest throne in the world,
we still sit only on our own bottom.
~Michel de Montaigne

I am feeling good right now—not only for being where I am —but for being who I am. I am a middle and high school English teacher. I just finished grading some forty-five sheaves of final exams—all of which are graciously full of metacognition's, a fancy term for a reflection. I feel good because every single bantering of my student reflections validates my inclinations and practices. I grade for effort, not necessarily excellence; I create an environment as demanding as it is fun, but mostly, I focus on teaching useful and practical skills. I model how to practice these skills and articulate how and why these skills are important to the unfolding of their respective destinies.

Or at least I think I do.

I am soon expected to meet my department head to discuss my "meeting of my goals" for this past year and to discern whether or not I achieved these goals. Like a fool, I practice in my head what I might say. I anticipate his wise, laconic responses and craft my own labored replies. It is a funny game. On the surface, it seems like a well-intentioned and useful exercise. My more immediate problem is that I can't even remember the goals I blithely penned so many months ago, nor can I remember how to access the "Folio" storing this precious cargo of my ongoing deceits. No doubt, I penned my goals to avoid any undue attention to me—safe words, fuzzy promises, and hints of an enlightened attitude—nothing unveiling the true deceit of my subterfuge, my unstated dreams lost in a mystic cloud of unknowing where all is settled and all is unsettled. At this late stage of my teaching career, I need to live beneath the hierarchy and find some noble serfdom to ply my trade in words—to step below the reaches of the pinging radar searching for my elusive self, if only to do me better—a betterment I am loathe to wear.

It is a cat-and-mouse game.

And a game I am destined to lose.

Ironically, if I lose, I win, for as Thoreau observed, "The only place for a just man in an unjust society is in prison," a philosophy echoed, too, by Ghandhi:

The dignity of man requires obedience to higher laws—to the strength of the spirit…They cannot take away our self-respect if we do not give it to them.

So, I cherish my incarceration in the dungeon of the poor, where the incantations of progress and proficiency are indistinct, muffled echoes—monkish chants droned in a strange language I cannot grasp with my ignorant paws, a language that does not lead me willingly into their new and strange faith or to stand in line with their legions of followers before a pantheon of shifting gods.

I do not have much to offer to the future. I am more at home in the past, dusting a humble cabin with a plume of feathers. I am an old teacher lingering in a school seemingly petrified of its present existence—a school hellbent on dizzying change, a change that is noble in intent but losing its bent to create honest, capable, and inquisitive boys. There is promise and merit in the visions of my overseers. They seek a common experience for all students, and I am not the one to stand in the way; however, there is also truth in my vision—a veritas I can't abandon unless I abandon myself.

Our school motto, *Sua Sponte* (which tenders as *"it is in your own hands"),* is slowly capitulating to a betrothed autocracy whose well-intentioned admonitions and edicts translate in my paranoid and irascible self as *"Hear me; do what I say, or you are a lost cause,"* which, no doubt, is aimed at teachers like me—an old guy with a stale brain and stubborn, misspent ideologies forged in the iconoclastic fire of my belly—but, despite the cage I am in, a teacher with dedicated, inspired, confident, and capable students.

I do not say this in a vainglorious way (though, more than likely, I do) even as I am proud to be who I am—if only for them —my students—if only for this proud moment on the cusp of another closing year. I feel good. I am alive and unfettered. The earth has not swallowed me; tradition has not dulled me; and change has not hobbled me. I am still my ineffable self. I want to crow like a rooster, bray like a donkey, and murmurate like a flock of grackles. My year is done. I have done no lasting harm and, perhaps, much good. My awkward band of brotherly students feels some memorable hint of pride and purpose for all that happened in this breathtaking slice of 8th and 9th grade time. I am energized by the entanglement of my curmudgeonly disposition, even as I subtly perceive that my social standing within the school is troublesome. I fear the future, but I am not yet defeated. I sense some wily hope will raise my flag above the maelstrom of the fray. I sing the inspiration of an old Scottish border ballad:

Fight on, fight on my weary men
I will only stop to bleed a while
then rise to fight again.

Yet, I am equally fatigued. I blindly hoped for something more validating in these last years of my teaching career of some forty years and more—a tithe more fitting, more appreciated, and more palpable to dust clean the mantle of my career. Once, whatever was called my vision seemed possible, tangible, and predestined. I was engaged by the future. I actually thought my difference could make a difference—some eyes might see and think, "Yes, there is something useful and practical in the deeds of that old miscreant." Now, however, my professional life is consumed with staying under the probing radar, eluding the prying eyes of those intent on doing me good. A stubborn foe, I cannot adhere to the edicts and ethos forced upon me, and like some revolutionary soldier committed to a stoic manifesto, I fight a futile battle against an entrenched and more powerful resistance. My banishment is a creeping, almost imperceptible degradation. Less and less, it matters more where I am and what I do. I do not play with the Lords of the Field. I do not dance with the courtesans in the ballrooms. There is no ladder threaded down into my dank, dark cell. Yet, from out of this cage, I sing joyously from the darkness of my soul. I yawp my *Mind & Heart & Soul & Being* to an eclectic cacophony of boys singing boldly with me in equal measures of curiosity, contempt, and compulsion in unrestrained choruses of unmitigated joy.

My school—this school I love—my friend, my comrade, and my family for some thirty years seem now a toothed foe spiraling into an abyss of conformity and acquiescence sheathed in a thin, dull armor cobbled together more for show than utility. The noble hierarchy has become the emperor with no clothes. The aged and dissolute are consigned to an abnegation of courage, dignity, and vision. Original minds and dwindling passion devolve into the entropy of dotted i's and crossed t's. It is a conundrum within a conviction. I feel a strange tug of loneliness. I cannot sense the profound within the babble and drivel of progress, so I plod on, go my own way, and hope to escape unscathed and unnoticed.

I am a common man with common dreams. I do not seek redemption. I do not need to be validated. I do not need monikers on my walls or shout-outs in department meetings or in all-school gatherings in our stately hall. I need freedom to tame my genius into a form kids can and will imitate and iterate; moreover, to understand, embrace, respect, and relive. Everything I teach in the course of any given year can be scribbled onto one side of a tattered notecard—yes, *"Give a damn and figure it out."* It is the only mantra I need, the only admonition my students hear, and the only lesson truly worth teaching. The world is not what we want it to be or can teach it to be. It is what it is—a messy, discombobulated mosaic of defeats and victories, odysseys between the Straits of Scylla—a whirlpool on the right, a six-headed monster on the left, and the only way out is through.

I need to be left alone, which, sadly, seems an anathema to our ponderous and predictable pedagogy. Our insistence on consistency and collaboration is at odds with common sense. We educate our students one day at a time, one way at a time, and one boy at a time. I am not a threat to anything or anyone, lest it be conformity and a misplaced notion of collaboration, nor to the dizzying array of administrators and perpetuators who insist on inculcating an ideology and pedagogy summoned from deviations of actual truth's, an expediency evolving from some short-lived meeting on a weekly morning, some accomplishment to lend their name to—but rarely an introspection of life lived and bursting out of the breadth and depth of their wisdom and understanding. It is a creed cobbled out of a shaky and myopic need for consensus, continuity, and conformity. The time they spend crafting my life might be better spent laying a foundation to withstand the heft and weight of true education.

I wonder if every teacher felt free to teach what they feel needs to be taught, a new magnificence would bloom in every nook, cranny, hallway, playing field, shop, stage, and studio of our school. Genius unleashed would create geniuses informed by genuine, enlightened minds—or at least gorged on passion and erudition—for how can we teach what we do not know, love, and express through the actions of our lives? Our school could imitate life itself—a diaspora of passions unleashed. Our petty prejudices and bigotries would seem benign to true and enlightened thought. A common dignity, respect, and revelation would supplant predictable, pedantic pedagogy. True education would happen out of the panoply of words and practices sown by teachers juggling their innate brilliance with insipid demands and tawdry expectations. It is what we do—and what we ignore —in our infinite quest to do well and engage and enliven the charge of being a teacher.

My ranting is not an oracle to denigrate, simple as it may be, but to elevate—elevate teachers to a position of *Dignity, Respect & Trust*. Unleash the prodigious potential and possibility bestowed upon this school. Call a spade a spade; weed out the extraneous clutter; and hold us accountable for our impact, not our personalities and predilections.

My goals for this year—and every year—are pretty simple, common, and mundane—to teach my kids to read better, to write better, and to think better. It is June of another year. They will leave unscathed. They will know the world before them. They have done their duty, yet sense with trepidation the swallowing whirlpool in a foaming sea, the raging monster on the beetled cliffs, and the maddened cyclops of the island. They will one day be alone. Odysseus' cunning deception has made us the eternal "Nobody." I can only tell them who I am and what I have been. I can't give them my future, but I can give them my now. I have no Athena beside me. My kingdom is my wit and wiles to persist.

My folios is my classroom—not an apology. It is a living, breathing, belching testament, unencumbered and free for all to see. The real folios of my students reveal and represent an anthology of striving and attainment—and all of it heroic and unforgettable growth. This false folio given to me in an earnest quest to tame my feral ways is a tattered rag compared to the actual me. While noble in intent and revealing to some, it is a shoddy, ill-advised parchment for me—words without meaning, inscriptions without courage; prescriptions without illness. It is four hands on the wheel and a silly document that in no way, shape, or substance inspires or informs what is dauntless within me—and what is dauntless within each of us.

I love teaching. I love the babbling of my days and the playful mocking of my studentry. In spite of this unmitigated, collective effervescence of joy, I fear, feel, and hear my castle crumbling stone by stone, bit by bit, gleaming nugget by gleaming nugget, whisper by whisper.

Please don't take this from me.

It is all I am.

I AM NO DIFFERENT, I THINK,

Than some hugger-monger farmer
Spading stubborn, clumpy soil,
Stooped and silent
In the first warm spring—
worn boots pressing hard ground
From early morning to noon.

> *Press. Lift. Turn.*
> *Press. Lift. Turn.*
> *Press. Lift. Turn.*

Every so often some root,
A stubborn tendril
Tethered to a distant maple,
Disrupts my rhythmic meter
And gives me pause enough to rest—
Long enough to make me wonder
Why I didn't just borrow Wally's gas tiller.

But I get back at it.

> *Press. Lift. Turn.*
> *Press. Lift. Turn.*
> *Press. Lift. Turn.*

At this rate I'll be done before supper.
Some sense of symmetry and purpose
Will yield a perfect scar
On a neglected patch of grass,

And some seed may yet be sown
Before I am called away
To a larger field.

.

THE HARD SELL

A defense of blogging

Taking a new step, uttering a new word,
is what people fear most.
~Fyodor Dostoevsky, *Crime and Punishment*

I am tired of the word "blog," and you are probably tired of me using the word "blog," but to me, blogging in English class is as obvious as mold in the petri dish in science, Fibonacci's sequence in math, declensions in Latin, gravity in physics, or cartwheels in the gym. There is an incontrovertible truth to blogging—it works. It works as a pedagogical tool in a teacher's chest of wizardry, not, as argued by many, some distant cousin to real and polished prose. This disinformation is an ongoing lie and misconception. Blogging is what you—the teacher—ask it to be and what you allow it to be. If senseless babble is what you want and what you allow, then senseless babble is what you will get. Twenty years of blogging in my English classes is proof enough that ownership and pride trumps all. Most kids simply want to have a living, breathing blog—a place their peers want to visit, read, watch, and leave gracious, supportive comments.

Blogging is about connection and community—not defiance and inanity. What artist, what writer, and what person is not energized by the notion of a community—however big, small, wide, or narrow you define community? Our genetic code is one big chunk of a mysterious algorithm seeking to connect in real and meaningful ways with real and meaningful people. A collective community of writers is greater than the sum of its parts—and a blogging community is the common in community —not a lone wolf howling in a desert landscape and surely not a rampaging anarchist upending sound curriculums and thriving ecosystems.

I know it is offensive when I wonder why we ask a student to bust their ass on a project, paper, or assignment that lives and dies in a day—a hard-wrought work we judge, grade, praise, or condemn and return as a shared secret between collaborators. I get why we do this. This was once a practical and sustainable model for a teacher and a student—and it is not so difficult to make the case it still is, but in the best cases, it is the mentor and the mentored striving for perfection together—the master and apprentice plying and learning the same trade. In the worst cases, there was no mentoring and no master, and in the average case, it was (and often still is) somewhat legible—but often not—indictments, corrections, and critiques scribbled in blue books between double-spaced passages, but lacking real and lasting passion on either side of the aisle.

When so much is wrong, there is little room for praise—not praise for the sake of praise but praise as recognition for an honest day's work. Honest praise, humble criticism, and good role models are the marrow in the bones of any outstanding student. This is what a connected community of writers provides to each other—not one voice speaking to one voice, but many voices speaking and connecting, each offering a singular harmony to the whole; moreover, you, as the teacher, command the symphony with waving arms and artful gesticulations. This is the opus you created. These are the students you guide, and this is the orchestra you conduct.

It can honestly be your finest hour.

If you let it be your finest hour.

One hundred and fifty years ago, Thoreau wrote, "Old ways for the old, and new ways for the new." I am sure he would be aghast at most of what the internet hawks purvey to carve out our leisure time as it barters away our precious time. I am also sure he would sense the opportunity to be close to the best the world has to offer. Like an imperfect tool in the hands of a true craftsman, we shape the wispy web in any way we want or need. As the old-saw goes, "It is a poor craftsman who blames his tools." As teachers, we need to retool ourselves, remake our classrooms as shops, and teach in new ways. There are new ways better than the old ways.

There. It has been said—there are new ways better than the old.

I hear hemming, hawing, and screeching in the fetid air of the hallways, warily arguing that the old ways still work, and I know they work—and some of us have spent decades perfecting better modes and methods in the classroom. No freaking iPad, Chromebook, malcontent, or chiming phone is going to change what you know, feel, and believe is best for your students. You won't change if only because you really do give a damn about the kids—not because you are the lazy, ill-informed, pedantic, paper-pushing artifact the tech-savvy might have people believe. But if this is you—if you are the one with a visceral reaction girding your heels in the sands of change—open the door just a bit and cultivate some change in your life.

As much as we despise the messenger, change is coming, and this change is not as radical as you believe. It is, in fact, common sense, a wise use of time and resources, and sound educational psychology. As teachers, we need to relearn and rethink our approach, or we risk irrelevancy in the classroom and, worse, in the minds of our students, who are, after all, the ones entering this brave, new, and screwed-up world bequeathed to them.

I have a friend over at MIT who has spent the better part of his professional life developing a radar to detect beyond the horizon. Would we steal this same radar for what is emerging over the horizon in education? Imagine the fads, trends, and standards we could have avoided. That little blip—that first blog on the screen twenty-years ago—now looms with greater permanence, resilience, and relevance than any of us foresaw in our unfolding dreams.

But even blogs—my precious blogs—are only one component of what is now possible. With a bit of guidance, direction, and support, those same kids with a funky little blog can now have a funky and incredible website, a portfolio that includes an embedded blog, and much, much more. This website can showcase an entire folio of the possibilities of writing and multi-media—essays, stories, journaling, research papers, podcasts, videos, poetry, reviews, travelogues, presentations, slideshows, polls, interviews, and editorials—really, "anything" presented in digitized form is possible, and it is equally possible to share what you want to share and not share what you do not sense you are ready to cast into the sea of humanity.

This portfolio is the beginning of each student's unique and empowering digital footprint they leave upon this world. Who among us doesn't sift through a shoebox full of old family pictures? Who doesn't like to find a tattered letter from an old friend or lover in some Converse shoebox? And who doesn't put that precious cardboard crate away carefully and tenderly, cognizant of its special and eternal value?

Why deny any student the opportunity to collect and collate their life and their works in a way they can keep, share, curate, and remember?

Why not encourage blogging?

Why not try it?

LIVE A LITERATE LIFE

Read. Write. Think.

My life is the poem I could have writ,
But I could not both live and utter it
~Henry David Thoreau

The poor go to another's orchard to steal a taste of fruit. The less poor plant their own orchards and harvest their own fruits, while the poet, the richest of them all, tills a higher ground and grows a more perfect fruit, but then must give the harvest away, for no one can steal or buy fruits that never bruise, fall too early, or wilt in the heat. This fruit of the poet gives more than sustenance—it cleaves us from the inexplicable and binds us to the possible. A poet's life is a vessel of humanity, and in their words thay carry the collective dreams, haunts, wonderings, visions, and perceptions lifting any who read or hear out of the mud and muck of a sultry existence and into a more transcendent experience—an uncommon experience of common life, yet so few of us actually read poetry even as we sense the greatness of the poets and their poetry.

The act of reading has little in common with being a literate person. Educators, psychologists, social scientists, and pundits decry the scourge of illiteracy but seldom define the framework of true literacy. Making sense of vowels and sounds formed into words arcing into a story does not imply literacy. A literate person appreciates the power of words shared between beating hearts, searching souls, and deft minds. A true reader keeps a bookshelf on one wall and a trashcan in the corner. The insights of one truly thoughtful, capacious person outweigh the benefits of reading a pile of supercilious, self-aggrandizing opinion pieces or trolling through the detritus of a hundred shallow websites. I have a good many friends who are not avid readers but who I sense are profoundly "literate." To be literate melds thought to reflection—at least enough to question, churn, mull, and distill subtle thoughts towards a universal clarity creating something noble out of a passing insight.

For there to be true literacy, there has to be discernment, discipline, and doggedness. For the wise but unread sages of the past and, to a lesser degree, the present, their lives were and are the legacy left behind—a legacy that continues to inspire, inform, and enlighten the path of any given day. Neither Jesus, Buddha, Black Elk, nor Mohamed set out to "write a book." Each of them lived their lives in concert with the wisdom of their thoughts and capacious visions hoisted from the depths of their incantations of unwavering belief. They each spoke their truths and let loyal scribes and bards listen and ink their words into written testaments of faith.

To argue that reading literature is the only gateway to wisdom and understanding is utter classist deceit and intellectual arrogance. Thoughts put into words and actions define literacy. The peril of teaching is knowing what should be learned but can't be taught. It can only be experienced. It is something you either do or you don't, but you are, to coin a new word, the "experiencer." By hook or crook, I am going to give you—my wide-eyed students—the opportunity to experience a literate lifestyle, meaning you are the reader, writer, listener, watcher, thinker, philosopher, poet, raconteur, creator, and creation.

But first, you must recreate yourself—some of you more than others. You must take conscious and concrete steps to willingly live and embrace a literate life. A literate life implicitly accepts how and why well-crafted words power us out of the "mean and moiling" life that so exasperated Thoreau. Begrudging your potential limits the possibilities and options life presents. It needs to be more than just poetry and classics dropped on you through my intransigent obsession with the past.

You live on the edge of the brave new world hinted at by an erudite visionary a mere generation ago. Ironically, the technology unshackling your generation literally opened wide the doors of learning for anyone who remotely gives a damn about cultivating truth, yet it also sucks the weak and timid sycophants amongst us into stagnant, vapid, and self-centered lifestyles whose only reflective moments in life are basking in front of a bathroom mirror or in the brief moments between loadings of a new "Call of Duty" game.

You have a chance to do something amazingly cool and real with your life. Do not attach daily journal writing to a list of chores, but rather as an opportunity to mold yourself into a more literate person. Write every day, or you will not grow as a writer.

Amazing seeds are scattered in innocuous journal entries. Read, watch, and listen to better yourself and deepen your appreciation for the power of words. Don't eye your couch as your lover and watch TV or movies to veg out and escape (though sometimes a dumb movie is just what we need); rather, watch a movie more thought-provoking; read a book that endures for a reason; or read a book someone recommends to you because they glimpse the seed of your potential for a higher faculty. Read the Op-Ed editions of the paper; go to websites encouraging mindful reflection more than mindless consumption. Listen to different genres of music in different ways. Learn and practice the skills of good writers: narrative paragraphs, life reflections, literary reflections, short stories, and poetry. Gather where thoughtful people gather. Make yourself a more active part of our writing community. Seek out writing nudging you towards your artistic sensibilities. Watch Ted Talks, history channels, nature channels—anything that fills you more than drains you.

Time is made, not given. It is on you to find the time to think and create. If you don't have time, make time. Find a way to create thoughtful moments. Sit silent; take solitary walks; and always, always, always spend the needed time to reflect and reshape what you did or did not do. Be curious and explore thoughts playing themselves out in the field of your experience.

Your life is an orchard of endless opportunity. Prepare the soil. Sow and tend what you plant. Cull the weeds and wait for the rains. Time will bloom the flower.

A perfect fruit will fall into your hand.

This fruit is your poem.

A POEM BEGINS

In a silky wiry mesh
Cradled on a barky limb, stirred
To a plodding life, nibbling
On leafy forage—oak,
Maple, catalpa and wild apple;
Reluctant, unsure,
Reticent and wondering
If gangly paper wings
Will lift her away
From the orchard
Of this—this
Unlikely,
Magical
Birth?

JUXTAPOSITIONS

How sadness begets joy

Why will you not wait for me,
when I am trying to hold you,
so that even in Hades' with our arms embracing
we can both take the satisfaction
of dismal mourning?
Or are you nothing
but an image that proud Persephone
sent my way, to make me grieve
all the more for sorrow?
~Odysseus, *The Odyssey*

Sometimes reality gets the best of us. My reality right now is sitting at the bedside of my mom for the last few days of her life. It is horrible, beautiful, and sad, yet incredibly meaningful, purposeful, and profound. It is strange how I go about the most common of pursuits while sitting by her bed in her small room. I watch the Pat's game, work up a comma test (which I am sure you are going to love), and laugh with my brother and sisters about our shared memories—and some (up until now) unshared memories. On Friday, mum said her last words to me: "Will you go with me?"

Though it was not clear where she wanted us to go…

I said, "I'd love to, but... I got a pile of your grandchildren to raise the way you raised me."

Her last words to me: "Okay then. Bye."

And that was it. Her last words...

Later on Friday, she rubbed my arm softly as I sang "Red River Valley" to her. On Saturday, she moved her finger a few times while I held her hand and recited the rosary for her, messing up the prayers and words as I have for the last fifty years. Today she is all but gone, yet somehow, for five lingering weeks, she has defied every doctor and nurse who looked at her and said, "Soon. It will be soon."

But we know now that it will be soon.

Very soon.

Soon enough for me to rush home at midnight just for some internet access to let you know I have not forgotten about you. I wish I could be trawling the rich waters of your blogs right now and see and comment on what you have been writing. The earnestness and honesty of your words are a powerful antidote to sadness—a needed reminder echoing the ebb and flow of life pulsating in the timeless rhythm of the universe.

I will not be in school this week, but I will post some work for you on Tuesday to get you through the week, though a break from me is more deserving. I'll be back soon, and we can dive back into *The Odyssey*—the book of books that so shaped the course of my life—a book whose very foundation is the power and love of family.

I am one up on Odysseus. He never got to say a fitting goodbye to his mother, Anticlea, wife of Laertes. She died grieving for her long-lost son, lost, she thought in some lonesome sea. Though you might not be in the habit of doing so, give your own mother, father, sister, brother, or friend a hug. Free up some words to show your love. You'll never regret it. When the time comes that you are in my shoes, you will have already created a beautiful memory—a gift to sustain you in the hardest of times.

My heart pounds with pain, yet my sadness cannot defeat me, nor will death defeat my mom.

I sit and watch my mom dance her final waltz with inexorable rhythm and purpose.

My tears are as real as my tomorrow.

ME & ROCKY

Ignore me, and you will succeed

Take your foot off the brakes,
but keep your eyes on the road.
~Fitz

Once, back in my days as a logger, I cut through a towering White oak. I didn't realize the trunk was hollowed and heart-rotted until my chainsaw screamed too easily through the monstrous tree. After the mad crush of limbs, leaves and tree thundered to the ground, I noticed blood on my saw and splattered on my legs.

But not my blood...

While cutting the tree down, I inadvertently massacred a whole raccoon family—a mom and seven incredibly small babies. I was pretty bummed about it all, but while sacredly moving the family out of the stump, I noticed the smallest ball of fur hobbling away on three legs.

A baby raccoon survived. I gently scooped him up and named him Rocky after The Beatles big hit "Rocky Raccoon." Blind and bare, he fit into my shirt pocket with room to spare.

I drove him home in my battered logging truck. My kitchen became my field hospital. I put him in a cake pan filled with straw and warmed by an old desk lamp. I was not even sure how to feed it. Its eyes were still closed. I heated milk from my goats in a pan on the stove and sucked warm milk into an eyedropper, and as luck would have it, after several attempts and childish cajoling, Rocky became my first suckling child.

For the first few weeks, warm milk was all Rocky could handle, but as time went on, he grew into a fuzzy little terror who would eat almost anything and learn to do most everything. He learned to open the refrigerator door. He figured out how to lift the toilet seat for a sip of water and open the cabinets. He tore my feather pillows into his own unkempt bed. No space was impenetrable. No task was impossible. He stole the chickens' eggs as if thievery answered his birthright. He slurped my cheerios in selfish abandon. He curled on my remaining pillow and cooed a raccoonish warbling beside my restful head.

In the mornings, while I milked the goats, he would lay on his back and paw the air with his single front paw, imploring me to squeeze the fresh milk all over his face. I sang old sea songs to him and wrestled him in mock battles. I felt like a young dad doing everything a dad needed to do and be. I wanted to raise a noble raccoon who could live in two worlds—the wild world and my tamed feral world.

Six months later, Rocky morphed into a stout, healthy three-legged rapscallion of feisty raccoon. With each day, I was more and more confident he could live in the symbiosis of my suburban airs and the harshness of a wild world.

So I started letting Rocky outside on his own. He always came back. He walked the woods and trails with me, along with a bleating herd of goats and the wild cat who came one day and never left. We shared our kingdom. Rocky was king. I was Saint Francis. All else were our minions.

Except the cat—the mongrel stray who answered to no name and heeded no master.

Some months later, I saw a hawk circling overhead above the hay field. I saw a coydog skulking in the tangle of brush beside the woods. I heard the haunting cry of a fisher cat somewhere deep in the swamp.

I never saw Rocky again.

Maybe I let Rocky go too soon. Maybe I should have given him a better rubric for life, but living by a rubric is no recipe for life.

Do you really need a rubric for this assignment?

MAYBE GOD SCATTERS US

Torn from bags of clouds—
A callous hand casting
Dry seed from a windy sky
Blown willy-nilly
Into some small crevice
We have to call home,
Tended or not,
In the disparities of fate.

I am not your son.
I am just the flesh
You force me to wear.
My roots are shallow and bold
And cling madly into shabby soil.

I stare into the cold waters,
Down the leaf-shorn banks
Of the Assabet
Towards the dam by the mill—

Damn it all damnation,
Still my useless quill—
I cannot craft a parable
Out of suicide.

STONES, WORDS & WALLS

Bringing clarity to chaos

I'm not ignoring you.
I'm busy building my empire.
~Moosa Rahat

Language is the gift and the tool enabling us to appreciate, understand, and express the complexity and nuance of our inner and outer lives. Language builds upon itself. It evolves as we evolve to breathe the newest air into the universe. The right words bring clarity to chaos and echo long in the halls of existence. Those who listen will be enlightened and will find new strength to face another day. Those who read will be entranced by the mysterious alchemy of a shared language. It is this sharing of words that begs our focus. We need to let the words we use bubble up from the broth of shared experience, and as like minds congregate, you will find your audience as much as they will find you.

Robert Frost once wrote, "Something there is that doesn't love a wall." But I ignore his lament and twist his actual intent. I study every rock wall I see. I love these walls lining the fields wending through the forests of New England. I even worked off and on for a number of years building stone walls with John Bordman—a brilliant and ornery Yankee insistent every wall be a "testament to eternity." I was young, rough, and unfazed as I tried to learn everything I needed to learn about this "piling on of stones."

From early on in my apprenticeship, John would leave me at a worksite for hours on end to pick through a mountain of stone, stumbling and groping for stones suited and destined to fit together and make a fitting wall. I placed my stones and squinted at them from a distance (just like John) to see if the hand of gravity, and not the vanity of man, placed each stone in its rightful and eternal place in time and space.

Invariably, John would return with opera music blaring from his truck. He would calmly and quietly destroy the better parcel of my day's work. As critical as he was of society, he rarely crushed my dainty ego by criticizing my efforts. Instead, he would say things like, "Damn, it's hard to find good stones in this pile!" In the same breath, he would add, "But it is all we have to work with." Then, with an intense flurry, he would craft a magnificent wall—a wall crafted to last for centuries—walls built out of the materials at hand, walls only a true connoisseur of stone walls can appreciate.

It was not long before building stone walls took its toll on the body and fingers of a fledgling folksinger; however, in my world of metaphor, I carry those same stones with me as I struggle to build a song, a poem, a story—or this. Words are the stones we work with, and the more stones in our pile, the more readily we build the wall of our dreams. It is equally important to know that a pile of good stones does not necessarily make a better wall, just as a thousand new vocabulary words won't make you a better writer.

John Bordman never went out and bought more stone just to have more to choose from; instead, he bought or scavenged "good stone" in the first place—stone from walls edging the fields (and what once were fields) all over New England—hand-picked stones culled from the wisdom of his experience—big, solid, interesting stones long weathered by the storms and ravages of time—stones covered in moss, lichen, and ancient ballads sung to young lovers.

We do not need obscure words as much as we need good words. We need to recognize good words. If our experience of life is limited and shallow, our big words will only impress small minds and alienate the truly wise. We need the experience of words used well, words used in elevated writing, words used in great speeches—words we hear and read and feel in meaningful ways—words we hear and read and sing and work to bring sense to the senseless.

An effective vocabulary demands attentiveness to precise language. It means embracing the world of words used well. It means turning off asinine TV; it means measuring a book by the possibilities it presents, not by its rank on the best-seller lists; and it means discussions informed by wisdom and decorum—not polemics or politics. If you are a writer, enter your writer's space with an open and disciplined mind. The wall will build itself.

Writing is—and always will be—rough stone on rough stone —words placed intentionally in repetitive, purposeful cadence onto a nest of eternity.

Learn the craft of words.

The art will follow.

SWING, DAMMIT, SWING

You only hit what you aim at

Every strike brings me closer to the next home run.
~Babe Ruth

What is so commanding and important about this literary analysis paragraph assignment tormenting so many of you? Maybe you won't be spending your life analyzing literature. Maybe writing literary analysis is just some loathsome academic exercise and ultimately no big deal in the greater scheme of your life.

Or maybe it is a big deal.

You will always be measured, remembered, and assessed for the clarity of your thoughts, for your ability to cut through the clutter and discern the true essence of truth, and for the magnitude, breadth, and depth of your thoughts while you convey this truth. Your way with words is the fulcrum to measure the weight of who you are against what you are. Your "way with words" ultimately defines how you are perceived and evaluated. Learn to write and speak well. It is not a dream to be toyed with; it is an action perfected by sustained action embedded in the power of language—the only real and memorable way we communicate with each other.

I am simply a teacher, albeit an annoying demagogue who insists you grasp something just beyond your desperate reach and, frankly, just beyond my reach as well. I am sure it frustrates you as much as it frustrates me. You are as close to reaching it as I feel I am teaching it, so we have to keep playing this game of cat and mouse and trust that some epiphany lurks in shadows around the corner, and your work and mine are not in vain or an exercise in vanity.

This literary analysis business is a lot like a baseball game: if you even manage to crack a hit every three times at bat, you are considered a star. If you manage to hit a home run once—just once—every ten times at bat, you are feted as a hero destined to be celebrated and remembered in clarion exultation through succeeding ages. Every foray into the box pits you against yourself. Do not let yourself be remembered as a timid dolt. No one is impressed by batters content to swing in a batting cage or by players who wait for walks or for easy lob balls dribbled remorsefully into the infield. We are impressed by the possibilities of the moment.

It is Carpe Deum time—or go home time.

The game right now is on the line. The bases are loaded. There are two outs, and you are down by three. It is all up to you. It is your moment. The ball is straight down the pike.

There is no tomorrow.

So swing, dammit, swing.

TEACHING FROGS TO FLY*

The parting is the hardest part of fate—
The slow untangling knot still left unwound;
We pause as if the hour is too late
To divvy fair the treasure we have found.
Our words like fingers pointing at the moon;
Whose light reveals the shadows you did teach;
And this hard goodbye seems to come too soon—
The pulsing tide returns you to our reach.
With each soul you shaped the morphable clay
And lay to rest the fickle thorns of time;
You gave us all an ordinary day
Below some harsh summit we could not climb—
I've never asked, but I've wondered how and why
You somehow managed to teach frogs to fly.

Lorraine Ward, in memoriam)

WINDSOR MOUNTAIN

Home is the place where, when you have to go there,
they have to take you in.
~Robert Frost, *The Death of the Hired Man*

I am sitting here at summer camp in what the kids call "The Enchanted Grove," centered in a swarm of deer flies swirling an antiquated dance around my head. I am sheathed in a bug net, draped like a veil around my head. I am not bothered in the least, and the swarm of flies adds a degree of sharing to the experience. I realize I am never truly alone.

This grove is a small patch of wood in the middle of a field, a tangling of popple, white birch, black cherry, and some long ago wilded apple trees growing in and around a good-sized granite boulder—around which my daughters (and a wonderfully crazy visiting artist) built a small deck last year out of pine slabs discarded from Bob's bandsaw mill.

"Here" is Windsor Mountain International Camp. Here is where we have been coming to as a family for the last several years. As a visiting "artist," I am considered enrichment staff. My four older kids are campers. Our three little ones and Denise are honorary and beloved guests whose playground is the entirety of camp, stretching from Windsor Mountain, past Black Pond, and into the great swamp and the Red Pine Forest. There is magic here. Our 1978 Bluebird motorhome looks more like a part of the landscape than a stout, thirty-year-old hulk of steel and chrome. As much as anywhere else on earth, I belong here. We belong here.

In the same way, everyone needs to belong somewhere.

I look back on my life with thankfulness. In sum, there is nothing I regret and nothing I would wish to change if it altered any degree in the here and now. If I could excise out the idiocies, the hurt, the profligacy, and the inane without mortally wounding the core of who I am and the essential beauty of this moment, I would do so a thousand times over—only a fool or a saint would do otherwise. My life has always been a confluence of opportunity and willingness, much of it down the road not taken, much of it proudly and stubbornly iconoclastic.

The irony is how settled I have become. I am here after traveling the oft-taken road—the long-beaten path of marriage, family, friends, community, and common labor—and it feels (and is) more rich and real than any dream I conjured in my halcyon days of youthful adventures. No doubt, I use my embellished and impeccably practiced stories to entertain and perhaps edify, not out of wistfulness but because I am acutely aware the well of memory is more important to the present than to the past—an enlightenment I never realized before. I do now, and that, in itself, is thanksgiving enough.

I have seven beautiful, wild, and unadorned children who run, play, fight and need to be told a hundred times to quiet down in their tent at night. I have Denise, an equally beautiful, strong, and loving wife who intuitively understands how family is entwined and nurtured by common experience. She knows with a quiet look what and who needs mending, what and who needs unraveling, and what and who needs to be left alone to heal in the soothing balm of contemplative time.

More than anyone I have ever met, Denise knows and maps the charted and uncharted majesty of marriage, friendship, and motherhood. She knows this camp is but another piece of the mosaic we bear forward in constancy—our shared journey mentored to the next generation.

This day is but a stolen moment—and I know enough of the cruelty of time to live solely in words—so I will head out to find Denise and the kids. They are probably making their way back through the darkened camp in a game of flashlight tag and dibs on tent space.

The moon tonight will be the most beautiful they will ever see—a full summer moon sparkled with fireflies and memories, family, and community.

Yes, this is where we belong.

BE A PUNK

A poet's manifesto

Poetry without form is like tennis without a net.
~Robert Frost

Free-verse poetry is not, as many assume, poetry without rules. It is a measured, thoughtful, and deliberate crafting of ideas and inclinations into words, lines, spaces, stops, and breaks intentionally placed and willfully constructed to heighten tension and calibrate effect. Free verse is a heroic effort to condense the power of the words into something deserving to be called poetry—and, with all due respect to Robert Frost, you can play tennis without a net—if you are disciplined enough to create a net only you and your reader can see and feel. Free-verse unbinds the poet from the trappings of convention, but it also binds the poet to an oath—an oath that seeks the absolute truth of an individual poet's vision of what is and what is not poetry.

Free-verse is the current end—or perhaps a plateau—of what is considered poetry. It is the culmination of numerous paradigm shifts in poetic thought. As I write this, there is probably some punk kid sitting in the corner of a stuffy English classroom initiating the next shift or movement in poetry. Maybe you are that punk kid. Maybe you see the universe of words and the possibilities of arranging those words in a different and more compelling way. It is what Walt Whitman did with "Leaves of Grass." It is what Allen Ginsberg did with "Howl" and T.S. Eliot did with "The Wasteland." There is no compelling reason, come the next time, it can't be you—but only if you give damn and only if you crawl out of whatever cloak you wear in your cocoon of ignorance.

Poetry is an action. I can call myself a free-verse poet because I have slogged through the mud of being a free-verse (for the most part) poet. The more you read poetry and write poetry, the less able you will be to resist its transformative power, but the more you stay away from poetry and the less you write poetry, the more likely you will live a diminished life.

If you really want to know who I am, was, and dream to be, read my poems.

If you really want to know yourself, be a god-damned poet.

Be a punk.

Don't be afraid.

SOMETIMES I WONDER

Does every day deserve a poem
When common words sung coyly
Seem more than enough
To capture the tenor and notes
Of our daily songs?

Do we really need poetry
Against an onslaught
Within a torrent
Of syllables lisped
In endless succession?

Do we really need to see
What is hidden
Beneath the rubble
And deconstruct
Something as simple
As stones in a wall
Or echoes within a well
When so few
Really care?

APPOPHOBIA:

(n) A lingering fear and distrust of apps

Always do what you are afraid to do.
~Ralph Waldo Emerson

We have evolved into what we are because we have somehow learned to balance mistrust and wariness of danger with a counterbalanced willingness to explore and exploit the rewards of equally dangerous undertakings and adventures. The stories of our histories would be tepid and soon forgotten if not faced with dogged struggle and valorous perseverance, revealing a greater truth, wisdom, and courage to live in a higher state of existence. If we do not accept and embrace this reality, we might as well relegate ourselves to a more degraded and ignorant self.

This is mighty high-sounding talk leading into a discussion of apps on an iPad.

But it is what it is.

Every folder on my iPad is essentially a toolbox to store useful tools. I never let any one toolbox contain more tools than can fit on the cover screen of any folder, many of which I seldom use, but some are essential to my daily workflow. It is no different than the toolboxes I use when teaching a shop class or managing the various projects I undertake at home.

I have a toolbox for plumbing supplies and tools. I have a toolbox for painting supplies. I have a toolbox for woodcarving. I have toolboxes for working on my car, bus, and boat. All of these are kept in my workshop and in my shed, along with benches, shelves, vices, hooks, and hangers.

So it is with my iPad.

No one has ever said to me, "Fitz, you have too many tools in too many boxes in too many places." I simply have what I need and what has evolved to serve the purposes and tasks of my everyday life. Still, I often journey to Tom Cummings barn, Bonesey's garage, or Hatrack's shed to "borrow" what I need and what I know they have in their toolboxes.

So why the incessant hubbub about too many apps on a student's iPad? If any app is useful to them or to me as their teacher, it is a useful app, regardless of how often a specific app is used. My shop students routinely come to the shop, a bustling lair filled with all manner of tools, most of which they have no idea how to use. The funny thing is that my varied sea-chests of tools never seem to bother them, their parents, or the school. Every visitor to the shop intuitively trusts that what I own is a useful and necessary part of a dynamic and well-equipped shop, and many of them are dangerous tools—way more dangerous than GarageBand, Quizlet, Photoshop, or iMovie.

Appophobia is as equally senseless as it is crippling to those gripped in the paws of the enraged bear of progress. The plaintive, whimpering call to limit these apps is led by malingerers with no clue how to use and exploit these tools for academic benefit. They see some unsavory app and declare it useless. They lament that learning new apps is confusing and distracting and proudly go their Luddite way. Using this logic, we should throw out quadratic equations, the Krebb's cycle, the causes of The Civil War, and the proper use of conjunctive adverbs. We should ban backpacks with more than three textbooks, any loose sheaves of paper, and calculators with any kind of trigonometry function. We should not give a lecture more than five minutes long or occasionally ask kids to just remember the assignment—as in, remember the conversation we had at the end of class.

Imagine the horror when the first pencils with built-in erasers tumbled off the assembly line. Mistakes disappeared with a simple flick of the wrist. Behind the curtain of correction, tortured sentences morphed into gems of clarity and conciseness. How could teachers ever know what students did and did not understand? How could teachers discern the genius from the dim-witted? How could teachers allow textbooks to supplant the power of their masterful oration on any twist of subject matter?

Education is like a shark— if it stops moving forward, it dies. If education does not move in the direction of its prey, it ultimately weakens and suffocates. If we put restraints on a teacher putting new and dynamic power into the hands of their students to forge a new and better way of learning, then education itself withers into frivolity. No fish is caught without first stirring the water. We must embrace the messiness of learning as the tailings of a miner's labor.

Which brings me back to this iPad of mine tapping away in the stillness of a late September night. It is my poet's hoe, my miner's pickaxe, my carving chisel, and smoothing plane. My iPad does what I need it to do at this given point in time. In a few minutes, it will be the final chapter of a good book. Tomorrow it may record my songs, film my video, craft my essay, fill my journal, create my quiz, model my discussion, post my assignment, paint my canvas, and grade my homework—and when I don't want it, need it, or feel it is not useful, the app simply disappears.

Click…

Back into my shed, my toolbox, or some dusty shelf...

The iPad is not a tool, a device, or a thing. It is an enabler of possibility. Apps are not a panoply of evil undertakings; they are merely shovels and spades helping us dig deeper and faster and cut our corners as clean and square as Mike Mulligan and Mary Anne.

Apps are not the problem.

They are a solution.

Much like a pencil, a pad, and an empty page...

THE NATIVE LAND

And I can see that something else died there in the bloody mud,
and was buried in the blizzard. A people's dream died there.
It was a beautiful dream.
~Black Elk, *Black Elk Speaks*

Yes, we screwed over the Native Americans. They were overwhelmed by a slow and then inexorable emigration from Europe, Asia, and Africa. Disease, destruction, distrust, and disaster became the reality for the native tribes of North America. It is a sucky series of sucky chapters in a world FULL of suckiness. It was opportunistic subjugation and deportation—the exacting measures of a more powerful group over a less powerful group. It was not, arguably, a calculated genocide, but it was, and is, a genocide of epic proportions.

The brood of assimilation masquerading as troves of treasure-seekers swarmed the early waters of America, seeking the bounties of unmatched fisheries and seemingly infinite lands. This land—the preordained land of explorers and settlers— became their next point of domination. By the dint of perceived manifest destiny, the newly crowned America became the fledgling frontier to conquer and vanquish in a misguided quest for divine purpose and destiny.

The world was suddenly smaller, and the harvest too enticing to resist. America became the land to embrace, enslave, and subjugate by all means possible. There was no moral purpose aside from the expedience of cultural grandeur and deliberate domination. If not the Portuguese, it was the French. If not the French Empire, it was the Spanish Empire—or the British, Dutch, or German Empires—carving a never-ending quest to expand the tentacles of provincial duty and cultural expansion.

But the people—the moiled and soiled people coming to the "New Land"—did not clamber on boats in Europe with the sole goal to screw over and claim America. They were, for the most part, escaping religious persecution, hopelessness, and despotism.

The Irish did not leave a land of joy; they escaped the ongoing genocide of their population by an overwhelming, occupying power. The Chinese escaped a life of serfdom to again lead a life of poverty—but it was better than entrenched servitude. The French were promised boundless lands in distant colonies. The African populations were incarcerated in America—bartered and sold as chattel by their own countrymen to dickhead slave-traders and then to greedy plantation owners and dissolute farmers.

Very few anybodies came to America to defeat the Native Americans. The thirst for dominance infused a bothersome and expedient necessity to keep the dreams of a new life and a new frontier alive. The streams of settlers escaping world unrest, persecution, and poverty flowed into the only sea able to hold them all—and that was America. The people in the way were the early settlers and, yes, the native tribes and nations. Generations kept coming like rush hour into Boston. The roads could barely contain the influx of cultures competing for the American landscape. The shit hit the fan. No one was left unscathed, but the native peoples suffered the greatest ignominy of all—the decimation of their way of life, a culture nurtured, graced, and distilled by countless generations before them, stolen, defiled, and ultimately destroyed by invasive species from distant lands.

Anyone with any wit about them understands history as a complex and intricate organism eluding precise analysis, and while it is convenient to have our inbred truths bundled into simplified and catchy phrases and political polemics, those truths are rarely self-evident. Our narratives, spun out in self-righteous outrage and indignation, ring of dull, myopic bantering and virtuous theater. We think we listen, yet we only hear the common cackle of like voices in the same grassy field. No one hears a different voice, except as a common threat—and the cackling beckons a cacophony of righteous hate masquerading as symphony.

The native genocide is something we have to own, even if just in our history books and public narratives. That said, we can't simply get rid of Columbus Day and call it "Indigenous People's Day" without giving this new day empowering meaning and actions. We are obligated to start remaking what is intrinsically wrong. It means giving back some semblance of land, dignity, and status to the native people.

I know it seems impractical and impossible to fathom, for the scale and magnitude of the crime are beyond comprehension. I do not believe the sins of our fathers are equally our sins, but the sins of our nation against the native peoples make a mockery of liberty and justice for all. If we do nothing, we are a lowly, shameless, sham of democracy.

I am intellectually ill-equipped to know the viscera of my thoughts with any sense of cogency. I am the dull twit who sees a bird in a snare and says passively, "We must do something." But if we do not do something, we are nothing more than dry spores in a vacuum of space—useless dollops of flesh, bone, and blood taking up space on our inherited nub of Eden.

But what can we do to undo the snare? We won't give away our homes, our communities, and our lifestyles to atone for the ignorance and brutality of our forbears. Most of us have no idea of our lineage beyond great-grandmother Sally, so who do we blame and what do we do that won't chomp more than a pound of flesh from our lives—lives by and large lived gracefully, fully, and magnanimously? How do we move away from mere contrition to palpable recitations of action?

I would argue for you—the singular you—to start right now in whatever way you can. Learn the histories of the native peoples of your stretch of forest, mountain, seashore, or plain. Learn their names, their leaders, and their tribes. Learn about their nations and their allies. Learn how they lived, how they raised their families, and how they maintained their physical and spiritual communities. Learn their stories, songs, and dances. Learn everything you can about who you need to give back to. Who are they now? Where are they now? Do they even exist?

At least then you can stop pretending to care, and maybe the word reparation won't sound as much like revolution.

Words without reparation are not atonement. We are, by nature, possessive. We don't easily give up what we believe is rightfully ours. I certainly don't want to carve up my small space on earth to give to a total stranger, no matter how noble I feel about the cause. There are, however, sizable chunks of public land around me where I walk my dog, go kayaking, or simply take a hike. There are literally sizable chunks everywhere. Some of these must go back to the ancestors of native peoples. It is another huge chunk of breath to also say, "And do what they want with their land."

And a bitter pill to swallow.

But it really is not our land. We may love our land, cherish our land, and even preserve our land, but the lineage of native land arcs back to a more ancient owner, far enough, perhaps, beyond the memory of even the native people. But it is right and wise to assume that for millennia the land was settled, stewarded by serendipity, necessity, and often force, by the Native Americans. It is their heritage and our duty to at least think of reparation—as if reparation is even possible.

I am not demanding we tear down our cities, towns, homes, and the dream of America. I am urging us to begin the process of restoring dignity and righting a wrong through recognition, validation, atonement, and, when possible, reparation. There needs to be a palpable way for the mosaic of Native America to weave itself back into the fabric of modern America—to be recognized as the progenitors of America, not mere footnotes of regret and sympathy.

The Native tribes must be validated through the unvarnished lens of history as wise and noble races who lost a righteous fight, not as victims of a preordained fate. We must atone for our sins against them by creating real opportunity, real education, and real life on our lands and their lands through incremental, illumined, and insistent reparation.

As I write this, I am more appalled by my ignorance than by any sense of enlightenment. I am more pauper than prince. My thoughts are strange and disparate seeds; I do not know how to furrow, sow, or reap.

Out of this gaggle of words, I can't find the truth.

I can only try.

And so can you.

THIS NEW SPRING BEGS ATTENTION

And shivers its literal timbers.
Cold, wet and pleading,
Scarred by winter winds
Pasty snows and frozen time.
My small field and patch of woods
Is now a monument to aging neglect.
Shorn limbs and branches hang high,
Tangled in the sugar maples
(Widow makers we called them
Back in my logging days—
But that is a poem for another day).

Even the last ash is too far gone
And will have to come down.
We already lost the towering White pines
To heart-rot and beetles.
The fruit trees never took
To the shade and droughts,
And only the black cherry, neglected
In a sea of blackberry brambles,
Grow unperturbed
In stoic obedience to tropism.

Always a lazy poet,
I find something else to do
And stoke the fire inside
And steep another strong coffee
And tune my old saw
And scrape out the oiled dust
And clean the jets
And sharpen the chain
And lube the bar
And convince myself
The trees, too,
Can wait another day.

THE TIME & PLACE OF A WRITER

Don't finish before you start

Writing is a struggle against silence.
~Carlos Fuentes

This is the time—the dog days of summer—when writing becomes more of a chore than a pleasure. The hot days and humid nights do not lend themselves to creative and articulate thought. The day is too full of enticing and entrancing possibilities, but because writing is part and parcel of my daily life, I need to create a time and a place to write that works for me, no matter where I am or what I am otherwise called to do.

When I am at summer camp with my family, I set aside two hours each morning from ten to twelve o'clock. These are the hours I am not teaching any classes or running any activities. I know I can find some cool shade and uninterrupted time beside our bus to tend to my dreams as a writer. Maroghini, a Jamaican drummer at the camp and author of many books on drumming, found me there one morning and said, somewhat ruefully, because his morning time is spent caring for his child while his wife worked at camp, how he wished he could find a time and a space like mine. So I invited him to join me.

Maroghini now comes to the bus every day with his four-year-old son, Amri, who happily plays for those two hours with my five-year-old, Tommy. Even at their young ages, they sense this is daddy's time as well, and though they spin around and through and under us with cars and trucks and planes and songs, they are as welcome and unobtrusive as a pair of butterflies searching for a sweeter nectar.

Maroghini and I work quietly and intently. I relish the wistful moments we take to stop our work and share with each other what we are thinking and writing. Sometimes it is only a simple comment or question, but often as not, it evolves into deeper and refreshingly philosophical talk that shifts and sifts the direction of my writing. When the lunch bell tolls, it always seems too soon, but it is as sacred as the time we spend writing, so we stop what we are doing, regardless of the point we are at in our writing. This stopping point gives me the remainder of the day to think about the direction of my writing. It gives me new ideas and phrases I can weave into my writing when I return, which is usually after the kids are in bed and Denise is settled and serene in her precious reading time.

The dark hours of the night add mystery and magnificence to my writing time. I sit outside under a single, swaying lightbulb and let the moths and mosquitoes keep me company. Denise might join me for a short while to give me a needed and always welcome break from my work. She is amazed I can sit outside while she spends her few moments with me swatting and batting away bloodthirsty battalions. Her invariable toast before heading inside is usually, "I don't know how you can stand it out here," but as lovers do, she understands why I am out there, and she always gives me the time and space I need. She understands my writing is my "work" as much as anything else I do, though my paydays are measured and tallied in a more celestial register.

Writing is work. There is no way around this reality, and until we realize and accept this fact, we will be disconnected from our potential as writers. Few of us have the nerve to call our boss and blithely say, "I just don't feel like working today," and expect a sympathetic and encouraging response. We go to work because we have to go to work, and hopefully we enjoy our work as well. Nonetheless, it is still work and our responsibility, so we go to our labors through the thick and thin of life. Many of my friends assume I write because writing comes naturally to me. What they don't get is that I go to my writing "unnaturally." With seven kids to raise and enough side jobs to make the taxman suspicious, I carve my writing time out of an already busy life. I love the summers because it is easier to carve those hours out of life, but I try and need to do the same, even in the most compressed unfolding of the year.

Creating the time and space to write is the first step towards becoming a successful writer. Do not measure success by the beauty and volume of your writing pieces; measure it by the yardstick of time. Do you put in the time you need to put into your writing? Are you ready to slog through the mud when words have to be pulled from the same oily muck? Are you ready to cut, shape, and polish a rock into some semblance of a gemstone?

Experience tells me when I am overly fatigued by a writing piece—when the value of continued writing is outweighed by the excessive baggage of junk I am creating. When this happens, it is noble and wise to head down a different road and work on some other batch of words. If the house is full of kids and friends distracting me with their exuberance at a time when I need to be writing, I won't force the moment; rather, I will use this more leisurely time to proofread, edit, and revise. Every writing piece benefits from a revisit to focus on structure, content, and form, and it doesn't need long stretches of reflective thought to accomplish this.

Build time into your day. Create the space and place to be a more efficient and productive writer, despite whatever chains and excuses hobble you.

Use your time completely.

Resist the temptation to be finished.

Or you will be finished as a writer.

THE DEATH
OF ORIGINAL THOUGHT

A difficult conversation

Let us know and conform
only to the fashions of eternity.
~Henry David Thoreau

I proffered up some lame excuse today to get myself out of an afternoon workshop at our school on "How to Have Difficult Discussions." I did catch the tail end of the conversation, which only affirmed my choice and deepened my fear that we are fast approaching the death of original thought. The constant parsing of words, the sanctimonious passing of creed, ideology, and conformity, coupled with the determination of a committed few to pursue their committed agendas, dilutes the power of the individual within a sea of collective drivel.

Through a shaky indoctrination of agendas, we obligate an acquiescence to ideologies at odds with common sense. We allow ourselves to be judged and juried by colleagues outsourcing themselves to schools desperate for a new culture or some emerging paradigm of diversity, equity, and inclusion we can somehow layer onto our incorrigibly white and wealthy heritage.

I am not appalled by the message or by their words. I agree with their message. I am happy enough to work at a school that is at least trying to willfully change, grow, and evolve into a better and more inclusive community. I am, however, appalled by the purveyors of pedantic pedagogy who subjugate individual will, genius, inclinations, and passions to conform to a predictable and shallow paradigm of stilted, skewed, and self-aggrandizing superiority packaged and peddled by a myopic few—and peddle they do to the tune of thousands of dollars to educate us with the potent magic of their wares.

The facilitators of our afternoon sessions seem like decent folks who are well-educated, balanced, thoughtful, and fluent in the rubric they created for us. They are utterly unfazed by the paltry cast of recalcitrant antiques unimpressed by articulate skullduggery—those hardy few unwilling to play in their game, who by and large keep their mouths shut, not out of fear but from a weariness of the wagging fingers twitching in the front row, the muttering incantations decrying the dinosaur ways of the old guard—us pitiful protectors of dying tradition, misplaced focus, and misguided values.

By the end of the session, I was none the worse for wear. There is some solace in knowing how to act and how to respond when a moment tips on its crisis. There is a certain grace when wisdom guides a moment of indecision, and there is a collective betterment when magnanimity lives and grows outside the confines of philanthropy. Maybe it is grace, but more likely it is my animal instinct to simply survive in this new savannah of education. Though I am sure I appear dumb and doltish, my head is remarkably alive.

I am not steadfast and stubborn. I am alive and flailing. I am a convoluted map of conflicting actions, and for better or worse, I am the axeman of my own tree, the arbiter of my soul, the destructor of my destiny, and the calculator of my conscience. I am a heady man who wants to live fully-fleshed as a person—a corporeal mixing of viscera, bones, body and being carving a testament to eternity out of matter of my choosing. If my heart, soul, mind, and body wants, needs, or prefers a new identity, a new leaning, or a new religion, I will not ask your permission, approval, censure, praise, or condemnation.

We consider ourselves enlightened scholars and educators, but we base our new pedagogies on dry and shaky foundations balanced precariously on one side of a complicated equation. The voice of true genius and uncommon wisdom is an impediment, not a virtue. Dissent and reason are judged as recalcitrance. Opposition is equated with ignorance. Conformity (though never phrased as such) is the only common good.

The old pantheon of God's is upended, supplanted by new committees, new departments, and new initiatives—as if they—

and only they—are the indispensable few. Dutiful department heads are charged with the unenviable task of changing the school culture—our steaming ship of balky tradition and insistent inertia carrying us forward to a brighter future—but who, in doing so, wittingly and unwittingly, condemns and undoes years of thoughtful decisions and actions manifested out of the exuberance of invigorated and enlightened experience.

Wisdom is seldom new; tradition is rarely stale, and progress is more noun than verb. Give me something new, and I will listen.

And change.

My difficult conversation is not with you.

It is with myself.

TONIGHT I SAT QUIETLY

While Hatrack and Ted
Discussed quantum physics
And dropped words
From capacious thoughts,
From the ruminating cud
Of bellied speculations
Like murmuration—
The critical transition
Where mass moves in unison—
When flocks, schools and herds
Heed some blind impulsive force,
Turning, weaving, avoiding
Each other—like electrons
Infinitely separated—
Like words in a poem
Moving towards
And away from,
And sometimes beside,
The unmoved mover.

TO READ OR TO WRITE?

Can one exist without the other?

Good writers rarely make good poets,
but good poets usually make great writers.
~Fitz

Forty years ago, in 1981–1982, I went to Beijing Teachers College in an exchange of "scholars," a moniker that in no way, shape, or form befitted my contributions to academia. We were the first group of American students to study in mainland China since before the communist revolution in 1949. I was not a particularly good student, but I loved living in China —especially when China was a more rural country than now. Few cars plied the streets of Beijing, and only one high-rise building, the Beijing Hotel, dwarfed the skyline at ten stories high. It was the gathering hole where the few foreigners, business seekers, and reporters in the city lived, stayed, drank, and dissipated their days and nights away—or so it seemed to me. The Chinese people, aside from the communist party elite, were invariably poor but always gracious and welcoming. Few seemed unhappy. One night, while visiting Zhang Hong Nian, a poet, artist, and friend of mine, I asked how, in the face of such daily hardship, the average Chinese person maintained their dignity and sense of humor.

His bemused answer surprised me. "Because China is so old compared to your America. We experience history through stretches of thousands of years. We have lived in the dark, and we have lived in the light, but America has barely a few centuries of history. You are yet to have an equal balance between Yin [darkness] and Yang [light]." He went on to poke fun at our American individualism and our unquenchable thirst for wealth and happiness while he searched for acceptance, stability, and tranquility—even while in his paintings he captured and exposed the harsh reality of life in China, yet painted in subtle ways the communist cadres might not censor from the panorama upon his sweeping canvas.

Zhang Hong Nian's notion of life was almost too much to wrap my pea-sized brain around, but I did love the idea of a universe guided by a balance between forces where something only exists in relation to something else existing: good/bad, up/down, high/low, light/dark...

And then I thought, 'Reading and writing?' I realized this pairing could not exist without the other. I was annoyingly proud of myself. This epiphany was the first philosophical thought I ever dwelled on for more than thirty seconds, but it was the power of reading and writing—of engaged reading and writing—that so transformed my life.

In this raucous era of my life, the imbalance tilted towards reading more than writing. Reading was easier. Reading did not require much thought, and it was (and still is) pretty damn enjoyable. Although I wrote a lot more than the average person, it was still a mixed bag for me. I possessed little confidence as a writer. Aside from a few enduring and endearing friends, I never shared my writing with anyone. I wrote for reasons I'll never really know. It is only recently that I started to share my writing with a larger audience—like you.

The weird thing is that I don't read as much anymore. I write much more than I read. Maybe it is because reading occupied so much of my earlier life, and I am now just starting to balance the Yin and Yang of my literary self. Maybe the limitations of time squeeze my day into priorities, and reading is not always one of those priorities. Sometimes I wonder if we need books as much as we used to need them. I know it is sacrilege to question the power of books, for writing—actually putting words on a page—was a transformative evolution in thought, and books are probably the most important invention of mankind.

Followed closely by the rubber worm.

But books are an invention, not a creation. A book is a tangible tool—a tool that has served a distinct purpose for centuries. Books led our way out of darkness and ignorance.

Books carried our stories, our religions, and our histories. Books taught us how to build, create, and even understand the universe. Books, speeches, and conversations cornered the market as the sole proprietors and purveyors of knowledge. Now, however, we get access to words through countless other inventions. We watch TV, the news, movies, dumb reality shows, and YouTube videos; we make our own videos; we chat with words and listen to NPR, Ted Talks, sports radio, and murder podcasts; and all the while we are inundated with advertisements, warnings, and outrageous opinions as we click away at the staggering number of options on our screens. By most metrics, we are more engaged with words than in any other age or slice of history. But where are the geniuses? Who are the icons of literature? What sly and cunning resources do they mine from the core of existence?

There are plenty of words and plenty of books out there, but are they good words? Are they good books? Will they endure into another generation or into the next millennia? Are they all yin or all yang? Are they worth the exchange of life given to them?

Probably, and probably not—hence, my insipid vacillations. My mind is more hobbled in darkness than bathed in light, but the simplicity of statistics begs that there must be more readers than writers; however, there are no new books without new writers, and there are no "good" new books without new, thoughtful, brave, and insightful writers digging deep into the bowels of the human condition, writers who train probing and promiscuous eyes to see further with stunning clarity, conviction, and power. So books win while writers rule, and in the tenuous balance of literary dependency, the forces of light and darkness keep each other alive.

So I lean on my pen.

I have no fame as a writer, and my audience is mainly students intent on escaping alive from my clutches. I know they will soon be gone, so I write to them, for them, and because of them, as if they are all characters in *The Great Novel of Fitz's Life*.

And they are.

I have an obligation to my students to create and shape a literary balance in their lives. I need to snag them in the snare of my classroom and pass along some ripening fruits of wisdom— but just long enough to fill their primitive gullets—and then set them free, lest my bias, baseness, and bigotry tip the fulcrum of their universe.

They are kids with hearts and minds as deep, complex, searching, and real as any of us bored and berating adults. We give them school, and they respond with diligence and duty. They live for sense and purpose, and we give them a litany of facts. They want freedom, and we cage them within walls and expect them to claw their way out. They want affirmation, and we give them exams and assessments. They want their own words, and we tell them to edit and revise.

I say, "Give them their words and let them go play on the windblown fields of the empty page. Give them books, and let them read without the sword of Damocles hovering over their unkempt heads. Shout from the sidelines, but do not diminish and coach away the joy of the game—this game is their lives and the heart of their infinitely perfect mind, soul, and being.

Let them seek, find, and create their own balance of Yin and Yang, not our conception of balance bleeding out in our own lives." Yes! They will struggle, but they will persevere. They will succeed, and they will invariably fail. There will be a precarious balance between happiness and sorrow, hurt and healing, loss and love, and fear and courage.

Give them a world of words and books and trust.

Set them free in an ocean of words.

And take a deep breath.

THE OLD TOTE ROAD

There comes a longing never to travel again,
except on foot.
~Wendell Berry, *Remembering*

I clabber down the old tote road towards the Red Pine Forest, leaning on my staff, skirting boulder-strewn ruts and small gullies carved out by two days of heavy rain. It is less than two miles or so from our cabin; still, Denise gently implores me to wear a pouch with an iPhone and an epi-pen. She knows my scattered mind, and she remembers how I once poked a yellow jacket nest with the stub of my staff and had to run like an enraged bear through the mad tangles of this New Hampshire forest.

I am wiser now, but no less scattered.

I don't know why I am drawn to this daily amble. There is nothing special here—miles of mossy stone walls slowly sinking under the detritus of a hundred years or more of leaf, moss, and deadwood edging what once were fields, overtaken now by massive White pines, ashes, and beeches weakened by blight, Red oaks, and Sugar maples. The forest floor is an impenetrable bramble of hobble-bush, scraggly sycamores, ferns, and bog. Here and there are old foundations, small and square, meticulously laid, dug into scrabbly hillsides, yet somehow hardy, cursing men and sturdy families lived in rough cabins and spent their days cutting timber, carving fields out of impossible ground, wrestling massive granite stones to clear their fields, and set the lines between each other.

My epi-pen and iPhone hang on me like effete sophistry. I do not even recognize what bird is calling who for what reason. Certainly not me—this morning intruder stopped by the great swamp sucking waters from dark woods. I scan the shores for moose. I know they are there, along with black bears, bobcats, deer, fisher cats, skunks, and raccoons. It is a fool's errand to think they would reveal what they know or where they lie at daybreak.

They, too, must have their walls.

The deer flies attack me like I am their last supper, but I learned long ago to dress for a summer hike as if it were mid-winter—heavy boots, gloves, denim—a shroud of mosquito mesh covering my head tucked deliberately into my sweaty, gently heaving breast. They do not bother me, incessant as they are, any more than they bother any other swatch of warm flesh breathing slowly in this still morning air lingering with warm, low fog.

If not for these flies, I would have to share this trail with gobs of humanity bent on an easier hike. These tourists will come in the fall when the weather is cool and mad dashes of color are ripped from the trees and overlay and soften this worn trail.

But they will not truly know this trail.

Only once, I met another hiker—an old woman with a willow basket and an old camp saw. She seemed unnerved to see me clothed in my normality and revealed in a wispish voice, "I am only here to find some black birch to make my tea." I offered her some extra mesh to shield her from the storm of insects, but she replied firmly, "They do not bother me." A few steps later, I looked back. She was gone. The mystic in me imagined some ancient Margaret searching and fettering this lonely bower for her illicit lover, Tamlin—but she probably just strode away faster than the flies could fly.

I've never seen her again.

At a certain point, the tote road splits to the left and cleaves around the massive swamp filled by innumerable freshets, springs, and small brooks—the gorging water filling Black Pond to the brim, a small pond as clean as a night sky but black as tea, steeped in a broth of bitter New England leaf. To the right, another tote road arcs into a smaller trail, wending many miles inland into forgotten land. Another small trail traces three more miles to Trout Pond. Every day I remind myself to someday bushwhack the stubborn, overgrown path, just to be one of the few who can say, "I have been there."

But it is the Red Pine Forest calling me. The vague entrance to this cathedral of trees is marked by a small, mossy boulder. I duck under the arches of young beech, saplings who will never grow old in this forbidden place. The Red pines are an odd anomaly within a feral woodland, planted in straight lines by some Yankee dreamer plotting a handsome fortune in telephone poles—seemingly hundreds of piercingly straight spires interlaced by an equal number of deadened timber, holed by pileated woodpeckers and mawkish jays. Some large branches, widow-makers to loggers, hang ominously on trees ravaged by wind and storms—stubborn trees who died trying.

I sneak in as the sun is rising, bending under an arc of evergreen beckoning me into the mysterious grove. Like the immigrant Red pines, I feel strangely out of place—as if I, too, am not welcome here. I am Narcissus staring into his vain pool of water, drawn and entranced by fleeting, corporeal beauty, but I am not trapped here, unlike the Red pines, stoic to the last.

I watch streams of light bolt in flashes of geometric entropy scanning the soft needled floor. I feel a murmur of wind and a cackling crow urging me to leave quickly—or die.

And so I clabber back home along the old tote road, coddled by deer flies, swarmed by mosquitoes, kindred to the moose and the old Finns of these woods.

I accept there are things I may never know.

THE INSECURE POET

I will annoy and impress you at the same time
And write a poem with a jackhammer—
And to let you know my poem needs editing,
I will cut down the whole line
Of towering White pines
Lining my side yard.

And though it sounds fine to you,
I will replace the muffler
On my old station wagon
And set the gaps on the spark plugs—
And drain the crankshaft,
And lube the kingpins,
And for the sake of trying

I will add on a new porch
And tear it down before nightfall.

I may even need
A whole new septic system—
One that can handle
This torrent of wasted words.

Passing cars will slow down
To see my gaudy Christmas display.

Though wrapped in insecurity,
At least one poet
Will be called
Industrious.

CONVERSATIONS ON A BEACH

In the end, only words remember

Conversation. What is it? A Mystery! It is the art of never
seeming bored, of touching everything with interest, of pleasing
with trifles, of being fascinating
with nothing at all.
~Guy de Maupassant

I walked to the beach with the kids to watch the sunset on the coast of Oregon at Manzanita. After whiffleball, tic-tac-toe, and beach tennis, the younger kids ran over and sat with me, leaning like gangly dolls against pieces of driftwood gathered around a roaring fire. We watched the sun set. We watched other untold fires glowing up and down the long plain of sand that rose into massive cliffs swirling in wisps of fog. Kaleigh stood alone, a hundred yards away, knee deep in the rhythmic return of surf, her silhouette slowly melding into the coming night. I wondered what she was thinking.

It was thirty years ago, when I was not much older than her, when I last walked this beach and stood where she stood. I slept by windy fires and wondered where life would take me, or where I would take life. I never imagined I would be huddled with seven tired and crazily perfect kids after twelve years (to this very day) of a crazily perfect marriage, talking with my kids about the difference between choosing to live simply without a lot of money, which is not being poor, versus not being able to make enough money to take care of yourself or your family no matter how hard you try, which is poverty.

We noticed the lights of the cars winding along Route 101, curving slowly along the sides of the cliffs. I couldn't help but brag, "Thirty years ago, daddy hitchhiked from right here all the way down to and through the Baja of Mexico."

They never see hitchhikers now. I had to tell them all about hitchhikers.

Pipo asked why I didn't just drive my car. "I didn't have a car. All I had was a backpack, a sleeping bag, and the three hundred dollars I saved working at Rick's gas station in West Concord. Plus, I wanted to hitchhike. I wanted to see how far I could go with three hundred dollars."

Always curious, Pipo continued his inquiry, "How far did you go?"

"Not as far as I thought I could."

"Did you run out of money?"

"Yes, I did."

"What did you do?"

"I did anything people would pay me to do."

Margaret asked, "Did you ever beg?"

Pipo reacted with what was probably a visceral reminder of his childhood in Haiti: "That's not polite, Margaret."

"No, I never had to beg. I just found people who wanted some work done, and I did the work. When I had enough money to move on, I started hitchhiking again. If you choose to be poor, you are not poor."

With his ubiquitous thoughtfulness, EJ said, "If you can choose to be poor, it's too bad you can't choose to be rich." He laughed at the possibility.

Charlie wondered, "What did you eat?"

"My favorite meal was Milky Ways and a can of Coca-Cola."

EJ countered, "You said that you lived on baloney and baked beans."

"That is another story."

Charlie wanted to know how many stars dotted the Milky Way. I smiled. "There aren't any stars. There's just chocolate and caramel."

"No. Really!" He got up and did a cartwheel and a handstand—his common response to any piercing conundrum.

Tommy asked, "Did you have to brush your teeth?"

"Oh yes, all the time." My reassurance was all Tommy needed to hear. He curled deeper under my jacket.

Emma, our stoic philosopher, quietly tossed more wood into the fire. Her questions are forever her own.

Pipo needed more: "Are we ever going to be rich?"

"We're rich now—in kids, bedtimes, hamburgs, and nighttimes on the beach."

"Fitz! You know what I mean."

"Don' worry. We're plenty rich enough."

The cool wind blowing off the Pacific drove Emma, Margaret, Pipo, and Kaleigh back to Aunt Mary Ellen's cottage. EJ, Charlie, and Tommy stayed with me. In the increasing darkness, the waves grew larger and more filled with towering mystery and dark foreboding. Charlie broke the elongated silence. "Mason asked me last night if I would go to Toys 'R US with him. But I said no."

"But I thought you love Toys 'R Us?"

"I do, but I knew you wouldn't let me go. You never let me go."

EJ laughed with wisdom larger than his ten years. "You don't have to go to Toys 'R Us to get toys."

"I know, but I do like Toys 'R Us."

Tommy perked up from his cocoon on my lap and cooed, "I like toys."

In the true spirit of the constantly churning and changing explosions in his head, Charlie shifted thoughts: "If hot chocolate only costs a dollar-fifty, why did you get mad just because I had two hot chocolates?" That meager meal was three days ago, but I'm sure, for Charlie, it will remain in the present as long as it remains a conundrum to him.

EJ laughed again: "Because two hot chocolates cost three dollars, and there's nine of us, and nine times three is twenty-seven dollars. That's a lot of money!"

EJ's logic seemed to satisfy Charlie. "My friends think we're rich because we have a big backyard, a bus, and a boat." He connected his thoughts quickly: "Are we going to go sailing this summer? I want to go sailing."

We have an old wooden sailboat cradled in Tom Cummings' side yard all summer—and probably will be all winter as well. It is a solid, funky old ketch designed by the equally funky designer Phil Bolger, whose philosophy of sailing is to give the common person a chance to get out on the water. I wondered if they sensed the wistfulness in my voice. "Next summer, we'll go sailing." And we will, I'm sure. This was our summer to scrimp and save for a trip to Oregon. My head is still racing through the pile of bills preordained to meet us at the door in a few days. Somehow the bills will get paid, and we can always dream of somehow getting ahead of them.

I turned my eyes back to the sound of the breaking waves, fearful I would lose this sacred moment. Charlie brought me back. "I'm glad we are not rich. Rich people are not always happy."

"And poor people are not always sad." I lifted Tommy off my lap and shook the sand from my clothes. "Wow! My legs are so long they reach all the way to the ground!"

EJ jumped up. "Mine too. And my shadow is chasing me."

"Mine, too."

"Me, too."

They ran through the dunes, wending along a trail they only remember from today, drawn instinctively to the light of the fourth house on the right.

I hear them counting, laughing, and running.

I walk slowly down the same street.

And pull the sinking moon behind me.

A CHINA JOURNAL

Streams of consciousness

*I was performing my ritual of sipping tea,
shooting flirtatious glances and planning murder.*
~**Mingmei Yip, *Peach Blossom Pavillion***

Part I

The dull staccato throbs in light rain on a dark night. Unseen barges make their way up the Qian Tian River —concrete shores marked by the arch of the bridge, the spans of beam stretched on beam, the impeccable symmetry of streetlights broken by a stream of impatient headlights—the bursting aorta of commerce and hope revealing Hangzhou.

Or is it the torrent of humanity flowing east and west and north and south around the antiquities of West Lake? Lovers. Couples in every configuration and every intent. Families dragging or being dragged. Packs of friends so hip and cool and daring. So much unlike the China I remember—my China in the early 80's—soft wool coats, blue or gray. Mao buttons and short-visor caps. Bicycles hauling human compost towards distant gardens outside of Beijing.

I fall just as easily into reverie as anticipation.

The grey fog and swirl of mist on West Lake outlines the shadows of rowing prams and party boats decked in imitation of palaces lost to time. On a far hillside—a bare shape of a gray palace on a gray background. Somewhere within sing the lusty cries and plaintive words of crazy Li Po, drunk again and strewing words with practiced and meticulous abandon—picked up by stooped bodies and weathered visages carried and thrown with feral joy—skipping stones stretched across still waters. Heavy, fluttering weight borne down by inescapable gravity:

The birds have vanished down the sky.
Now the last cloud drains away.
We sit together, the mountain and me,
until only the mountain remains.

Right now I am happy to my bones and as lonely and weak as a man can be. I scroll through pictures of my family and share them with the sky, a sultry cloak of a murky heaven heavy enough to fall—the dirt and smoke and stench of progress. Each picture tugs at my heart. I am not built to be away from home— Tommy scales a rock wall. Emma plays her ukulele. Margaret her guitar. EJ fixes his VW Beetle. Charlie juggles a soccer ball. Kaleigh collects seashells and beach glass. Pipo washes enormous pans in the camp kitchen. Denise sits in the backyard—our blessed perfect backyard—holding a chicken as delicately as she holds any of her own brood of children. I cling to them as wildly as wild can be. I will dare anyone. Any time. It is not a test I need to prepare for.

The craziness is the contrast—this city of millions and millions and millions and millions sprouting steel and glass and brick in every configuration of a weedy architect's dream. I should be happy to be here, but I long for the simplicity of my back porch—morning coffee with Denise. Kids busy. Friends who call. A slow jog. A bulb needing to be changed.

Only a fool would or could argue with me.

Jet lag wakes me in the middle of the night. I read Joyce for an hour. Is my head Daedalus or Bloom? What does he mean by that? … It is too easy to confuse work of the head with work. Real work. What do I need sleep for? Dave and Rob—my American partners on this trip—are still asleep. Long in jealous sleep. Or maybe like me—eyes wide-awake, curious if the sun ever shines in this city? Maybe stuck in fogged memories brushed in Song Dynasty waterstrokes. Rounded bellies, curled navels, insatiable smiles surrounded by calligraphy'd words. China is not a country who etched its history on cave walls. Everything flows and dies and recreates itself in an unending cycle of births and deaths measured in massive ticks of time. For me and Dave and Rob at least, it is three days of incessant rain, mist and curiosity; still, I am a "silent claw scuttling across the floors of silent seas."

Yet, we laugh as much as men have always laughed at the vagaries of Fate in this country, a country who created the word *Fate*. We are ecstatic with our luck to be here. We scrounge like beggars for coffee in the morning. We force ourselves into taxis like hobo's stuffed into flimsy rucksacks. We teach the new elite of China—the sons and daughters of scion and opportunity. Kids only, and no different, as if God only has three or four molds to work with—here is your intense child; here is your dreamy child; here is the child hobbled by a dull mind nurtured in like-minded fanaticism by parents deluded by assumptions of perfection, and here is the kid of the world—the ever-real world —the everywhere world—give me love; give me hope; give me joy; give me space. Save me from yourselves.

We work alongside the young and restless torn by conviction, inclination and duty—prey to vanity, pretense, boldness and unplumbable magnanimity in equal measures. We call them by English names chosen in blithe randomness: "This sounds good —I like this name—this is easy to remember—many famous people are named Richard." I want to scream and say we are not so lost we can't remember the tongue-twisters of our youth. It is as easy for us to say to say "One sly snake slid up the stake and the other sly snake slid down" as Liu Guo Ping or Ren Qi Wei or Sun Zhu or Zhang Hong Nian. I like your name. I want your name. Your real name. There is no other way to begin.

Just tell us your name! and maybe the BBC won't report every unfolding day on the gulf between us, on what our misunderstandings are, or on how we need to understand history. We are all ignorant, damn it, in every way, yet we are also transcendent in every moment—if given the chance. I do not want to meet another ex-pat who has been here for three years— or five years—or ten years, for they have nothing to tell me but their story, and as perfect and real as their story may be, I will measure their story against their own ignorance—and, unsurprisingly, we are surprisingly equal. I need to know the wisdom of my backyard is as expansive as any unboundaried world. If not, why seek peace? It is unattainable. We do not need travel to suffocate bigotry. We only need to love and accept one thing that is not ours and build from there.

The young teachers from the school where we are working—Arvin, Angie, Addie and Ray—walked us around West Lake tonight—a quartet of twenty-somethings who are the pillars of the new China They are modern, ancient, vulnerable and imperturbable. Arvin, in almost manic ecstasy, tells story after story of the history, the meaning, and the reality of every turn in the path with spontaneous bursts of broken English and untranslatable Chinese. Angie and Addie and Ray recreate the meaning, but not the ecstasy, blessed and cursed as they are by the temperance of subtle, humble and defined lives.

We feast in some palace by the shore. Table after table full of men downing small shots of incredibly strong liquor. "Gang Bei," time and again—standing like warriors around a magnificent table. Sometimes a table of their wives locked in the chatter of tradition. Sometimes a table like us—a few friends; a few guests and toasts and laughs in a broken dance of broken language cobbled into some kind of understanding. It feels like defiance, a changing of the guard. Sit with your wives, dammit! Yet, I was jealous of their camaraderie of tradition.

We men, regardless of culture, rarely change.

We watch a Chinese opera performed on dark waters. We sit in the night in a pouring rain surrounded within a sea of flimsy blue poncho's. I love my poncho, our collective firmament, for it makes me as Chinese as the rest of the crowd—my blue tarp like their blue tarp. My Mao jacket and their Mao cap. I want to gasp like the crowd at every cool shift of scenery—of tens of feathers running across the surface of the water—of lovers floating on ancient barges never quite touching prows—of ominous risings and fallings of girded columns of steel rising out of the waters of West Lake. Instead, I squint like an engineer trying to figure out the mechanism of reality making people gasp. I regret this has always been—is—my fallback—this doubting distancing me from the lure of wonderment. I want to be lost in amazement.

Yet, I was only gifted by the delight of engagement and deconstruction—the lost twin tower of faith.

Tonight, like everything, did not end. It was truncated by everything that truncates. It is absurd I am still awake. Wisdom and experience plead with me to let go of the night, but I can't. Louder than the wisdom of experience is the voice of Du Fu: *"Upstairs the scholar lets down his white hair/ He faces the wind, breathes the fragrance, and weeps."* The poet's guttural cry croaked infinatum. Not unlike the barges—some conveyance I do not see—a sound, merely, in a gray night, but I feel the dull, throbbing staccato notes—the predictable heartbeat of diesel reassurance lurching into the strong, moiling and unceasing flow of tomorrow.

Tomorrow is already here.

Part II

A day can be perfect. I have to believe this.

Today was. Is. Is was a day in China.

The sun breaking through today after yesterday's typhoon. Lazy walk to the coffee shop. Practice Chinese with young cook dreams of more tells his long story. Reassure him—yes—as good as anything in america. Wished really wished Denise was there. Our every Saturday Sunday trips to serendipity cafe in maynard reborn borne in hangzhou city.

Sweet, strong coffee. Cool clean breeze off sidewalks scrubbed clean by yesterdays torrential rain. Kids running from store to store. Buy muffin there. Fruit here. Dough sticks from roadside vats bubbling oil. Dumplings steaming in scalded trays. Creamy warm milk in plastic bags fattened with sugar. Running skipping hop back to grandmothers. "The waiguo ren [foreigners] spoke to me!" I feel incredibly alive. Placed. Placid. Content...old men sweep leaves torn from spindly trees lining pungent streets with brooms cobbled of broken branches and bundles of lashed twigs. We nod to each other like it is a universal tongue. Yes. I get it. I understand without words stammered out of meagre vocabularies. Life transposed on life. Strangely I miss my motherfatheruncles long gone and imagine them beckoning from the park benches steaming in wet morning heat…wisps of smoke rising to balconies draped with flowers laundry tv sets bikes slipping into alleyways filled with poverty love confirmation…always always always a confirmation celebration of age. Dignity. Grace. Acceptance.

I hear Mister Toe's taxi and incessant horn in morning traffic like the bellowing from barges on the pulsating sighing unrepentant river. "Come, come. Sorry. *Dui bu qi*. Sorry. I overslept…" We. Rob. Dave. Me. Cram our oversized bodies into an impossibly small car. More beeping weaving avoiding. A mass (a liturgy almost) of traffic people bikes scooters busses trucks. A city so huge expanding towering with belief in tomorrow acceptance of today democracy of common life. We are all here. We are all here. It has to work. It has to. It does. It really does. It stretches the clothes of my perceptions preconceptions prejudice anticipations. I wear the disbelief like a shawl in the rain. In the tangle of work obligation progress crossing dodging maneuvering there is no anger—no words to take back regret amplify justify. No righteousness, fingers, pissed off anythings. Simple reassurances no one is alone. Listen I we you are here. We are not travelers. We are embedded like silk in a fluid tapestry. We are was is.

It has to be a word—isness. We are dropped into the *isness* of what irretrievably is. We are dropped into a warm busy teeming broth of humanity. We shake like dogs on muddy banks and run to our buildings. Work. Work. Work. It is all work. It is all family. It is all friends. It is all there is—a jigsaw of sameness oneness isness. It is a common world of commonness. Fair and unfair in the same accepted fated breath. My head still can't wrap around it. I am an American. Damnit. An American. I let go of worrying if it matters. The private goal is the collective goal. I am not sad detached wandering wondering. I am going to work. I am going to do what I need came want should must do.

The kids are waiting for us. Us. Me. Rob. Dave. Old americans. Proud americans. Proud americans come to teach preach perfect tentwelvethirteenfourteen-year-olds and young startled dreamy suddenly beset by reality sweet loving accepting yearning teachers. A few days ago experts now we are common and is. Three waiguo ren clambering laughing going to have to work. Three teachers going on a Sunday field trip to pick grapes on a farm—a muddy farm outside the city clung between city and mountains. Purgatory. God on one side. Maybe both sides. Maybe purgatory is perfection. Maybe. But today is action not reflecting dust of yesterday. Old peasant women lead us to grapes in groping heat smiling pointing painting coaxing cajoling. Their faces wear long march Mao hunger I have been there and there and there. There too. We nod our vocabularies in gestures and broken guttural primal vestal sounds. The kids meanwhile are kids. kids. kids. Nothing is unreal, unexpected, overdone impressive. More isness. Love. Compassion. Ballets of energy stories leaping stretching reaching towards bundles of fruit— putao, yaomei, pinguo—grapes, strawberries, apples: Sameness. Isness. Happiness. Yes. True happiness. America. China.

Sadness, thinking, wanting, remembering (screaming almost in a vacuum) for my own children to just be here. Not there. Engulfed awed renewed in new hampshire summer camp. Cool clear waters. Stars plucked out sky summer camp. Away. Happy without me. For me. Because of me. Alongside a clay shored quiet stream I share pictures of my kids with these kids—my students—precious precocious indefatigable youth. I need them to know I am as real their mothersfathersunclesaunts. Each image turned and studied like a textbook. This is what we all learn. This is what we all learn—love. Today's lesson is love and picking and dancing and remembering and wanting and being indefatigable youth. Infinite tomorrows and yesterdays cloven and jammed into the impossibly small taxi of today. Beeping horns of love in every direction. These are my children. My children in america. They were born when you were born. Cried when you cried. Woke in terror-filled nights like you. Laughed in school-yards like you. Jammed into expectations like you. We them they are together altogether the crazy world of stitched cultures woven by old men and old ways with broken dreams and unbridled ignorance—children together altogether born again in games of minecraft, tag, hide and seek, pushing unwanted food away, grabbing devouring celebrating…They are born and will be borne. Within. Without. Beside. Before. They are. Need to be. Every thought every action every dream. My family is our textbook of love. Denise is the mother. I am the father. Here is our universe. Our textbook. Endless flow of sometimes words sometimes action always love always is. Isness of opportunity chance fate desire hammered in the mystic forge of love determination persistence stubborn clinging to flotsam idyllic isles key-wests of dreams words nods limits distant horizons figuring out giving a damn…

In the city again playing team tag in an empty mall detritus of progress. The children lead me hide me cajole me protect me old and vulnerable behind columns arching over western sloth: armani, hilfiger, levi, scotch, shoes, handbags. Lean away as if this floor is a diseased ward—typhussed smallpoxed malarial—a story cried in bold decay and impeccable ruin. We win the the game. We win the running man game—we us them me the old teacher. Old Laoshi. The youngest kids. Smallest kids by far. We won, I said, because we did not attack. We protected. We won candy. Winning was all the mattered. Grabbing devouring celebrating turned over to parents eager for harvard princeton mit. Turned over to endless days nights life of work homework absolute perfection. What is your favorite game Shelley? (I asked her on Friday) I said—you must have a favorite game. I do not play games she said she meant it lived it was it and today she played as if there was no tomorrow. Just the isness joy release of a penitent shorn of sin. I pray. I really do. I pray today has enough rebar to sustain the weight of her play. Play Shelley. Play. Parents maybe only happy she says goodbye to us in english. We. Dave. Rob. Me. We are from Boston. Good schools in Boston. But today. Today was a better school. A mystic forge. Orb resting on pinnacle. East. West.

I wished I shouted—You should see the small towns. Go to the small towns. It is all I know. All I can teach live pray do. It is my *is*. Go to the mountains clinging to your horizons west of the city of hangzhou. Small villages pocked by endurable endless persistence perfection of patience forbearance love. Do not go to shanghai to the east. It is too close to boston harvard princeton mit. Pick grapes strawberries apples. Fresh fruit. Pithy flesh hung on bones. What Mao could not let be. What we you can't taste. Rich soil. Soil fed depleted fed depleted fed depleted. Irony.

Displacement. The high huge glassy towers of hangzhou sucking in the countryside. Families cleaved apart at the juncture of sinews. Depleted. Fed by wisps of dreams promises borne on trains scooters carts sodden shoes. Here is heavy coal diesel haze parade of weaving dodging fate of progress regression progress regression. Dreams. Unforgivable dreams. Trapped. Living. Celebrating. Coins trapped in mud. Sledge hammered into mastheads of concrete steel glassy towers beaked cranes endlessly lifting dream on dream on dream with spindly cables. The captain speaks. The ship sails: straits of Skylla. Ahab. Odysseus. Hydra. Whale.

The only way out is through. We. Rob. Dave. Me. Resist exhaustion easy to return home to sleep morph ourselves into another taxi-cab to the markets on hufang jie—the street near west lake—mad market of many everything every pedlar ever peddled. I try to film the scene and spin slowly. Then delete everything. It tells nothing really of what the scene is doing to me in me through me. More *isness*—the isles of what I feel.see.touch.taste.hear—senses synapses bursting lighting arcing thought to thought sense to sense. I find myself drawn to old china—old artists patiently waiting for anyone no one someone to pay 300 kuai for a ten-minute portrait flash in the enormity of life. I just say, *wo mayo nemmo duo qian* I do not have much money and try to summon words palpable breath memories from them to me. Some kind of connection not nod-like real conversation between souls and not cultures. They smile and get it. No painting is real. Really real. Just the finger pointing at the moon.

But not the moon itself.

Not the moon itself.

Not the moon itself.

Perception. Illusion. A color slide in kindergarten. Real. Not real. Perception. Illusion.

The wizened ancient woman sitting waiting on a bench with me waiting on the bench warm smile big laugh looking at me and sway-smiling in the closing hours of the day while menwomanchildren pass by stare munch—crabs four to a stick spitting out pulpy entrails brittle shells. Whole fish speared on skewers eyes pleading smothered gasping in air bellies ripped quickly skewered over fire. Sucking duck heads taste good really no boiling in languid bath of oily broth. Squid boomed and tied flaccid tentacles clove hitch bowlines fast to spar of death continuance birth and rebirth. Depleted. Fed. Depleted. Fed. Joy. Everywhere joy. Families. Lovers. Friends. Eat. Drink. Twist their ways through pulsating crowd hawkers beggars who always find me. African engineers diplomats. Some few americans who too cool maybe want need to avoid me or maybe just embarrassed to be american mistaken for tourist. I am your thorn. I want to call your bluff expose the absurdity of your truth. I am the proud american who says hey first who always never turns my head down sideways askance. Practiced feints. Enervating avoidance. Are you alive as me? I want to say.

And then this old woman lady maybe once madame on shady bench makes me more alive sucking vestigial memories wisdom lessons pain loss everything humanity wears probably like (or is) Penelope and me maybe I have returned to hearth destroyed by vagaries of fate. But no gods to praise thank remember resist blame. My temporal *isness*. Her eternal *isness*. My fraud of words no match for hers—Go. Go. *Man man zou.* You. You go slowly. Through life? This wending street? Next stall bench store hawker home? I do not take any more pictures. I look for Rob. Obscenely tall american god. Dave's loud laugh cleaves the market like a village on the edge of the mountains. The waypoints of this journey descent ascent. Drawn to siren songs. Us. Them. We and eddie and bill…We are in orbit around each other sucked in by gravity of familiar mutual assured levity and forbearance. Necessity. Will. Mere inclination.

Together we laugh and laugh and laugh. Trundle. Limp. Like old beggars under sacks knocked kneed backs bellies twisted by raw fish frogs roe jellyfish snake chewing sucking bones fat sinews of fated fowl flesh noodles grain liquor. I am a child twirling in an arc bound to them following them completing them each other. We are untethered box cars wending climbing towards hazy mountains draped in wispy belching of young factories insistent on more and more for them and we and me always wanting never really resting on a pinnacled orb. West

Lake first sun in days floating outside gravity. Sidewalks stretching cars busses people skirting going to ignoring beckoning the sun reminder of impermanence setting into west lake antiquity.

Out of tune street singer croaking swooning moon river beside crazy intersection maddened crazed by plastic steel sticky tar of importance. I have to need to want to do grab his guitar. Please. One song only. Crazy foreigner. Proud american. Lean on me I sing and mean it more than ever in pub club grass engulfed gazebo in small american town. I am an amalgam of vanity pretense sorrowful primal need to be will be heard. This is me. This is me. This is me. One song only and leave flattered full of plastic importance towards dissolving sun woven into perfect random intersection of elm sycamore willows leading beckoning drawing us to the lake. West Lake. Like faith. Unerring assurance of the improbable happening before us. Rob the improbable god. Dave's unerring laugh and me scrunched on impossibly small bench lapped by ancient waters temples herons cleave the sky. Carp swirl to the surface. Cicadas scream from lowing branches.

We. Rob. Dave. Me. We are a small sea. Mouth of river. Still cove. Like Rockport. Walking Denise and Kaleigh on seaweed slipping outcrops. Like here. Dribbling stream awed and attached to dynasties. Histories. Stories. Mystic forging of lost regained recreated fables follies earthed and unearthed. Meticulously recorded guarded preserved in amber. Tradition. Remembrance. Disassembling the moment. *Isness* of this day. This perfect day.

Xenia. Peace. Disbelief fate-luck circumstance. We are the same stream melded out of all waters retreating returning cleansed. We buy soda from a machine. Check our phones. Remember to remember something. Fed. Depleted. Locked and freed by common things needs even dreams. We. Rob. Dave. Me. We hail a cab and return home.

I am a speck in this night. A single lamp in a concrete tower trapped high above the qian tang river. I do not have the power of the distant barge—dark shadow in moiling water carrier of mystery reality actual substance. *Isness*. I'll go to sleep and dream —simple dreams unfettered dreams. Cranes. Skeletal steel wires pulleys resting on unfilled towers tentacled to muddy earth earth sucking shores sheathed in mirrors dated in hope need want. Escalators ascending descending everywhere. Hades. Heaven. Home. Solid places. Joy of with for in spite of because of kids. Indefatigable. And maybe please please please always release me from vanity terror of myself just give me me and you and your love—*Isness*. Perfect perfected solidity of remembrance—This…

Part III

Today it was a temple built into the mountainside west of West Lake. Mr. Toe drove us out there. In most ways I just follow Rob and Dave. They seemed to have read the guidebooks, figured out a reason to go—and then we go. Sometimes Arvin or Sherry tell us where we should go, and if we agree (which we always do) we are led, tutored, fed and returned home with rarely a finger touching a wallet—meals of endless courses, strange foods, many toasts. Nothing ever to regret.

Tomorrow, Dave and Rob are heading to Shanghai. I had no and have no real interest in going. I fear it would put my head in a death spiral of confusion. Hangzhou itself has already left me dizzy and unsure of my steps. It is fun, however, to listen to them plot and plan like it is some navy seal mission. A calling. Must be completed in an eight hour time frame—and it does. They are groping for China in every real and palpable way they can. Tomorrow is our next to last day teaching at the Wahaha School. And then we head home, our bellies filled by different feasts from roadside stalls. It seems we have been here so long. We worked every day and scrambled through every busy day, except for the day of the great typhoon—which did not end up being so great but at least a day off. I miss Denise and the kids and wonder how/why so many people I know can just leave homes with an alacrity and insouciance of stoic acceptance of fate. I know it is obligation and not desire, but I wonder if they feel the same knot —the same unsettled feeling. Or maybe Denise and I are just not used to being apart, like swans bound by common strands of DNA. We have had the same wallet for close to twenty years. Our doors have no locks. Our keys are always in the cars.

Every night, I sit on a sixth floor balcony of a thirty-story luxury apartment building, maybe smoke a bad Chinese cigar, read, write, and think—all the while in awe of the city spread in front of me. My time here is pretty much uninterrupted time. It gives me space with few concerns or obligations, and so I have been experimenting with my writing by heading down what may seem—at first blush—a pretty strange path. In Part II I tried to elevate the level of a of a journal entry simply by using a more elevated, slightly maddened poetic voice—calculated images, a healthy dose of double dashes, an inner voice barking was/is as weak and reflective as I was and am—jet-lagged, isolated, searching for meaning and reality beyond the obvious.

It is energizing to let all hell break loose. In a calculated way, I tried to recreate my head with all of its diasporas, phobias and non-sequiturs intact. An astute or simply intuitive reader might take me to task for borrowing from James Joyce in *Ulysses* or Walt Whitman in *Leaves of Grass*. Another might think it pure self-indulgent blather; while another might just think it strange, pointless and illogical. It is, however, as deliberately crafted a piece as I have written in a long while. I am strangely protective of my words, as if those words are dull and imperfect children— loved because they are the progeny of my spinning spirit and unplumbed soul.

Whether heaven or hell, I write out of habit and a conscious choice to recklessly probe the edges of what is true and unfettered writing of self. I am acutely aware of the limitations of my intellectual depth and breadth, so I am constantly searching for what is real in the moment, for in my moments no one can rob me or question the validity of who or what I am. I can never capture this present experience of returning to China in a traditional narrative (like this). My head twirls in a broth of synaptic sensing. This entry is not mine. It is yours—a dumb-downed genuine story but incredibly lacking in totality—a counterbalance to the excesses of completely letting go. It is a making of sense, not a recreation of actual experience because the "actual" odyssey is a disparate flotsam of immediacy. In any given moment I am here and there leaping forward and back through the incongruous totality of everything I am and was and long to be. Every word typed to this page immediately places these words into a distant, inviolable past, though physically counted only in milliseconds.

This then is my apology, not my anthem. Please accept these travelogues as such. I am not trying to be vague or cloy or clothing myself in mystery. It just is, as Thoreau once wrote, *indivisible from its essence.* I am not obsessed, but I am convinced the only test of words lies in the reaping, not the sowing. If somehow you—my rare reader—will linger a bit longer in my fields and sense a greater bounty coming, then, and only then, have I succeeded as a writer.

My temptation is to explore the particulars of the people here—the people who embrace us with utter and complete magnanimity—as somehow representing the people of China. This would be so easy and convenient for me, but, really, all of us are just slices off the roast of life. The awkward politeness and sculpted awarenesses of our first days here evolved through Darwinian mutations into something not cultural, but true, universal friendships honed by the wheel of hospitality sourced out of the well of humanity.

Tomorrow night, Arvin—a forty-something science teacher who has made it his life mission for for us to appreciate the antiquity of China (and not to measure it by the polluted, overgrown, chaos of everyday life China)—has invited us to his house tomorrow night to have dinner with his parents. He wants us to see a China not toasting us in city restaurants, bars or classrooms, but rather in a home in a small village—a single stretch of family eager to welcome us through the over-sized door of hospitality. I fear he will spend more money than he has, and he will micro-criticize every action he makes and every natural imperfection lost, found and returned in the reality of anything called "home." He is a man who is impossible not to love, who is insecure in any given moment, who fears his goodness is misplaced or misunderstood though to me it is never misguided. He is a man whose eight-year-old boy is everything— as in *every thing*—to him, a reality which snares both the magnificence and myopia of China.

The one child policy in China [since changed to two or sometimes three] creates children too precious for freedom. Everyone here accepts, lives and lives the logic of the one-child policy, but the manifestations imply an approach to cultural norms seldom broached in the history of earth and put into continual practice and decreed by law upon untold millions of people. All of my students here are "only-children," and in varying degrees they act like only-children, but more so their parents are acutely aware their child is their *only* child—their "one shot" at a legacy; hence, there is little to no room for error. As Shakespeare wrote: "That's the rub." We—parents of the world—constantly measure our success as parents through the portal of our children. I do it all the time. But here it taken into an uncharted sea whose shoals are dredged by the unyielding claws of a proud and ancient culture lorded over by the insensate paws of a massive, controlling government.

My ramblings aside, I am over-joyed to be invited to Arvin's home. So much of my time in in China back in 1981-1982 was spent in homes—real homes—squares of mud, brick, clay and tin set in sprawled alleyways with common latrines and single pots and pans set on small coal stoves preparing paltry feasts. I miss that simplicity, that connection and that validity.

I returned home after my first trip to China and spent close to ten years in a small log cabin, graced with an outhouse, a simple stove, one pot, one pan and a cold water well flowing until some cold night in November when the pipe would freeze solid, and then I would wait until it thawed on some warm day in March and slurped back to life. I consciously tried to live with little, though I could have scavenged an entire kitchen from the swap shop at the Carlisle dump. Arvin's home may well be the face of the new China—the China reinventing the yardstick, the China emerging and sometimes bursting out of a generation resting under leaves like the cicadas, but now chattering in maddened choruses in every grove of tended trees.

I am speechless and stunned by the skyline of the city. I can't comprehend the reality. I drive the streets and crane my head in disbelief and can only wait for time and space to give context and some infantile understanding that justifies my claustrophobia of words cluttered and pressed together. These are the new temples swathed in carbon haze. They will be gone long before time has recycled them into something new, not the truly ancient temples carved out of the hillsides along West Lake—not the homes of godly emperors served by scores of eunuchs, peasant farmers, concubines and foot soldiers. I do not feel as if I am embedded in a new dynasty. I only sense the impermanence of something inherently unsustainable. The skyscrapers seem more like Towers of Babel paling in comparison to the mud homes of my memory.

I am exhausting myself. My head is now only one of many on the Hydra of my intrinsic self. In a few short hours, I need to be in front of my students who only need to know I care about verb tenses and sentence structure. Any success I have as a teacher is in how well I have learned to wear the proper head at the proper time, so my students will never sense or fear the fulness of the monster lurking in front of them. My teacher-head is only a toothless rag of fur and broken appendages my students stuff in their backpacks and carry through life—if only to shape dreams to help them sleep at night. Dreams stretched in every horizon.

If a teacher is not also a dream, he or she or they is no better than a book carried and shuffled across hard desks—a vague remembrance—listless as beach sand. Mud scraped off old boots.

I am not making sense.

I am making real.

MAKING IT WORK

EJ and Pipo squat in the driveway
And poke their heads through
The wheel-well and pass
A half inch socket and WD 40
To my bloodied hand.

I shout out to them:
"The transmission cooler line
Is completely shot,
And the thread
On the flare nut
Is stripped bare—
It turns, but won't catch,
Into the radiator.
In short: we're screwed."

I hear them giggling,
Splashing in the oily cold
Puddle I am soaked in.

While Pipo runs to get
The extra red hose we used
To fix the heater on the bus,
I send EJ to get the cement
We used to fix the gasket
On the wood stove.

In my sarcophagus
Under the old Buick wagon,
I fumble through my pockets
And find some hose clamps
That just might work.

EJ slathers the flare nut
In an icing of black glue.
And so Pipo can use
His beloved tape measure,

He cuts me a piece of red hose
18 ½ inches long—exactly.

There is no turning back now.
I cut out the old line
And jam the flare nut
Into the fitting
Until it sets.

Everything is dead serious—
Pipo lays on his belly
And fits the 18 ½ inch hose
To the cleanly cut ends
Of the cooler lines;
EJ takes his flathead screwdriver
And tightens the hose clamps
While I keep
The damn flare nut
From moving.

And in the stale air,
Beneath a 1988
Buick LeSabre Wagon—
Soaked in mud, love,
Oil and anti-freeze—
I am the luckiest man alive.

A LETTER TO THE LAZY

Thoughts from the island

*We often miss opportunity because it is dressed in overalls
and looks like work.*
~Thomas A. Edison

Dear Huck,

Is there any room left on the island? I hope so. I just got back
from four hours of singing in a crowded, noisy club. I'm tired
and kind of grumpy. I'm not sure why. Maybe because I could
barely hear myself sing, or maybe it is all the moaning and
complaining from my 8th-grade class about my weekend
assignment, which they say is" too much and too tough "and so
unfair—but, damn, right now I need a break from everything.

I think about you all the time. You've got it made. You sit
around all day, smoke a pipe, catch catfish, snag drift logs, and
talk with Jim. Hells bells, I could even deal with the rattlesnakes.
Sorry about Jim and the snake. I know you didn't mean for Jim
to get bit by some snake, but it was still pretty stupid—and mean
—though I know you thought it was going to be funny. It is
strange how easy it is for any one of us to screw up.

Kind of like with me and my students'. I did not hope to get
a bunch of them all mad and annoyed. I really didn't think
taking a walk in the woods and sitting for twenty minutes writing
a letter to you was a big deal, and I didn't think reading a good
book for an hour was work at all. I actually thought it would be
kind of fun and interesting—or at least different.

I hope I have time to walk this weekend. You will probably
walk around and sit whenever you want to sit, and you will, like
you always do, think. I know you can't keep from thinking. You're
always thinking. But Man O' Man, you've got a lot to think about

—more than I'll ever have to think about because your thinking is probably mostly worrying, and Jim's worrying is probably worst of all. If you get caught, you'll be whipped by your drunk Pa, but Jim will get whipped, tarred, and sold down the river.

It makes me feel stupid to worry so much about how mad some of my students are right now. I bet some of them will stay so mad they won't get anything out of the assignment; they'll just be mad the whole weekend. I'm sorry if some of them do not seem like they care about you in the letters I asked them to write to you.

They all think they have busier lives than you. Teenagers are like that. They're busy, alright, but just lazy busy with stupid stuff. Seeing as you got so much extra time on your hands, maybe you should write them a letter. I would, but I'm afraid they'd tear it up and throw it in the trash.

They're really good kids, mostly, but I worry sometimes about how they will handle the really tough times in life. Those times will come, but they do not know it yet. I mean, my assignment ain't tough like you got it tough. It will just take some time. I don't imagine Jim has had free time in his whole life, which is ironic because he isn't free.

He is already a slave.

I guess where you stand depends upon where you sit.

Sorry for the long ramble. I'm wicked tired. I really don't want to go to the island. I was just saying that.

Tell Jim I say "Hi."

And be real careful. It ain't so nice here either, sometimes.

Good luck.

You'll need it.

Sincerely,

Fitz

NATHAN

A shortened life, well-lived

I would rather walk with a friend in the dark,
than alone in the light.
~Helen Keller

After my oldest sister Patty died suddenly and too young, a friend said to me, "Sometimes God takes one to teach many." In that sense, my small part in Nathan's rich, deep, and varied life as his teacher has been turned around. Nathan is now my teacher—our teacher—and in this unspeakable and implacable tragedy of loss, we are now his students, and he gives us now—and will give us forever—profound, immutable, and indelible parables to learn, speak, and embrace in our own lives.

As quiet, polite, and reserved as Nathan lived as a person, his mind was, in every sense, *a mind on fire*. He lived a life in love with the possibilities of words; he lived a life alive to the possibilities of nature, and he never—ever—gave up on the possibilities to find truth, meaning, and purpose in life.

It is no surprise Nathan was a kindred soul with his mentor and friend Henry David Thoreau, both of them so inextricably linked by a common love of the soil, rivers, ponds, fields, scrubby woodland, history of Concord, and, more especially, Nathan's beloved hometown of Lincoln.

It is an honor to be asked by Nathan's family to share a few passages from *Walden*—a book Nathan not only read but re-read and lived many times over. He took it to heart when Thoreau wrote:

> *Moreover, I, on my side, require of every writer, first or last, a simple and sincere account of his own life, and not merely what he has heard of other men's lives...*

And so Nathan did what few can do. He became a writer in every sense of the word—a writer brave enough and dogged enough to search for eternal truths rooted in the muddy loam of common life, and, in doing so, became the thinking person's philosopher Thoreau so ardently sought:

> *There are nowadays professors of philosophy, but not philosophers. Yet it is admirable to profess because it was once admirable to live. To be a philosopher is not merely to have subtle thoughts, nor even to found a school, but so to love wisdom as to live according to its dictates, a life of simplicity, independence, magnanimity, and trust.*

Simplicity, independence, magnanimity, and trust are perfect words to describe the essence of Nathan's life among us.

Nathan lived as a seeker of wisdom over knowledge, and while he was an amazing student and scholar, he was never the boisterous classmate shouting out a naive and impulsive answer to a vexing question; instead, he chewed his cud and explored the question, then intently, quietly, and humbly embedding his own fully reflected answer into his equally quiet and humble life. He did not care what others thought. He didn't seek accolades and recognition. He cared more about how and why he should live— and how we, too, could, can and should live our lives. Like Thoreau, Nathan did not live a secret life; rather, he sought to live a fuller and more mystic life in his own inimitable and iconoclastic way.

> *In any weather, at any hour of the day or night, I have been anxious to improve the nick of time, and notch it on my stick too; to stand on the meeting of two eternities, the past and future, which is precisely the present moment; …To anticipate, not the sunrise and the dawn merely, but, if possible, Nature herself!*

As I sit here reading my own tattered copy of *Walden*, it is hard to discern who is Henry and who is Nathan, for their words and lives are enmeshed and linked in silky threads of solidarity. In these final words, culled from *Walden*, I hear, feel, and see the strength and magnanimity of Nathan's heart, soul, mind, and being.

I would not have any one adopt my mode of living on any account; for, beside that before he has fairly learned it I may have found out another for myself. I desire that there may be as many different persons in the world as possible; but I would have each one be very careful to find out and pursue his own way, and not his father's or his mother's or his neighbor's instead

I went to the woods because I wished to live deliberately, to front only the essential facts of life, and see if I could not learn what it had to teach, and not, when I came to die, discover that I had not lived. I did not wish to live what was not life, living is so dear; nor did I wish to practice resignation, unless it was quite necessary. I wanted to live deep and suck out all the marrow of life, to live so sturdily and Spartan- like as to put to rout all that was not life, to cut a broad swath and shave close, to drive life into a corner, and reduce it to its lowest terms, and, if it proved to be mean, why then to get the whole and genuine meanness of it, and publish its meanness to the world; or if it were sublime, to know it by experience, and be able to give a true account of it in my next excursion.

God is now with Nathan, guiding him on his next excursion through the woods and down the river, and while his death leaves us with inexplicable and implacable heartbreak, his life left us with a perfect and enduring parable on how we might live, enrich, and perfect our own lives. He left us forlorn, but not alone. Buddha once said, *"Do not mistake the finger pointing at the moon for the moon itself."*

Nathan, you are a full moon shining in our eternal sky. Your light and inextinguishable magnificence will lead us through this dark and lonely night.

And in the final words of *Walden:*

"The sun is but a morning star…"

THE BOTTOM LINE

Around my cabin they are dropping trees—
The tall White pines that sentinel these woods,
That crack and thud before being dragged
To the landing, and then bucked and loaded
Onto a top-heavy pile of harsh truck.
Every so often the machines will stop.
I hear the loggers gam and cuss and curse.
"For Christ-sakes, these are all shit-full heart-rot."
Pissed beyond pissed they went and bid so high
For what the mill owners will smile and laugh.
The slash is piled high and the ground scarfed.
I dip my pen and turn back to my work.
Piecing together the best of our wood,
None of us will make a killing today.

WHY READ THE ODYSSEY?

I close "The Odyssey" one last time
and the night closes in on me.
There is no Athena,
no pact of peace,
and I am no king.
I am suddenly alone,
curious and free.
Humbled by the day,
I face the darkness
with a strange and enduring calm,
ready to make my way
back home again...
~Fitz

Read well. Read deeply. Read often. This blessed trinity sums up the greater part of what is basic to an understanding of a complex and evolving world. To read well, you need to read closely, think imaginatively, and allow yourself to be challenged intellectually, emotionally, culturally, and politically. To read deeply is to search for meanings, morals, and messages embedded in the images and actions within a text. It forces you to decipher the metaphors that cling to the twists and turns of plots, or it prods you to understand the spartan logic of a philosopher's mind as he or she lays out a reasoned reflection on the conundrums and constants of life. To read often and well is to place reading before the lesser pursuits of the day. Second only to the feeding and sheltering of the body is the feeding and nurturing of the mind, and there is no greater food than a piece of great literature.

Not all of you have the courage to read a great book, and literary timidity is a travesty only to yourself. Some of you have already blocked the gates to the greater reservoirs of your mind.

How then can I teach you anything? How can I expect you to be moved when you are anchored in your safe and shallow harbor? Don't touch a book if it hasn't touched you; don't waste eternity with an idle mind.

"But," you say with exasperation, "you give us these books, and you compel us to use your choices, not our choices. How can we be touched when we are force-fed what to read? How can there be romance when there is no passion?"

The angst of my mystified students is justified, for what healthy teenager is loathe to rebel against the directives and edicts of a misguided teacher?"

Therein lies the rub: What if the teacher is not misguided? What if, on the contrary, your teacher is well-guided by life, instinct, and vocation? How could you not listen? Why wouldn't you listen if there was some measure of hope your teacher could guide you to a greater understanding of life than you ever dreamed possible?

At a certain point in my life, I let Henry David Thoreau be my teacher. Only then did I realize my cynicism and laziness hobbled me and distanced me from accessing the opportunities created by reading great works of classic literature, and so I began a forty-five-year adventure of reading what are commonly thought to be great books—and I am still barely out of the harbor.

My first real book was *The Odyssey*, and I'm damn sure it will be the last—if I have any control over it. Life is too precious to chatter and blather with fools and strangers. If you are unwilling to face the challenges of *The Odyssey*, go back to your social media and gossip with the idle minds of your generation—and mine, for that matter.

If you are afraid to become a man, don't become one.

THE CONCORD WOODS

The Stewards of Diversity

*Our ability to reach unity in diversity will be the beauty
and the test of our civilisation.*
~**Mahatma Gandhi**

In the early 1980's, I started a small-scale suburban logging company with my friend Sandy, which we named "Loon Cordwood," and for a few years we were rare birds—logger in Concord. We cut down trees and sold the wood, mostly as firewood, but often as logs for lumber. It was hard work and stupidly dangerous, yet strangely satisfying—and we did, surprisingly, survive our incompetent idiocies—mine more than Sandy's. We cut trees that needed to come down. We were mainly hired by the wealthy to manage their woodlands, and the landed gentry could get the tax deduction for being so noble with their wealth. Before we got to their woods, some well-educated forester would plod the woods and mark with an orange blob of pain the trees destined to the saw mill or consigned to firewood to come down. The foresters mandate was to keep the woodland healthy and sustainable. Other times, our mandate was to cut clean entire acres and clear land for a new Concord mansion, a horse pasture or some tacky, posh development.

There was little nonsense in Sandy. The woods were a workplace to go to and get it with our fingers intact. He could tell the value of any given tree from a hundred yards away, He a could drop a tree in the opposite direction it leaned, and he could split a cord by hand in less than an hour. We were a mismatched pair, yet we got along well and many board feet of lumber passed through our chains. As I wrote in a song, "We had pockets of cash, and a piece of the sky," but at the end of every month never any discernible profits. What we had, we split evenly, and when we split after a couple of years, there were no grudges, only stories to tell and retell.

At first, I was the romantic logger. I wanted to be tough, work in the woods and drive loud trucks. We worked in stifling heat, numbing cold and drenching rains. After a spell, I found myself more entranced by the woods themselves and not trees I stole from the woods. I liked "managing the land" as a dreamy apprentice to the forester. I was not a ravager of the woods, but rather a worthy steward of the forest doing the satisfying work to keep the woods a healthy, vibrant and sustainable ecosystem. The foresters talked of the need to create diversity in the woods to sustain a new generation of trees and undergrowth, for without a diversity of trees and brush, the forest would fall prey to the blights and diseases of a "monoculture," a sameness where one blight of fungus-borne could decimate the whole forest.

Being a sucker for metaphors, and long out of the logging business, I can't help but relate this to the ways we live our lives. Without diversity, we too will fall prey to the moral diseases and blights diminishing our humanity and killing off the better part of a healthy, vibrant and strong society. Every community is in some way a woodland—a mix of species begging a vibrant mix to reach its fullest potential—and we, as the foresters and loggers of society, must work to make a healthy, codependent ecosystem happen. For our own survival, we must nurture the greater woods and encourage other trees to grow alongside us—in spite of our pride in whatever towering or scrubbish tree we claim to be.

There is no vaccine for prejudice or bigotry—only deliberate work and effort to encourage diversity in our own lives. Without diversity, you know what will happen. We all know it, even when we choose not to see it. But we do see it, but avert our eyes from the scene of the crime. With blinders stripped, we see it everyday, in our lives, in our schools, in our professions and in our acceptance of each other—but only if our eyes are open and our hearts and souls are willing. I grew up in Concord neighborhood, back when Concord was still dotted by middle-class neighborhoods, working farms, and some kids who actually ended up in the state prison—and not always as guards. I lived a childhood that was almost mythic in its magic, but I always sensed it was not "real." The Sears, the only black family in Concord, lived around the corner from us, and they had six kids too; their yard was exactly the same acre as every other yard in a sea of yards. Their dad yelled at them as loudly as my dad yelled at me. They bolted home when the street lights came just as fast I bolted home. It seemed real to me, but I have spent a good part of my life trying to figure what *real* is and have not pierced the bubble of the conundrum. What does real look like? Is it real I teach at a mostly white, wealthy and privileged private school— as in hyper-privileged? Is Concord any more real or less real than it ever was? Have I made some deal with the devil for the sake of a job? Am I pious enough to tell someone else how to be pious?

Am I a fraud, a spinster or a beacon of hope?

When I was logging the woods, the scream of my chainsaw and the crashing of trees in the woods disturbed the neighbors. My work as a noisy woodcutter disrupted their lives and their comfortable notions of what "their forests" should be, but it was not—and is not—and frankly, never was their forest. It is our forest, and if we don't tend to it, our communities will fracture, our country will dissolve, and what a hell of a place to leave to our children.

If you haven't noticed, it might be because you live in Concord or some iteration of Concord. The people chanting for change are not only on the latest news. They are beside you, above you and below you; their roots are inextricably entwined with your roots, and you cannot disentangle from them. We share whatever water courses through our communal sand. We fight for the same sunlight. We live, die, breathe and grow with, for and beside each other. We, they, it is our future, and if you can't embrace this continuum, at least accept it; otherwise, your life and your way of life has a looming time-stamp—a sell-by date vaguely marked, yet definably stated.

Diversity is seldom a choice. It is inseparable from our nature. What makes us common is balanced by what makes us uncommon. Denise and I did not seek diversity in our family. It simply happened. We have a son from Haiti who lost both his parents to Aids, who lives with an incurable and ultimately fatal disease, who was a six-year-old kid pulled from the binds of his siblings to live in this strange and forgiving land. We have a gay son who married to his Scottish partner, who finally "came out" and found the joy and validation of simply being who he is and was and always meant to be. We have a daughter who is a victim of sexual assault and who now works tirelessly with other victims of sexual assault. We have another daughter who suffers with Misophonia, who is literally allergic to the most common sounds of life. None of them have the luxury to be diverse. They are who they are—real people living real lives because of—and in spite of—all working for or working against them. We have four other children who undoubtedly wrestle with their own demons and flirt with dancing angels—as do their parents. We are a typical family because we are atypical. We do not consciously celebrate our differences—we celebrate being a family; we accept being a family, and we do the work (sometimes imperfectly) families do.

The inexplicable evolution life drops us in fields of diversity. If we do not embrace this diversity, we ignore the calling to be fully human; we lose what it takes to be real, compassionate and accepting, and ultimately we lose what is most precious in our lives. I am no paradigm of virtue or enlightenment. I may not like the gangly White pines lining my side yard. But I love that they are there. The scrubby oaks and tangles of brush make my hike through the woods more tiresome and difficult, but they are the saplings of a future and greater forest to leave to our children, and, whether you are ready or not, our feral forest is what we leave behind to future generations.

See your bigotry as bigotry and just get on with it and calibrate your change. It is the edict of evolution to evolve and change. Open your eyes and open your god-damned heart. make the best of our puddle. Appreciate it. Nurture it. Sustain it, but above all, accept it and all it encompasses.

We can never be satisfied with what we have, but only for what we might have.

And should have.

DECEPTION

Because he fished
in mountain stream
with tied fly
he'll never bait
worm to barbed hook;
won't mess
with shallow topsoil
and grubbing.

"Naw," he says,
"It's like camping
in your backyard."

I drop my worm
and sit—maybe
bump it on the bottom.

He looks like the cover
Of an LL Bean catalogue—
A crouching shadow
On a rocky shallow
Stuck in a frame
Of a setting sun.

He rolls a silent loop
setting dry fly
on calm water—
the back cast
and the set.

But today it is my fish
small perch
we'll bring home
fry in flour and egg
and give him shit—

"You and your split cane
and frigging oiled line."

THE NAGGING THING

The common code of humanity

Disobedience is the true foundation of liberty.
The obedient must be slaves.
~Henry David Thoreau

There are not many more nights like this—cool enough to sit outside on the back porch and warm enough to think. The kids and Denise are long asleep. I welcome my call to duty, or at least I answer the call with stoic acceptance. During the school year, these long hours are my sacred time—a gift to tidy up the maelstrom of schoolwork—grading, posting assignments, playing the catchup game, and assuring parents , all of which is the numbing reality for most teachers.

I think…

I consider myself a good teacher. I love what I do and what I teach. My school is supportive, and it has the resources to help me do what I want to do in class. If I feel any angst, it is the gnawing reality of teaching at a wealthy private school striving to be in touch with the times and changing and evolving with the whims and dictates of a seeming Fate. We are not, nor can we be, where we should be, but we are heaving and leaning upward on the downhill side of the boulder. We are working to increase our diversity; we recognize the various traditions of a myriad of cultures; we teach good moral values; we demand decency and respect in all circumstances; our pedagogy and curriculum are enlightening, empowering, and prepare kids well for…

This is where my questioning begins.

As much as I want to think I prepare my students for "life," I fear that, in most cases, their simple access to a privileged lifestyle is all they really need to succeed. I look at my own seven children, all doing very well at what they do. I have four in public high school, one in a public college, another who graduated from a public college, and one, my youngest Tommy, a 7th grader at my school. It has always nagged me that I could not give my own children what is a birthright to the majority of my students—students who take private music lessons, who hire tutors at every turn or bump on their road to success, who travel the world and give presentations on safaris, or who join service projects in remote villages, or who simply and unaffectedly talk about second homes on the Vineyard, Nantucket, or St. John—or their ski houses in Vermont, Maine, and New Hampshire. They are, by and large, good kids and not bratty or self-important in any way, shape, or kind.

Just privileged. And privilege, as with any gift, comes with baggage.

As a school, we "honor diversity" in a staggering number of ways, yet our hands are never dirtied by true difference. There are no girls. There are no children with severe handicaps or special needs. We struggle to find the right fit for black and Latino students bussed out of Boston and Lowell to our gilded suburban enclave. We honor, but cannot seem to inculcate, our *dream* into the web of our *reality*. The majority of our students are children from wealthy families. Their opportunities in life are blessed and informed by a quiet acceptance of this blessing. Mot of us probably wish we were more wealthy than we are, so perhaps we are in no way better—just unlucky—and cursed by the fate of our lineage that began in some pot-holed mill town or a hard-scrabble homestead somewhere on the periphery of a proper world.

So I teach, I sing, I give guitar lessons, and I tutor. I build things, dig gardens, and write loose screeds of bland prophecy. Somehow, I cobble together a good life for my family. The harsh twist is that I am always leaving my family to give to other kids the same blessings I wish I could give to my own kids.

I hear Bob Marley singing,

Winter's here,
And I'm still standing there.
Summer's here,
And I'm still standing there.

I don't want to think of my kids waiting in vain for my love, but they get it, perhaps more so than me.

My students, wealthy or less wealthy, are guiltless of any sin —and I wouldn't even know the poor from the less poor if they didn't drive to school in eighty-thousand dollar cars. But the classroom is far from the parking lot. Whoever walks through my door is who I teach. Whoever walks out of my door remains a mystery. I hope and trust I can create a better life for all of my students and not incarcerated them in the preordained cells of society.. On the next day, I hope again, stumbling and mumbling like a drunk out of a bar. I do not recognize myself. It is just strange.

My actual life is detached from the lives of so many of those I teach, so I implore my students to find enduring, universal themes in literature and in their writing, if only to help them see they are not so special—that no one is special. We are inextricably linked and bound by the common DNA of humanity. We are heirs to all that makes us human. I need my students to see each other—and me—as just another branch on a common tree, born from the same tangled rootstock. I entice them—and I hope embolden them—with stories of my own notable academic failures. I tell and retell reckless parables of my odyssey through life. I share my poetry and songs and share my stories of my 8th grade crush and a summer spent trying to get her hand to brush against mine.

I am a wacko teacher, code nine. I am also an old, traditionalist relic. My honesty is the only gift I can possibly give to you—my students new and old. Every other gift is cardboard and ribbons. Perhaps they will remember I taught them comma rules or how to whittle a bird out of a scrap of soft pine. Maybe they cried in class… Maybe they laughed at death… Maybe they will see this and say, "Fitz was full of shit." Maybe…

But there are a lot of maybe's in life…

I pray, dear students; do not listen closely to me.

I fear I'm full of something.

JOURNAL ENTRY #1

Only you can make yourself a writer

Not until we are lost do we begin to understand ourselves.
~Henry David Thoreau

We are what we are, and we are what we put into words. Above all else, and despite the challenges, we discover who we are through the process of putting substance to the subtle murmurings of thought.

On most nights, after the work and play of the day, after the kids have stopped homework, chores, and Fortnite, I come here to this chair, open my Day One app—and start writing, usually with no set plan other than to simply write, and in writing maybe discover a bit more of who I am, what I care about, and why I am.

I am rarely amazed by what I write, but I never cease to be amazed. My journal writing is never wasted time; it is life added to the day—energy created by expending energy—a cool twist to the laws of physics.

Our minds are a labyrinth of caverns holding infinite treasure, untapped in greater measure until we sift through what lies within us. These clicks upon a screen are the same as scratchings upon a page—common words made uncommon simply because they are mine, not yours. They are my testament to eternity—dry seeds to plant in your imagination, to root in your soil, and to give food for your thought, be it a few scrabbly berries or a harvest feast, for to write is to share, and sharing our words evolves into the sustaining grains of humanity.

At its worst, journaling is a jumbling pile of disconnected ramblings void of a unifying theme or coherent purpose. However, at its best, scratching words in your journal every day beckons and leads us to the fresh starting point of enlightened literature—masterpieces of craft wedded to universal, infinite wisdom. Like any craft, we need to start with a few simple tools, a bit of discipline, and a willingness to perch by a workbench—to chip, mold, and practice until something worth remembering is created.

And then you, too, will never cease to be amazed.

This will be a year for you to remember, if only because I will taunt and haunt you time and time again to open a blank page and fill it with your soul. In time, you will lose the disconnect between what you think and what makes it onto the page. In the end, the "doing" of writing is what separates the good writer from the bad writer. No amount of my teaching will make you a great writer; only you can make yourself a great writer. Only you can tap the power already within you.

There are only two rules in my class: "Give a damn and figure it out." I won't expect you to do what you cannot do. I will, however, ask you to do many things that stretch the limits of what you think you can do, wish you could do, or never imagined you might do.

I won't try to hobble you nor try to defeat you. I will set you free in a playground of words and let you practice the game of words—words spelled out in the unfolding of your indefatigable lives.

The games you play are your games, not mine.

This is my journal entry, not yours.

Now write your own...

IT IS BEACH DAY AT CAMP

And I woke up to The Beach Boys singing
"Let's Go Surfing," and now
Everyone has gone surfing—
Off to Hampton Beach
In six school busses:
Two hundred campers, fifty counselors,
And several gallons of sun screen.

Here in an emptied camp
I am a washed up gunfighter
In an old western town
That lost its gold fever.

A devil's heat mixes
With New Hampshire humidity—
Milo pants on the porch, snapping
At wasps and deer flies
Swirling with impunity
Around the cabin porch.

I am my rare old self:
A grizzled sloth
Hung on a sagging branch—

A lazy poet on a lazy day.

There is nothing to do.

It seems even the words
Have gone off
To another place.

DAN ZANES

The magic of a mentor

If you have built castles in the air,
your work need not be lost; that is where they should be.
Now put the foundations under them.
~Henry David Thoreau, *Walden*

A new artist came into town, and though I had some vague idea of what Dan Zanes looked like from the various album covers of his music I own, I was still struck by how much "presence" he commanded. He ambled through a common dinner line at Windsor Mountain Camp as if he had been there all summer. His impish grin framed under wild shocks of graying hair, belied his career as a rock star from an 80's rock band and his current renown as a folksinger with a Disney Channel. Dan was not new to camp. Some decades ago, he worked here in the kitchen, washed dishes, cut fruit, and, from what I heard say, sang a lot of songs. During Dan's days as a dishwasher, the camp was named Interlocken. A big arts and music camp in Michigan claimed the similar name Interlochen and sued for exclusive rights to the commonly pronounced name. Though our camp was Interlocken first, the big guy with deep pockets usually wins; hence, our camp is now named Windsor Mountain International Camp—a summer camp for kids from around the world nestled on a beautiful hill of a mountain sidled by a dark wilderness pond in the wet woods of southwestern New Hampshire.

I would bet, pound for pound, Windsor Mountain produces more music than the big Interlochen, and in my mind, probably better music—real, unaffected, and persistent music. Dan was visiting us to relive old times and revive old music curated over decades of campfires. His arrival here is a scene repeated almost daily at camp. For as long as I've been here, the gravel drive up

One World Way is a virtual turnpike of funky, offbeat characters showing up for several days of artistic enhancement. All are greeted with the open arms of equanimity and a collective magnanimity powered by the enduring ethos of camp. Everyone noticed Dan Zanes as another artistic savant of some sort, but few realized the depths of his contributions to American rock and roll and folk music, so I was pretty much alone in my idolatry. However, at the time, I didn't realize how profoundly an aging rocker turned children's folk singer would plot a new course in my life and change my ideas about creating and performing music.

Old dreams die slow and often imperceptible deaths. We imagine the possibilities of life until those hopes fade into the impossibility of reality. And so it is with my music. My once grand dream of pushing the frontiers of folk music as a writer and performer is now a steady, predictable, and somewhat rewarding role as a low-level folkie in the small circle of New England's folk scene. I also know that if I stopped playing tomorrow, the ripple of my absence would not reverberate on any distant shore. This in itself should keep me humble, but I reached into my reservoir of pride and approached Dan with the hubris of a beaten lion. I introduced myself as a worshipping fan, but he seized the opportunity to show how much he already knew about me. He was eager to hang out and play music together. We set a loose time and an ill-defined place— somewhere in camp, sometime after all the kids lay asleep in bunks.

And so at ten o'clock at night, within a screaming buzz of mosquitoes, I sat on the steps of the dining hall porch, playing my battered Gibson guitar in the dark. I was too proud (or perhaps afraid) to walk across camp to the cabin where Dan and his wife stayed. Our plans were too loose to be presumptuous on my part. It was not long before I heard, "Hey Fitz," and there was Dan with his mandolin and a banjo. He sat beside me and started singing "Sitting on Top of the World." I followed his song with "Crawdad Hole" and "Salty Dog Blues." Back and forth, we sang the camp songs we love to sing. There were many songs to sing. We moved indoors and attracted a circle of counselors not on night duty. We played until the night seemed closer to morning—all old folksongs, all with refrains and choruses everyone could sing along with, and every one culled from the bulging chests of memory and experience. I was not trying to impress anyone. I just wanted to hold my own with one of the greats, but I soon realized Dan was not out to impress anybody either. He just loved the old songs—songs standing the test of time and Fate—songs I've been learning, hammering, and performing for the past thirty years in bars, at camps, and on makeshift stages. It was an old-fashioned sing with old-fashioned songs, plenty of laughs, and plenty of participation.

I walked back to my bus energized by my "jam with Dan." I regretted I had to drive back to Boston the next day for several small shows. I did not want tomorrow. I wanted another today. I wanted to sing again in a circle of friends, not in the corner of a bar, to the bus lines at a camp, or in a fancy hotel ballroom— which was exactly where I was heading this morning. I didn't want to leave. I wanted and needed to recreate this night again and again. And again if I could. I needed to keep the well flowing with song after song.

I slept restlessly and racked my head for the hundreds of songs I learned and unlearned over the years. I questioned my foundations and the loose cobbling of my life as a performer. I was once nobly convinced of the beauty of everything I sang— mainly folksongs, sea shanties, raucous sing-alongs, and long murderous ballads—and sometimes, though rarely, my own quiet and contemplative songs. The awareness of the intrinsic power of song emboldened me with the confidence to sing and play unabashedly, but lately my confidence has been slipping. I listen too closely when someone says a certain song does nothing for them or a certain song is a musical dead end—so much so that I try to win a crowd over with the tried and true, but not what I really want to learn, play, and perform. I haven't invited Barry Lyle over for years. I haven't opened a Guinness for him and sat with my tape recorder rolling, all the while cajoling song after song out of Barry—songs all but lost, save to scholars and a small band of balladmongers—Dan Zanes among them.

In the not-too-distant past, Dan was the lead singer for The Del Fuego's, a popular Boston rock band. I am not one to pry or preach to the past, but I gather the lifestyle reached a breaking point, and so he moved in the direction of playing folk songs for kids, albeit with a killer band of musicians. Dan has recorded seven albums of music. The best, in my mind, is a collection of sea songs. It is a mesmerizing stream of classic, traditional folk songs, many of them the same I sang for years playing in the Boston pub music scene. Dan recorded every one of these songs of the seas in rough mixes tinged with beauty and realism. He makes no claim to nautical experience, only to a love for the music itself.

Dan's music simply works for me and inspires me to rethink my pedagogy of what my music could, should, and will be. It makes me rue I never recorded those songs myself. I felt the same rueful regret when the "Brother, Where Art Thou" soundtrack came out, and more recently Springsteen's "Seeger Sessions," both of these recordings chockfull of mainstays on my set lists for years. But at least it makes me stop, sit, and ponder my next move—and move I must. Or fade away.

I appreciate my iconoclastic image, but I also recognize how much of my life was and is spent emulating people I respect, be it Thoreau, or Kerouac, or Bob Dylan, or Dan Zanes. I do not want or need to do what Dan Zanes does, but I do want to live with the spirit of his genius and integrity. I need to let go of some things and grab on to others. I need to follow Thoreau and live deliberately; I need to create experience like Kerouac; I need to tap into the well of words like Dylan; and, most importantly, I need to turn my ship in the direction of a new and distinct horizon like Dan Zanes. I need to follow my own song:

It's one step and you turn;
Two steps and you go;
There's many steps that make a mile,
And there's many miles to go.

This is my first step.

A BOY'S LIFE

Shop, Wrestling & Blogs

*Give the pupils something to do, not something to learn; and the
doing is of such a nature as to demand thinking; learning
naturally results.*
~John Dewey

When I meet former students of mine and reminisce about the good old days of teenagerdom, a hearty portion of my academic progeny remembers three things: woodworking, wrestling, and blogging. Wrestling and woodshop are easy targets for wispy memories of joy and fulfillment, but writing—one might not think so, but writing as a blogger injects equal shots of dopamine and testosterone into the husk of teenage boys. Suddenly they have a place to go and a space to do what psychologist Michael Thompson argues boys do naturally as the prime drivers of their intellectual and emotional lives—they compare and compete in a rich and tumbling quest to find their niche in life, to discover (often in heartbreaking ways) where they stand in the unspoken hierarchies of youth, where along the continuum of sexuality they lean, and where in the arc of life they are destined to travel. They balance on a precarious beam of life that pivots on a triangle of duties, dreams, and derelictions.

The lives of boys are a constant juggling act. They deftly defy gravity and keep the circling lobs of joy, affirmation, and purpose in the air. It is a hard game they play. The pressure of youthful proscriptions tangles them in weeds of kelp. They soon fall prey to confusion, doubt, and distraction. It is the rare teacher who can invoke the spirit of Athena to give a gaggle of boys the strength, resolve, and cunning to slay the six-headed hydra, navigate the Straits of Skylla, defeat the Hydra on the left, and avoid the gorging whirlpool on the right. Even the most detailed lesson plan created by sincere and worthy teachers can save the crew scrambling about the deck on the veering ship of the average classroom.

But woodshop, wrestling, and blogging do this.

Teaching woodshop for ten years is pretty damn close to waking up in heaven. Boys do not waddle and trudge to shop class. They bolt from the hallways of academia and burst through the shop door into a brothy and brotherly mix of sound, sense, and purpose. They have a box to build, a boat to craft, a bird to carve, or a sea chest to cobble together. They rise on the yardarms with palpable joy and intense purpose. They learn to use sharp tools. They learn to sketch dreams and temper those dreams with doses of reality. They clean the shop together. They unload bending planks of lumber out of my truck like a union of longshoremen. They do what all craftsmen do. They make things; they splay their tools on benches and saw, drill, glue, and sand. They make a godawful mess, and then they sweep, sing, snicker, and sing and snicker and sing again. They ignore the closing bell. They come to the shop before their classes and during recess, and once more as the afternoon busses arrive—like parents checking their children in the night—just to make sure their unfinished cobbling of wood is as safe and sound as it was left.

They sense the brevity of time and are never lost in musings of the coming weekend or loathings of looming homework. Every shop class is an incarnation of our wildest dreams for what is called project-based learning, and the best example has been right before our eyes since the heady day in 1929 when our school first opened its doors. Our school's founder purposely put the first shop among the academic classrooms. He wanted the boys to "hear the sound of real life." It is the pulsing drum and purposeful power of creation—an incantation of faith and a true apprenticeship for a responsible future.

Wrestling is a bird of a different feather. I often laugh that wrestling is where boys who can't play basketball or can't afford hockey come to spend the winter. Invariably, it is a motley crew unprepared for battle of any sort. Some few have been on the team for a couple of years and wear their hardened skins like knights armor (which it is)—proud of where they are, who they are, and what they have accomplished, especially compared to the new kids quivering in newly bought wrestling shoes. The first few weeks are the hardest physical work of their lives, yet few quit and few move on to a more idyllic sports alternative.

Their bodies bend and contort in ways they never thought possible. They ache when they go home and ache even more when they wake up the next day. Despite the pain, they persist. They see the more experienced wrestlers working twice as hard as them, practicing the same flashy moves over and over again in a repetition of a sacred dance—until stumbling repetition births intuition and every iteration begets greater perfection. The young wrestlers suffer more ignominious losses in a day of practice than in a season of soccer, but, over time, they lose less often; they begin to understand that losing to a better wrestler is no stigma, and defeating a weaker opponent is not a catalyst for celebration. They discover the virtues of dogged, determined practice, and all of this builds a more replete moral character buoyed by increasing physical strength and ultimately evolves into a metaphor, lesson, and possibility for every action in life.

But how the Sam Hill does blogging fit into the pantheon of pedagogical gods? Why do so many of my former students from my last twenty years of teaching English to 8th and 9th grade boys always—as in always—initiate their conversations by first asking, "Are you still blogging?" They seem aghast when I reply, "I just didn't get it going this year."

I am equally aghast at myself. I bleat and baa a tepid confession. I try to convince my weary conscience that it was just too hard this year to keep up with the blogging communities. Too many edicts from above put sand in my gears. I could not juggle the balls and dance the awkward step of conformity—something I literally forced my students to do in their youth. I force myself to believe I am still teaching solid writing skills, yet however skillfully I parse my words and thoughts, my cajoling's ring hollow. My words have no pith, bulk, or weight. Nothing in my dalliance with education rises to the power of simply letting boys write in their blogs. Nothing rises so high as sharing their writing in a community of peers—with myself an equal and humbled peer, waging my own battle with words.

Blogging simply works. Daily blogging evolves into a perpetual motion machine, and it is not long before I do not need to ask them to write—they just do. Everything looks cool, feels cool, and is cool. Every piece of writing, video, or podcast they post to their blogs affirms and reaffirms the competition and comparing that defines and delineates their lives. They want to win the admiration of their classmates, but more so, they want to be noticed, affirmed, and recognized for their unflagging efforts.

In the beginning, blogging resembles the first week of wrestling season—it is hard, grueling, and painful to get words on a page—especially as some have never received a word of praise in their lives for anything they previously wrote. They were beat by the kids who seem to write effortlessly, who somehow think of things to write about, and who never got a grade lower than a B in their lives, but these struggling students "see" what makes for good writing. They sense the connection between what they are taught about writing and what they experience as validated writers. They compare their work to that of an accomplished kid, and soon every sinew of thought in their prewired brains wants to compete. The words start to flow. They get some positive comments from classmates. [I do not allow negative feedback from them, me, or anyone else.] Every word of specific affirmation in the comments is a thundering bolt of dopamine into their visceral selves. Every new post is an opportunity to cull the bad and cultivate the new. More than anything else, they live the life of a writer.

They are writers. They have no choice. If they want to be a good writer, they need ply the trade of a writer.

Blogging is more than just a portfolio of curated work. I respect the power and purpose of a well-curated portfolio, but for my purposes, blogging in a community of writers is light years ahead of a "portfolio" of writing pieces. Portfolios are a fine way of collecting, collating, and curating the best of the best of whatever, but portfolios lack the life and the dynamic interactions of blogging. They lack the myriad possibilities of blogging. Portfolios are like dinner in a fine restaurant. Blogging is like eating pizza and hot dogs while watching the Super Bowl. Blogging is rafting a wild river. Portfolios are a trip to a museum with your parents artsy friend. Portfolios are like saying you love a certain poetry.

Blogging is reciting, "Still I Rise."

A colleague of mine once said in a department meeting (which I did not attend) that "blogging merely encourages "dumb" writing." I wish I was by his side at that meeting, if only to remind him I am also a teacher of writing and a writer—or at least sort of a writer—and to remind him I am also the wrestling coach. I would have asked him to share the last piece of writing he wrote and shared with anybody. I'm sure it was an email or a text message—and probably pretty dumb, too. I would remind him that I am still a shop teacher in heart, soul, and practice—though my new shop is a classroom littered with books, ideas, and iPads. I would show him my boys sharpening tools and crafting boxes out of words, shaping carvings sliced out of phrases—one eye on the project, the other eye on the plan. Writing well is a craft, not a gift. It can be learned, but not without practice, and not if I precut every board for them, square every corner, and spray the varnish for them. Imperfections are the glory of the creative process. The next iteration is for perfection.

And the next iteration is their gift to eternity.

So, yes, despite the seeming chaos, I do teach my students to write. I teach them to embrace their imperfections and dream of their future. This they can remember, and this they can set on the shelf by the duck that looks a bit like a swallow. They can sit at their shaker table, which leans precariously towards the window. They can fill their seaman's chest with trophies from soccer games and memories of their favorite blog post ever.

The best ever!

It is an early spring day today, and there are only two months left to flesh out the school year. I thought of tilling the garden and sharpening my chain saw. Instead, to relieve my angst, I am setting up a sea of new blogs—one for each of my students—to somehow redeem this year for my neglected band of brothers and for me.

I will rebuild my crumbling wall. I will give them each a blog, for I need, when this school year ends, to say,

"At least I tried, goddammit.

At least I tried."

THE FISHER

To cast far is to cast well.
I've always believed that
The biggest fish are just
Beyond my range
And lie in dark water
I could never swim to.

But experience is the wisdom
That has me now casting
Closer to shore,
Nearest the reeds
And overgrowth—a subtleness
Geared to result.

It's still early in the season
And the beaches are lined
With jars of worms
And salmon eggs—
Talk of bag limits
And hatchery trucks.

I'm glad though to see
The lines
With hooks and bobbers
Already hung up
In limbs of overhanging oaks—
Caught there by kids
Who swear and pull
And fall on their ass.

They see my fish and ask
Where they are
And how to catch them.
I tell them
They have the right idea
And just keep
Humming it out there.

SOUND, SENSE & IMPACT

Sturdy stones in the wall of time

It goes like this the 4th, the 5th,
The minor fall and the major lift...
~Leonard Cohen, *Hallelujah*

I should have some catchy opening line for this essay, but I am baffled for words to capture what I mean by "sound, sense, and impact," a phrase that defines how and why a song works—a phrase I spout too often. As a songwriter, I do the down-and-dirty work to make music that rewards my listeners with an occasional song standing out beyond the ordinary. However, the reality is that most people are attracted to the ordinary, not the extraordinary. My listeners are drawn to the familiar and predictable patterns of music they already love and wish to hear, so I won't go too outside "my" ordinary—not if I wish to keep my persistent and paltry audience seated at their tables.

I am in a rocky marriage with the music of my musicianship. I am more hack than prodigy and certainly no child genius. My foray into music as a songwriter and folksinger started in a sparse dorm room at Fitchburg State College, whispering the lyrics to "Hollis Brown" and softly playing Bob Dylan's two-chord dirge about murder and suicide. A guitar, my memory, and my voice are all the tools I need. My guitar is an old pickup truck whose only job is to haul whatever words my head remembers and carry whatever my voice sings.

I am not proud of the choices I made with music, for I never really learned music. I never put in the time or practice to study more than what suited the narrow needs of my precious lyrics and the stories woven into my coarse melodies. I never call myself a musician, but I do call myself a folksinger, for singing folksongs is what I do. If I need to create more polished music—

true music—I rely on sidekicks, mostly Hatrack Gallagher and Seth Connelly, who join me on stage and ply their respective trades on harmonica and guitar with astonishing skills.

Why now, in my ripening old age, this curiosity about music and its sound, sense, and impact? I feel too old to learn, yet too young to give up on the promise. My hands and fingers are gnarled by sixty-five years of life, labor, and mistreatment. They rarely do what I want them to do. I am a lame golfer playing my rounds with a hacking stick. I swing and flail with unnerving persistence, yet somehow I sink the ball into the distant hole and go home happy.

I write more songs than most might imagine. My journals are filled with songs—songs I trust are crafted with some semblance of skill and awareness, yet I also know the good songs from the bad. I sense when my words rise above the ordinary or sink into inanity. I sense, too, the forgettable tune from the memorable. If I am unsure, I slip those songs into my set while singing in a small bar here in town just to see if those songs survive on their own in the muckled battlefield of live music or if they should be abandoned to the fields of mediocrity. My friends are unswervingly honest. After forty years of playing at The Colonial Inn in my old hometown, my humility overrules my pride. I am not afraid to let a song die an early death. I simply move on, perhaps because I have not fully mastered, or even slightly mastered, the patterns of the music I create or, more likely, stole.

My original songs revolve around the same five or six chords that somehow hold my ballads together. In those heady times when I meet with some palpable success, it is as much an accident as an intentional gift of virtuosity. I am not, however, too old to change, too old to adapt, or too old to learn. My words —my sheaves of songs, poems, essays, stories, and ramblings— are stones in my wall of time, insuring some part of me will be left behind. But I am not yet ready for that distant future. My songs need sound, sense, and impact in equal measures, or they are merely the detritus of decay—scrolls of papyrus on a stormy ledge, torn and blown by the Furies, lost in the passage of time.

I live for tomorrow's star to rise.

SWIMMING UNDER WATER

The diaspora of thought

This is patently absurd; but whoever
wishes to become a philosopher
must learn not to be frightened by absurdities.
~Bertrand Russell

It is strange how happy I am to feel first flies of snow mix with a drizzling rain, misting over my conundrums of thought. Last night I went out in the cold of midnight to cover the boat. I bemoaned the predictions of a morning burst of snow, for it meant another day of waiting for spring. My visions of painting and scraping our wooden ketch in the warm sun of March are not quite happening. After tying down the tarp and covering the boat, I sat on the porch in a beat-up Adirondack chair I made years ago while teaching shop. Our porch—and this chair in particular—is my refuge. It is my lonesome valley, bouldered jetty, and foggy moor all in one. It settles the world for me, and it is a rare day I am not renewed to some degree by the simple act of sitting in this sacred ground and letting my thoughts blow, seethe, and settle in a pulsating, philosophical diaspora.

I could, or maybe should, fix this chair, especially as it now leans so precariously to the right that I must lean to the left when I sit down. The effect is even more pronounced with the old outboard motor leaning against it. Beside me lie the snowblower and bags of wood pellets for the stove. And then there is the battered clawfoot bathtub in the driveway I wrestled out of the back of the truck yesterday—and that was about as far as one sane man was going to move it.

It is another warm-weather project—strip off the old and layer on the new.

I imagine this is also the job of a philosopher.

I wonder about the job of a philosopher. I wonder if being a philosopher is to simply think wise thoughts and keep them to myself, but I also wonder if I am preordained to collect, collate, and curate these thoughts into a semblance of Logos and publish them for the world to accept as impermeable truths or cast off as vain and selfish reflections scratched on a foggy mirror.

The problem with logic is the formality and discipline it requires. The vague and varied thoughts must be wrought with academic precision into the confines of mere words—and words aiming beyond the realm of words and into the construct of pure intellect are misread as often as they are internalized and understood with any vestige of the philosopher's true intent and meaning intact; but, as I tell my students every day, "A bird in the hand is worth two in the bush," so the least a philosopher can and must do is to write—to write as simply and magnanimously as possible—to convey the subtlety of their thoughts to those who need or want to understand; otherwise, it is just philosophers writing to philosophers within the incredibly narrow confines of academia. The end product of their treatises is usually a logic so dense as to be painful to read and, in the end, rarely worth reading. The complicated exegesis is as much to me as dry sand as it is verdant soil. There is nothing palpable to form into shape. It is like trying to tie the wisps of a spider's web back together or clearing a muddy puddle with sloppy, groping hands.

We are all born to wrestle with blinders that focus and shape our individual and collective vision. I am comfortable with the limits of my vision. I find myself falling back on the same notion I spout too often: "Where you stand depends upon where you sit," which is probably why I like this chair.

Born into New England stoicism, I appreciate a laconic response to life. I have lived and worked broadly—if not deeply —and have come to love wisdom borne from listening to those who live in simple work and generous gestures. By opening myself to this mosaic of insights and asides, I find myself living in a palpable, if limited, philosophical sense.

Once, back in high school, I was picking beans at Pine Tree Farm with John, a longtime Italian farmhand. I complimented him on how quickly he could pick a bushel of beans. Stopping his stooped and incessant labor, he replied, "You reada' the books. I picka' the beans."

I return to that moment as often as I can, if only for the reminder that I cannot hold wisdom.

I can only use it for short bursts.

Like a kid swimming under water.

THERE IS IN AN UNEASINESS I FEEL

When I begin to think of myself—
My girded shell squeezing
Oysters in a jar;
My oily viscera
Jammed and joggled
Into impossible places.

My pancreas
Is never where it should be;
My tongue is a trapped
In a tangle of intestines—
My esophagus, cut cleanly,
Swirls in the diaspora.

My voice gargles and froths.
Even I cannot understand—
Guttural vowels,
Unutterable lisps and yawps.

Chomping embryos
Cannibalize each other—

Pulsing.
Mawing.
Insatiable.
Frenzy.

When I reach inside
The palpable stew
Everything slips from my hand,
And I am left with nothing
Stuck in my craw

But this poem.

THE VALUE OF A CLASSIC

Pry the blinders from your eyes

A Classic is a book which people praise and don't read.
~Mark Twain

All of you are, supposedly, reading *The Adventures of Tom Sawyer*, a recognized "classic" book, but what Twain says about reading classic literature is true—classics are books many praise yet few read—and few of us go thirsty to the well and gorge upon the greatest works of literature because... well, just because...

The dutiful among you simply answered the call of my dreary assignment. Some of you are skimming as much as possible to glean just enough to talk or write intelligently about the book, while the laziest of you are woefully putting off your reading for as long as possible before I compel you to write some meaningful screed about what you are reading.

And then—thank God for Sparknotes—you might even get away with it.

But only for a while.

Life has a way of catching up with us in some karma-like way—nobody willingly admits they are a shallow shell of a person masquerading as a viral host of knowledge and wisdom. We need to believe that how we live is not only sustainable but also healthy, vibrant, and real.

But how healthy can we be if our thoughts are only as wild and free as turkeys in a pen? How healthy can we be if the food of our mind is a mush of glutinous starch and sugar? Sooner or later, the fat settles in, the muscles fade, and a simple walk down the street stretches before us like an epic journey.

I hope what we are reading is as exhausting as it is energizing. I hope you sit down, read forcefully, and pry the blinders from your seething eyes and murky soul. I hope you will open your stubborn, seeking self to the possibility of a true and profound literary experience. I hope you sense the eternal value of a transient experience. I hope you will give a damn and try to figure out how and why these words you are reading are praised as classic literature. Is there anything here in this baneful assignment that a modern mind can see, use, and believe?

The Adventures of Tom Sawyer is not a classic because a coterie of fuddy-duddy English teachers deemed this book "required" reading." What you are reading is a classic because the words, plot, and value of Tom's journey are validated time and time again in and through the ravages of time and place. While the language is archaic, and often coarse and regretful to the modern ear, it also captures the timeless joy and bewilderment of our youthful spirit, an engaged, spirited search untamed by the passing of years and the evolution of our morphing moral codes.

Your book is a mountain, and you are the mountaineer scaling some unscalable mountain peak. Your indefatigable efforts take you to a higher peak than perhaps you have ever climbed before. Good books make this happen. Great books do it over and over and over and over again. At this point, you may be tempted to rest in a valley and be satisfied with a more narrow view.

I remember when my youngest son Tommy worked on his sixth-grade "Explorer Project" at school. His subject was George Mallory, the famed mountaineer who, when asked why he climbed the loftiest mountains, replied laconically, "Because it's there."

Mallory died on Mount Everest. He and his partner, Sandy Irvine, were last seen in 1924, just 800 feet from the summit. Mallory's body was found some 75 years later. No one knows whether they reached the summit or not, or who reached it first. We just know they tried.

Keep Mallory's spirit alive. Read your classic. The peak is yet above you—waiting... Keep climbing.

Because it's there.

TO A NOT-SO-SUBTLE RACIST

One of my earliest rebel memories was drinking beer with you on a summer's night at White's Pond. Maybe Michelle was there and probably Lana, too, and no doubt some other miscreants like us, killing time and wounding eternity, but, for whatever reason, that summer's night was transformative and still clings to my memory some forty-five years later, it being one of the first times I imagined my life did not have to follow the tried and true. There was no logical reason to go home before sunrise. There was no compelling reason or fated destiny to be a small-town Catholic kid in the mythical beauty of Concord on a warm Saturday night.

The world was my oyster—mine to live and breathe as my own.

That world is still my own. But it is not solely my own.

Don't get me wrong: I love your posts. I love your heart, soul, and passion, which is all too lacking in the world today. You obviously love our country and rebel when people shake its hard-wrought foundations and, to quote Bob Dylan, "rattle its walls." But—a big "but" here—you do not cut the board all the way through. The far edge is still intact, and your words don't fit into what you are trying to build with your seething hatred of the moment. You settle for less than who you are and who I know you to be. You don't cut your thoughts all the way down the line. You stop short of the profound meaning you are trying to share. I actually do read what you post. I think deeply about your point of view. I try to reconcile what I know is in your heart with what I fear is swirling in your head.

I've watched this video you shared on Facebook—this lamentable lament of insipid cowboy manhood you agree with and ardently praise—too many times. The video has some twenty-three million views and, regrettably, millions of likes. Nothing this guy says in the video is wrong. He has every right to share his thoughts—except he is a handsome, self-serving prig of a twit trying to stir racist slurry into the muddy hole we live in, and while idiocy is his right, it is in my mind intrinsically wrong.

Scarily, he could be just another me or you, albeit diminished by myopic arrogance burdened with patriotic anger masquerading as masculinity. I have traveled the whole country —and damn near most of the world—but I am a white, smart, tough American guy. No one gives me shit. My skin color is perfectly pale. My breeding falls into an acceptable lineage. I grew up in the right place. I have the gift of gab, and I am, usually, a good guy. Doors—big doors—open for me wherever I go. I barely have to breathe to live well and be accepted for who I am. I am treated as an ambassador wherever I wander with almost anyone I meet. But change my skin color, change the lilt of my tongue, change the perception of me—or just change me in any subtle or not so subtle and palpable way, and my experience of what it means to be American will change.

To cut through my wordiness, THE BOTTOM LINE is it must suck to be a black American—an American as American as you or I or my black son, but a full-blooded American who can never assume the implicit rights we have to say, do, or believe what we are and what we want to be or want to do. Black America is not "our" America. There is no "united" America in Black America.

The potholed road of the black experience is a frustrating continuation of perpetual wrongs utterly disconnected from what *they* experience and what *we* experience. We are not marginalized. We are not afflicted. We have our voices. There is no need to stifle other voices with bigoted righteousness. There is no biblical commandment standing in the way of their full-blooded freedom. The hero of your video is a sham and an illusion. He is a paltry yet poetically gifted affirmation of our inherent privilege to live our American dream in unencumbered and empowered ways.

You are an old friend, a good friend, and a friend with a deep and abiding soul. Do not go down this racist road. Do not swap your own thoughts with a bigoted, egotistical shithead. Give voice to a broader country and walk a wider and wiser street. Use your imagination and your sense of love and possibility to listen, hear, and sense the power of change.

It is all we have.

We need abiding respect and tolerant actions to cultivate, cull, and craft the impossibly elusive American dream. What we have is what we have to give away, and sometimes peel away, to forge a new possibility—a fledgling and difficult paradigm that needs to be, can be, and should be enduring, real, and utterly and completely American.

Find a real hero of a man.

Share his brave words.

There are plenty out there.

THE POETS CABIN

I have grown too familiar with these woods
And walk silently as if they're hallowed.
Crouching down in roots of upturned pines,
I hide in the tangle of last year's storm
And dart my eyes with a primitiveness
Frightened by voices I do not know.
I could run along the trail of the deer
Where it crosses the conservation path,
And sleep in the cat-tails by the slow river,
And hear the bass rise to the evening hatch—
I walk home feeling through gaps in trees
Drawn by the light and damp, smoldering, wood
Like I have a fur ball in my stomach
And need a place to be warm and covered.
I'm surrounded by log walls with gapped sides;
I have thought too long and am not skittish—
I am an obnoxious drunk out splitting wood
And scare even the jays who shake their nests,
Who cackle, call and whistle me away.
An old man clothed in a body of youth,
I yearn for a disregard that is real.

A MOST UN-ORIGINAL TEACHER

Set the scene, state the theme,
say what you mean, and finish it clean.

Good writers borrow. Great writers steal.
~T.S. Eliot

Yes, that's me. I am a fraudster, thief, and plagiarizer of the worst magnitude. I copy the very styles of classic poets; I steal from Noble Laureate novelists, and I copy words from every and any source I can. Even worse, I steal from myself. If you even dare to look at my journal entries from last week, there is such an uncanny similarity between them all that I fear my secret is out—I am not an original anything. I am a shameless old shop teacher using borrowed tools and stolen wood to cobble together a slew of sturdy sea chests, and they are only sturdy because I stole the plans from Captains' Bligh, Hook, and other Pirates of the Caribbean. They hold treasure enough that I can still pass as a writer—at least amongst the ill-informed and dim-witted.

So, yes, take a look at my journal entries, some of which I am quite proud of writing (unless, of course, you are opposed to my "formulaic" approach to writing). I am not a pirate in search of trinkets, so I will rarely waste my time searching for worthless treasure. I know you could care less about the events of my day (and, for the most part, neither do I), so I rarely write about my predictable and pedantic life—unless it sparks a search for a greater treasure—some timeless theme drawn out of some common experience that just "might" enlighten, edify, and energize me or some rare reader of my wit and wisdom.

Take a look, and you'll see me doing the same old, same old, in every entry I post. I am a manic fitness buff who does pull-ups on every door jam he walks under.

Why?

Because it makes me stronger, not weaker. Because my exercise is like a musician practicing scales, an artist practicing brush strokes, or a little kid practicing jump shots over and over from the same crack in the pavement on their driveway until the dinner bell rings and reality beckons me home.

I simply practice what I preach: "Set the scene, state the theme, say what you mean, and finish it clean." It works for me and might just work for you. If it works for you, disregard my admonitions and cull your own genius in whatever fashion befits your leanings.

When I *set the scene*, I attempt to write something worthy enough to catch a reader's attention—something leading logically to the dangled last part of my opening paragraph where I state my theme and at least point you (my reader) in the direction my paltry essay intends to go.

After this opening of the door, I *say what I mean* by weaving together some loose tapestries of paragraphs bound in some semblance of unified thought—musings not irretrievably painful, dull, and dissipating to muckle through.

I am vain enough to want people to like my writing with a squirrel's sense of curiosity. I want them to follow my thoughts around the track to the finish line, where I jolt down a *clean* one-liner—one last nugget to hold, think, and dwell upon before leaving my lair.

I am callous enough to disregard readers who don't really give a damn about what they're reading; otherwise, (warning: conjunctive adverb in use) I'd go crazy and could never be good, old, unoriginal me—the guy who cheats, steals, and connives his way into being called a writer.

Try it. Steal from me.

I don't care.

What was mine is now yours.

TURNED OFF

Keep it simple, stupid

It is desirable that a man live in all respects so simply and preparedly that if an enemy take the town... he can walk out the gate empty-handed and without anxiety.
~Henry David Thoreau

Sometimes, like right now, I long for a pile of papers on my lap I could speed through, grade with a series of checks and circles, daub a few scribbled lines of praise or condemnation, then drop your labor into a shoebox on my desk and say, "Here are your essays!"

But I don't have a desk. I have a cool classroom with a wide-screen TV, a huge seminar table, plenty of comfortable chairs, big new iMacs, and even a recording studio. I haven't used paper for any assignment in years. I post my assignments, grades, videos, and the literature we study online. I send out assignments via text, email, and an online calendar. I let parents into the loop in an open and ongoing way. It is a really cool way to do things. I get few complaints from kids or parents; I work pretty hard at what I do, and I get an incredible amount of support from the big bosses at school.

Lucky guy, me... But not right now.

Right now, I just want to turn it all off and return to a different time, or maybe just a new time. I want to delete my blog post from a few days ago and join the Luddites in prayer. Hell, I should just delete the whole damn blog and write the assignment on my board. (Though, damn, I don't really have a board—and god forbid the kids see my actual handwriting.)

Tonight, the power went off. The darkness is pierced by the few candles I could find in the pantry, and this calamity has brought my enlightened ship to a meandering drift in still waters.

I am stuck here with an iPad dangerously low on battery and an app that luckily works offline. I feel slighted by the sultry technology I've embraced so readily with my blinders on and oracles spouting. How will I face my anxious students who are expecting a grade tomorrow morning at 9:17? If word gets out, I know there will be smug satisfaction on the part of a few colleagues who will wave their piles of papyrus lab reports and essays in my face. Behind their smiles and expressions of concern bubble smug thoughts of suppressed and righteous glee: "Fitz finally got the comeuppance he deserves!" In my paranoia, I imagine one of them beside my house in the dark rain jamming a phillip's head screwdriver into my sparking Verizon box. This really is a shutdown. Thank God we are reading *The Odyssey*. At least I know this is just a test—an opportunity, really—to exploit the heroic side of my personal journey.

And I will get through this! Damn it! And I will grade those papers, and I will leave audio comments and clean little boxes full of canned and specific feedback because if not, then what? Will I have to swallow my pride and say, "Boys! Could you please print out these essays and have them on my desk before study hall?" (But, I remember bleakly, I have no desk.)

I hear my voice sauntering gleefully back to haunt me: "Boys, figure it out." "The only way out is through." "An excuse is like a crutch." "When the only tool you have is a hammer, everything looks like a nail." And oh-how-hollow my voice will sound as I pick morosely through my shreds of confidence, clarity, and misguided wisdom—like shards of broken glass from the tear-stained carpet of my "technology classroom. But my students are, after all, fourteen and fifteen-year-old boys. I could just bring in several dozen donuts and yell, Essay extension party in room B216!" Only the brilliant few would be offended. The dull majority will celebrate the unexpected strawberry-glazed rewards for the calculated sabotaging of my creed and mantra by a dark and looming force arrayed against me. The solution is elusive and calls me away towards a new paradigm.

One involving a book and a bed.

And a dose of humility.

ON WHAT REMAINS

There is something that always remains—
that held this dry boat
through a long hot season,
hauling sweet-water from deep taproot,
gorging the supple mane.
I chase your crazy dance
of one leaf falling—
its final defiant uplifting
before settling,
yielding to the slow current
of the gentle river.

The westerly wind,
blowing in from Great Meadows,
is traced in a rippling, catching
the brittle cupping
of your curled topsides
powering you before the gale,
leaving a wake
to make Slocum proud.

I jump at the chance to fall
into familiar language:

'You'll never grasp the wind'—
raw feed of sailors—
though you can know what it does:
hold it, spill it,
sometimes just hunker down,
leaving it still
as immutable as desire.

Today it is a simple broad reach
to the Merrimac—but be careful:
the current is wicked at the breakwater,
and there's no bottom that will hold
around the Isle of Shoals.'

It is hard sometimes
to always love
the wind.

Do you have any idea
what I am saying?

It is as sensible to me as an acorn.

I am the man constantly risking absurdity,
chasing you along the banks,
shouting practicalities
and heedful warnings.

Perhaps it could as well be
a recipe for a simple bouillabaisse.

Water is dear to me
and I don't know why—
another traitorous element
that carries you away.
(You see, I need to think it is just
as equally beyond your control.)

I chart a fear within you
that I will swamp you
with one clumsy step.
And we will be spilled
like burdened fisherman
from a Gloucester dory,
thrashing about in brackish water,
forgetting how well we know
the practiced strokes of youth.

Though I have succeeded well
in the ways of blinding oneself,
I am still as expectant
as the starkened oak
waiting out the carrying

of another season's young.

After it all,
when you are some leagues away,
I'll sit on the banks,
and with the messiness of a child
I'll fashion the silty clay
into a strange and sympathetic audience;
and I'll speak to them
in a surprisingly real and honest voice,
and tell them the story
of how the wind and water
conspired to take you away—
and how, in the wake of everything,
the river recovers itself.

Everything always does.

Though something always remains.

EMBRACE THE BEAST

Keep the magic alive

*A man either lives life as it happens to him, meets it head-on
and licks it, or he turns his back on it
and starts to wither away.*
~Gene Roddenberry

What do you really need to learn? What teaching and what practice will somehow stay with you? What amulet must you carry or what elixir must you drink to defeat the sloth within you and free you to play on the fields of the Lords? You are lucky my pity and forbearance took a soft pen to your recent essays. You might even think you are in some Mensa Society of good writers, and you are—save for missed, misused, and misguided punctuation.

But, damn, blame me. Don't blame yourself (though I wish you would). I'm your teacher. I at least thought I was—until I read your essays. I should have graded those of you in my class last year more harshly. It is only fair. I practically beat you over the head for three semesters with comma rules, hyphens, long dashes and semi-colons, brackets, and even the weird three-dot thingy…

If you have forgotten, I did not teach you well enough to remember. If you do not remember, I am a doltish parody of an educator, droning my forgettable formulas and pedantic dogma. What kind of English teacher can't teach what is basic and critical to good writing?

Me, I guess…

Experience taught me that when the average teenager hears the word "rules," they immediately start building a wall to keep my ornery rule out of mind and out of sight. It is too bad because "the rules" are what keep us going and keep our scattered ellipses of thought together in some semblance of logic and coherence. If we don't keep the flow going, the fun ends. Imagine Fortnite if someone hacked the system and no enemy could be blotted off the screen. Imagine the hissy fits of millions of whining men and boys across the world swearing into headphone mics when their perfectly placed snipe has no effect on the clueless avatar hopping across the screen.

Imagine soccer without goals. Imagine bread without flour. Imagine earth without a sky. Imagine words as any jumble of letters. Songs could blossom in any arrangement of notes, riffs, and patterns. Parents could choose their kids, and kids could choose their parents...

Where am I going?

And what does this have to do with punctuation?

Punctuation is a relatively recent invention and is merely a tackle box of lures and hooks to connect "thoughts" (clauses) and "fragments of thoughts" (phrases) and any series of elements together. It helps a writer mimic and reproduce the effect of an ordinary conversation—or a profound rendering of poetry or a stupid and insipid movie you wasted ten dollars going to see on an otherwise perfectly fine Friday night.

Punctuation keeps the magic alive.

As far as the written word goes, the rules of punctuation follow the laws of physics, and without them, nothing holds the strands of thought together.

Where does this leave you coming with trepidation to the assignment page? It leaves you in the sharpshooter's crosshairs of a cold, calculating, toothed teacher measuring the distance between himself and his unsuspecting students—measuring their capacity for genius; discerning what exactly will help them learn, remember, practice, and use "Fitz's Top Ten Comma Rules."

You will find my rules of punctuation" are a beast you cannot slay, you cannot avoid, and you cannot ignore. Your only option is to *embrace the beast*, grasp your arms around it, wrestle it to the ground, and hold it down until it is tamed. When it is tamed, morphed, and manipulated into a friend and ally, it will follow you like a devoted terrier for the rest of your life. *The Beast* will always be faithful to you, protect you, and strengthen you. Maybe then you can pen a letter of thanks to me, long since retired and living off the memories of students who actually gave a damn, figured it out, and made something of their lives.

Learn all the beast has taught you.

Then let it go.

You are now free...

THE WOKE

The fear of who and what we are

It is better to conquer yourself
than to win a thousand battles.
~Buddha

This is a tough one to put together. I know from the scuttlebutt of the hallway that I am perceived as a stumbling block to what we call diversity, equity, and inclusion in our school. Perhaps it is my fear that "they" are right —they being the anointed arbiters of change, not the quiet, stubborn misfits of tradition like myself—Huffalumps who continue to pursue an outdated pedagogy, marginalizing the afflicted and perpetuating an entrenched and primal bigotry.

Try as I might to accept the lexicon of those more woke than me, I can't, with any clarity or conciseness, bring myself to use this new language—a garbled tongue created by academics and sophists. If I change the lilt of my tongue, I find myself shrouded in ill-fitting clothes, gangly and unseemly on my aged and weathered frame. I feel like I am on a first date—I am nervous and unsure what to say and when to reveal my scarred and wary self. My words echo hollow and ring of pretentious falsehood more than illumine my soul to anyone curious enough to actually want to discern what is embedded in my rarified soul. I am a quantum entanglement whose nature is only revealed when visibly seen, heard, or felt. Until then, I am only particles of possibility—smoke and vapor, but not yet real. I am an odious scent untraced by the limitations of judgment; hence, the irony of being judged. The premise presupposes a linear response to the evolution of our values.

I am essentially unchanged from who and what I was this morning—but as Buddha says, "You cannot enter the same river twice," so whatever change I embrace is an indiscernible seed that may or may not find soil to grow in.

The final tally is whatever words are spoken about my life.

Perhaps if these woke warriors followed me on my own journey in the classroom, they would not be so fearful for my students. They would not be so quick to adjudicate the tenor, tone, and misdirections in my teaching—much less in my life. If they did, they might find a timid man more interested in the soil than the fruit. They might hear the stuttering lisps of my intellect; they might see the lingering fear in my flitting eyes; and they might sense my reluctance to wear any uniform that defines and delineates some treacherous enemy.

I am fearful of every clarion call to engage in an ideological battle. I would not know which dragon to slay or which flag to raise. I do not have the wisdom to know who I must include or exclude, who to raise on pedestals, or who to carve into monuments. It is a rare few I trust who are intent on doing me good, and I trust they know who they are.

I have lived some sixty-five years on this sodden, besmirched orb, yet I am still a restless, wandering savant bathed and polished by the sands of time, wearied by conflicting winds, drenched in the wretchedness of inexplicable loss, and consoled by everything making us human—because of and in spite of ourselves. I live in the arms of love—the all-embracing, transcendent power of our fragile, redemptive commonness.

It is everywhere I go. It is everywhere I have been and undeniably everywhere I will ever go.

I am dim and unwitting. I have no use for the blinders anyone clabbers on me. I don't grasp handholds or cling to any worn path. I feel the wind, sense the sun, and smell the sea. I know where I am less than who I am. I do not really need you, yet I am comforted and calmed by your presence.

Grab my hand and walk blindly with me. Imagine the absurd possibility before I am flung too far from redemption.

Oh, beautiful, drenched earth...

Our diaspora of humanity is our greatest gift. Woke, awakened, or enlightened, this diversity bleats out of the soil and begs for space to grow, flower, and fruit.

To share in this damned and blessed harvest of earth, we must abandon our lofty pedestals and first be farmers, fishermen, and wanderers.

And then we can teach.

FORTY REASONS TO LOVE

At the wedding today
Every couple is dancing—
Some twenty,
Thirty,
Or even forty,
Pairs

Twirling, shuffling, swaying,
Whispering, winking, sometimes
Just staring softly
As into those same eyes
Some twenty,
Thirty,
Or even forty,
Years ago.

Even the Peruvian waiter
Is tracing arcs around his tables,
Singing to his water-vase
As if he could possibly
Summon his own wife
To this field in Vermont
With a simple chant
And incantation
Of love.

It seems to be working.

The bride is too radiant to describe;
The groom swaggers
And bursts with disbelief
The bride is now
All his—and he hers
Forever.

God only knows
What the parents are thinking.

What diminuendo can bring this
To a perfect close?
What repeated cadences
Will signal the final coda
And let them finally
Sleep?

Denise burrows into my neck.
I cradle her head
Within my chin and palm
And whisper the words
The band is playing
To make them our own.

I know so many of the couples here.
I know their hard roads,
Broken dreams, promises
And tragic losses—
The vagaries of fickle fate,
The mortal coil
We are heir to unwinding, yet
All is lost, forgotten
Or forgiven
In the undulation carrying
This sacred dance.

I close my eyes and blur away
The only stern ones—
The wedding planners, hiding
In dark corners, barking
Muffled grunts, convinced
Their choreography is working
Magnificently
On this square plot of parquet.

But there is an edginess in them—
A drunk, tattooed cowboy
Is going off script,
And blows

Vape smoke into
Heavy, late-night air,
And the teenage staff
Has yet to trundle the coffee
To where it should be.

I want to tell
The whole assemblage
Not to worry.

We are all old hands at marriage
And can find on our own
Some twenty,
Thirty,
Or even forty,
Reasons to love.

RICH BEYOND MEASURE

Ah, but what is Wisdom?

I've never met a man who was truly awake.
I wouldn't know how to look him in the eyes.
Henry David Thoreau, *Walden*

Somebody once asked Thoreau if he would give a talk on the evils of alcohol and tobacco. He declined, reminding his audience he had never tried alcohol or tobacco, so he was not able to speak about the effects of either from personal experience. Personal experience generates our most powerful ideas and is the catalyst sparking our most profound actions. Retelling our personal experiences inspires our readers to look more closely at their own lives and delve into the mystery of their own leanings, strengths, and foibles. An experience retold is relived through the emotional and intellectual intensity experienced by our perceived audience. Our personal narratives are experiences retold for a reason—to recreate the emotional and intellectual intensity of the original experience.

If nothing is gained or learned from experience, there is nothing to write about. Your writing will be an empty exercise— a drag on you and a drag on your readers—if you can get anybody to read what you wrote. But if you gained anything, if even the tiniest granule of wisdom is mined from your experience, it is worth snaring in a net of words. Through the transformative power of words put to page, you amplify uncommon wisdom; you cull it from the herd of extraneous clutter and present your wisdom to your readers framed within a larger revelation of amplified truth and wisdom.

Ah, but what is wisdom?

I have sought this magic stone of wisdom for many years. Perhaps wisdom is simply informed truth, sensing the problem from every point, angle and distance. Perhaps it is the grain of sand holding the kernel of an unknown universe.

If you do not know what wisdom is or where to find it, you need to wake up; otherwise, you will never find what is truly yours. You will live a life prescribed and pre-ordained by others —strangers with no skin in the game of your life. If you choose the easy way through and if you limit the scope of your experiences, you will live a life hobbled by ignorance and illumined only by your arrogance.

The next stage of your life—high school through college—is when you will need to start making real decisions laden with real impact. You will need to look long and hard at the fork in the road and ask yourself the questions that will shape your fate and destiny. Do not grow old and wistful. Grow old and mindful. The only way to begin is to start now. The only way to erudite mindfulness is to be brave and take a bold step—tentative though you may feel.

You need to take the same dawdling steps with your writing. Write about your experiences, and you will gain experience as a writer, and if, in your life and in your writing, you keep your eyes on the road (the craft of writing) and your mind open to the journey (experience), you will become a better writer—maybe even a great writer—maybe even a philosopher bent on wisdom.

Great writers create literature informed by wisdom from which we—as readers—broaden and deepen the scope of our own lives.

Live. Read. Write.

Give a damn!

You will be rich beyond measure.

DANNY, JIMMY & ME

The conundrum of collaboration

A purse is but a rag unless you have something in it.
~Herman Melville, *Moby Dick*

I

Mrs. Roeber never seemed to let Jimmy go outside, which, to my thinking as an 11-year-old neighborhood kid, was why he was so smart. Most days after school, I'd rush two houses down the street and get Danny Gannon to come out and play. Then the two of us would go to Jimmy's house next door. If Mrs. Roeber answered, she would always be polite and say something like, "Jimmy needs to catch up on some science work. Perhaps he can play later." If Jimmy answered, he would usually be out of breath after running upstairs from his basement "workshop." He would plead with us not to give up on him—or at the very least, we should go out back and talk to him through his basement window.

So me and Danny would sneak out back and lay on our stomachs on the pokey gray gravel outside his basement window. Five feet below, Jimmy would be doing *his work* at his workbench. I always wished I was smarter, so I could do Jimmy's work for him and get him all the sooner outside to play. I was better than Jimmy at a lot of things, but those things never got graded, and most of those things I couldn't appreciate until "later in life." But, to my Tom Sawyer way of thinking, I preferred being outside and average to being inside and smart.

Danny was an outside kid and smart too, which always troubled me, but not enough to let it call my 'inside/smart; outside/not smart' philosophy into question. Danny's voice was always the warble warning us the sledding jump was too high, or the rotting branch would not support my weight, or those snakes would bite, or we couldn't run faster than a swarm of bees from the nest we just blasted apart with an unerring volley of sticks and stones.

Once we got Jimmy outside, he was like a mad scientist: "We'll just have to see how high Fitz can go on his sled" or "I'll distract the snake, so Fitz can grab it from behind" or "Bees have been clocked flying at 80 miles per hour."

Looking back, we were the gang who couldn't shoot straight, and we did tend to go our different ways as we grew older, but we still manage to reconnect somehow, and it doesn't seem like we are a day older.

It is hard to put into words, but Danny and Jimmy might not be the best of my friends, but they will always be the friends I need to remember. Just thinking about the three of us together is a window opening to a cool, autumn breeze—and the coolest thing is that the window is always there. It might be the only thing we actually had in common was living next door to each other, but we made it work; we made it real, and we made it last.

No choice. No problem.

We did it together.

II

Life was pretty simple with Danny, Jimmy, and me. There was no forethought in doing things together. It was more than just some manifestation of a primordial strand we responded to with a visceral enthusiasm bordering on mania. As humans, we are born to be tribal in nature. We expect and need to be a part of a community. We know in our bones and marrow we can't go it alone. There is no Huck without Jim. There is no Odysseus without Athena, and there is no you without some hand to pull you out of the muck you have made of your life.

Thank God for the primitive man patiently stalking some wily prey to have the primitive women scrounging for tubers, berries, grains, and millet, providing the bulk of their communal sustenance, leaving us lazy hunters to chew on the fat of the day.

Tethered as we are to some community, we do nothing on our own. We are bound by the strands of extended family and community. We breathe freely the collaborative atmosphere of trust and unfathomable magnanimity.

It makes me wonder why I hated group projects as a student. More telling is why, in my shaky wisdom as a teacher, have I changed my mindset and my actions?

Even as a teacher, I hated group projects. They never seemed like group projects. What seemed in theory to be group work was really some small industrial factory spewing its incessant belching of traditions in unequal and unsatisfying distributions of work and wealth—a parceling of talent where the smart kids were rewarded the lion's share of honors while the poor students (myself especially) were continually paired (usually by choice) with a misfit tribe of alike friends who accepted the inequities of the classroom as a normal and immutable reality of life.

Danny, Jimmy, and me went to the same schools. Jimmy was —and still is—brilliant beyond my wildest dreams. Danny, too, seemed way smarter than me and probably smarter than most of the smart kids, though his demeanor was tempered by a shy and steady reserve (which by default kept him from the brilliant crowd) that often forced him into our regressive and unrepentant tribe. As close as the three of us were bathed in the ecosystem of our townie neighborhood, our schools erected barrier after barrier to keep us apart, and those walls did an admirable job of keeping us separated. We only collaborated on our woodland joys outside of school. Jimmy was smart but not arrogant, and he never willingly sought the tribe formed around us in class, for when the academic birds of a feather were called to gather, he was soon surrounded by the peacocks and strutting roosters of Concord, all brilliant in their own ways, aspirations, and inclinations, while my tribe wore our C's and D's like gang tattoos on bruised and battered torsos.

Not much has changed in the years between now and then. My students now are at least grudgingly inclusive, but the iron curtains in our classrooms are still there—just more subtly erected. The academically accomplished kids are almost insanely driven to preserve the status quo—and if paired with the less accomplished, they will go to extreme lengths to do all of the work themselves. They do not want their brilliance diminished by the more doltish, less fortunate, and least able. They will labor far into the night to correct the sloth and ineptitude of their partners. It is an ongoing ignominy the gifted suffer in stoic silence, for "collaboration" is an essential part of the rubric— and, ultimately, their grade—and, in the end, they need to say it was a collaborative effort. Kids like me who simply sprayed red paint on a smoke-spewing model of Mount Vesuvius remained mute in the complicit code of the caste silence dictating our lives.

The rich preserved their wealth, while the poor squandered their meager chance to make a mark on the yardstick of time. The paradigm was etched in stone long ago—one law for the rich, one law for the poor. It is strange and telling how the rich suburban and private schools tout the quality of their students and teachers when, in reality, they are just exposing the quantity of wealth and resources at their disposal. It used to piss me off, but I remained satisfied in a smug and arrogant way that I, at least, saw through the smoke and mirrors. My brilliance had a short shelf life, for at that point in time I lived and accepted what Jesus said was true: "There will be poor always." I remembered this phrase as an acceptance of the inequity of life, not as a challenge to redefine poverty. For my needs as a teacher, I needed to redefine what wealth really is and how wealth is spread around a classroom. I needed to unearth and return the just inheritance to every kid I taught. I needed to see each of my students as a treasure trove of possibility. I needed to make everything my plucky students did together engage the passion of Danny, Jimmy, and me, hucking stones at a nest of snarling wasps.

Every kid has to have a pile of stones to throw at the nest and the legs to run as fast as they can; otherwise, there is no skin in the game, no shared risks—and, ultimately, no shared triumphs.

Every classroom in every school on the planet is a blessed and cursed mix of myriad possibilities—rich or poor, enriched or impoverished—permeated with a mix of talents, drive, will, and a sharecropper's dollop of abnegating responsibility. As a kid, I hated group projects, and this hatred gorged my inherent biases for the past fifty years. I sucked as a student because I was never a full part of the gifted group. I was a lesser satellite of a greater star. As a teacher, my groupings hobbled along like drunks, howling inanities to the stars. I saw the same inequities I despised in my youth perpetuated in my own lame assignments, yet I still kept unleashing the same six-headed monster on them—the beast who swallowed my childhood whole. I was stuck in the stream of my own inbred traditions, though I remained convinced I had nobly engaged my duty as a teacher.

Then came my epiphany.

I never really taught what the word *collaboration* means. None of us can grasp the wisps of confusion. In my blindness, I assumed we shared some common understanding of the common phrase—*to do things together* (whatever *together* really means), but while reading and teaching *Moby Dick* with my ninth grade classes, we found ourselves discussing the crew of the Pequod—and what a wild mix of nationalities and cultures manned this doomed ship—Native American harpooners, freed slaves, dreamy poets, adventure-seeking deckhands, re-tooled carpenters, sail menders, lookouts, blacksmiths, cooks, and mates from every corner of the world—all bound together in a common adventure with a defined purpose. Roles were delineated, but in the fray of the chase, every sailor was an equal; every man took to the boats and lathered the sea, thrashing bulky oars towards a common and fathomable goal. It was a seeming success—until the monomaniacal Ahab stepped to the deck and pointed the Pequod on a new tack in his obsession, come heaven or hell, to find and slay the great White Whale.

Collaboration then became my duty, my fate, and my new pedagogy. In parsing the demanding twists of plot in *Moby Dick*, my students initiated a conversation about what collaboration *really* is, and through the convolutions of discussion, we extended the metaphor of *Moby Dick* to define and delineate what it means to collaborate. Collaboration is a shared adventure with shared rewards, where every person is due their rightful share—the share agreed upon before setting foot on deck. No group effort is inherently equal, for our skills, aptitude, and strengths on any given project are too disparate—nor will the rewards ever be the same, for we will always reap in proportion to what we sow and tend and what we sign on to do, but the journey   and the chase itself—can and must be invigorating and rewarding for everyone.

No single person, no greedy shipmate, and no set-appointed captain should alter the common purpose of any voyage. Every person, low or high, must accept the mundane roles on quiet seas and rise from the forecastle or slide down from the masthead when all hands are summoned to the deck and onto the whale boats. Every sailor drops everything. In chanting song, they pull together in precise rhythm and chase the whale; moreover, barring death or dismemberment, every sultry or joyous hand needs to be on the mother ship for the length of the voyage.

The Pequot's crew hoped and expected to sail home to Nantucket bellied full of oily ballast—a bounty measured and assessed down to the last drop, and every part of her motley crew would know and expect and receive a fair share of the reward.

Now, I not only love group projects; I believe they are the heart and soul of my classroom. They are what binds us together as a community. They are opportunities to share strengths and work through weaknesses and differences. They implore us to recognize and respect the dynamic power of uncommon backgrounds pushing towards a common dream—not merely a goal. They help individuals find new and deeper sources of strengths never fathomed before.

But collaborative projects are not all roses and perfume. As a teacher, you must accept that projects inevitably take twice as long as you plan, and if you can't be flexible, you are no better than Ahab. At the same time, your students need you to be a captain who is stern and unforgiving, who expects duty to be dutiful, who gathers the crew on deck when need be, and when the ocean is empty, frees them to their chores without being meddlesome—but when the blubber of the whale is stripped and cut and boiled down in the tryworks, your classroom will be a bloody, oily mess, and, just as in life, people will bitch and moan and convince themselves their individual effort and persistence is what is keeping the boat afloat—and before any mutiny succeeds, call the crew on deck again and admonish them—and again if needed.

True collaboration is an honest day of hard, dirty work, not a bunch of friends pass off sloth as substance.

And when all is said and done and your students are tired, bloody, and bruised, give them their fair share of the split—

And reward them, dammit.

Reward them.

I DID NOT EXPECT THIS—

A cold night in early May
Drowning in a spring gale
Drenching downpours.
Silting sands
Petulant and moodful
Cut a chaotic mosaic
Swallowed and melded
By chomping waves
Barking and gnawing
Up stoic dunes curling
Hissing fingers clutching
Dissolving chunks
In a receding tide.
Headstrong grasses expect this
While my tame and wizened life
Keeps me at a distance
Spitting aphorisms
Taunting this angry sea
Backpedaling down
A glistening road
Looking back
To what I once was.

DIGITAL DAMNATION

The footprints you leave behind

Oh, it is excellent to have a giant's strength,
but it is tyrannous to use it like a giant.
~William Shakespeare

Someone is not just looking for you; they are searching for you. You are one regrettable statement or stupid posting away from your judgement, and hence your character, being questioned by an admissions committee, potential boss, or anyone else casually (or intently) searching your name on the web —and it is going to happen. The irony is that the only disparagement worse than a questionable digital footprint is no footprint at all. While there is some nobility in being off the grid, there may also be precious little else to set your particular genius and passion apart from the masses arrayed beside you, before you, and behind you.

A powerful and compelling digital portfolio puts your proverbial best foot forward. Your digital portfolio, collated and curated over the course of time, stands as a powerful statement of who you are, what you value, and what you have accomplished. A digital portfolio shows you give a damn, and you have been giving a damn for a long time. It is an abiding reflection of your inner character, your persistence, and your values.

As your teacher, a guy who has spent the last twenty years of my teaching using blogging communities, online assessment, and ongoing portfolio creation, it has been worth it. I love what you create. I love navigating your sea of blogs. I love to see, read, watch, and listen to whatever prophecy fills your screen—those tiny plots of real estate—those bits and bytes of a digital world that are uniquely your own. I love seeing you progress as writers and artists with every new post and every budding tangent of your imagination. You are bursting forth like sunflowers in windy fields, bending and bowing in intimate dances—waltzing's you might not even notice.

But if you do, others will as well.

I quote Buddha too often, but once more, "I am just a finger pointing at the moon, not the moon itself." You are the one who needs to find inspiration; you are the one who needs to be the captain of the ship hauling you to a distant port, and you are the one who needs to put into words what others can only imagine.

You have only scraped the ground of your blog's potential. Now is the time to turn the soil, plant the seeds, and tend your magnificent garden. This is my clarion call—it is what I pray to inspire when I ask you to create, collate, and curate all that is redeeming and redemptive in your evolving life.

To *create* is the miracle of thought put into form. To *collate* is to gather what you create. To *curate* is to perfect what you have created and place it in a living museum—which is your blog, the portfolio you are willing to share with the world.

In the end, it will outlive you, but it will inspire the generations you leave behind. It will echo your thoughts and shout into the void:

Yes, I gave a damn. I figured out who and what I am; I blasted and drilled through the hard rock of life. I left a footprint behind. I am not unsung.

I want to remember you. I want you to remember you.
So that's it. My song is sung.

The rest is up to you...

THE PROOF OF WORDS

Your final redemption

If you could say it in words,
there would be no reason to paint.
~Edward Hopper

Never measure the moment until it passes. Seth's wife Sue called Monday, telling me thunderstorms flashed around Nashville all day, and so the airlines canceled Seth's flight. Seth was down in the big music town, wowing the Nashville elite with his amazing musical skills. Seth asked Sue to see if I would cover his gig at the inn. I figured a Monday night would be a pretty dead affair, but I also figured it might almost fill the fuel tank on the bus, and Seth was in a jam, so what the heck? It was as I imagined it would be—a few tables of folks having dinner, seemingly unaware that music was a part of the fare as well— and me unaware what gift the night would bring.

After more than forty years of playing in pubs, I still fear the angst of imposing on people who are just out for a social drink or dinner. I still think long and fretfully about my first bleating song piercing into an already busy and satisfied crowd. I am still the awkward kid gangly in an ill-fitting costume. Every night in a pub still feels like a first date.

I win or lose the crowd quickly when my first notes hit the air.

As I set up my gear, the only person paying attention was a young boy nibbling French fries and slurping a milk shake. Parents appreciate when their kids get attention, so I started my set with "A Fox Went Out on a Chilly Night." The young kid laughed when "the fox grabbed the gray goose by the neck," and especially when the "fox and his wife cut up the goose with a carving knife—and the little ones chewed on the bones—oh."

Because he laughed, the parents laughed, and because he listened, the rest of the crowd listened. It is the same scene I relive so many times as a less-than-notable folksinger playing in the same less-than-notable pub I have played in for decades. I have few regrets, for some "thing" always happens to redeem even the hardest, most toilsome of nights.

But tonight brought a different redemption.

A couple in the far corner requested "I'll Fly Away." I shook my head slowly, feigning limited knowledge of that classic gospel tune—a tune I've probably sung some 3000 times. By bar standards, it was a hit, and my small crowd of people stuck with me the rest of the night through the good (and not so good) of my repertoire. Between songs, I queried each table about where they were from and why they came to this Colonial Inn. "To see you, of course," became the polite, mocking, and endearing reply.

After I finished singing for the night, the last table left was a couple in the far corner. They invited me over, and we talked until closing. We started out reminiscing about folk songs and lyrics that somehow rise above the ordinary—lyrics that capture the raw parts of our psyche and nourish reflection—lyrics we are drawn towards and leave a listener pondering and awestruck. I wondered aloud how a good songwriter finds their words. The husband quickly replied, "You only know what you think by first writing it down." As a writer, his words hit me in the sweet spot. The phrase hooked me in, like the fox on a chilly night hooked the young boy.

I asked him, "What do you mean by that?"

And the magic began.

I don't remember their names. I know I wrote them down on a napkin somewhere. Jordan, I think, is his name, and Sally (maybe?) is her name. I know he is a professor of psychology at the University of Toronto, and she is a professor of writing. Jordan told me William James first coined this thought, and he added how his own research and his teaching validated what James wrote is true—*you only know what you think by writing it down.*

We talked, mused, laughed, and wondered aloud. I don't remember everything, but I walked away inspired by their words, their collective wisdom, and their gift of newfound friendship freely given. I drove home thinking of words and how words purposefully put into form are needed to fully understand our joy and sorrow and our journey through life.

There is something palpable and real in words put down on the page that breathes those drifting words into a steadier life and a deeper meaning. Meaning is born of expression, not simply reflection. The seed is sown in the depths of our private meditations, but the plant—and hence the fruit—is born to give form and shape to those meditations. You can't point to a newly sown garden and say, "See what I've planted!" You must first put in the labor to make those seeds sprout and flourish. Only when the field blooms rich in fruit and flowers will the gardener share the bounty of their labor. Sally added that her research proves that writing about the joys and sorrows of our lives makes us more physically healthy.

So, say goodbye to the gym and grab a pen, not a dumbbell.

Writing helps us overcome our fear of the unknown. It creates the necessary distance from what is hard, troubling, and moiling in our lives. It helps us see the foreboding monster within from the periphery of a safe distance. You might know your fear of bees is somehow related to your stepping into a bee's nest as a child, but you've never written about that experience. You have never truly reflected on that hard and revealing time in your life. Through writing, you may not overcome your fear of bees, but you can put your fear of bees in perspective. You can sense the rational in what was once irrational.

You move forward, not back.

This is not to advocate running for a pad and pencil every time life gets tough. Tough times often need tender time—and sometimes a long, reflective time before the rawness can be fully expressed in words. Knowing when you are emotionally ready to write about a difficult period in your life is part of the process; hence, writing must be a part of our lifestyles—not a medicine only reached for in times of need.

Through writing, we will know when we are ready!

After my father died following a long illness, it was a cathartic exercise to write a eulogy for him. I was prepared for his death. The process of writing his eulogy was easy. The words celebrating my dad's life flowed out of me like a mountain stream. But when Patty, my idolized older sister, died suddenly, I was devastated. There were no words I could say. No one even asked if I could write a few words about her. I couldn't. But, with the balm of time far enough behind me, I find myself writing about Patty often—she was my pillar, my earliest mentor, and my collaborator as a writer.

Years later, I now share the fullness and joy of our lives together as if she were an old friend yet living beside me. I laugh when I talk of her—as if she is knitting a sweater in the next room. I now understand how the magnanimity of her life did not die or diminish with her early death. It is relived and reborn in the words I write. The once bitter memories echo in the halls of my valley and are filled with poignancy and meaning, gifting an added depth to my ongoing, truant life.

In the same way, writing about common experiences brings joy and celebrates what is most real and eternal in our own lives. It shows us we are on the right path. It keeps us on a rhumb line towards the truth. It gives us a moral and intentional framework upon which to drape our lives. I am often smitten by envy when I read my wife Denise's blog. It is full of stories about family life in our home. She manages to find the enduring meaning in a passing moment; she draws inspiration from an offhand comment out of the mouths of babes, and she always finds—and stays focused on—one powerful theme driving her warm, wise, and witty thoughts delivered in unfettered and unvarnished prose.

When I am tired, grumpy, and out of sorts, I go to her blog —not because I am seeking comfort, but because I am energized and informed by her words. When I am full of hope and optimism, I go to her writing because it keeps my optimism and hope alive. Denise is proof of the power of the moment. There is no need for a lag in time when celebrating a joyous moment, as may be needed in a more difficult time. If it is worth a picture, it is definitely worth a few words, too.

My conversation with Jordan and Sally was cut short by the bartender, Subhas, flicking the lights on and off in mocking annoyance. We said our goodbyes and echoed assurances of future visits—visits I am sure will happen.

We sucked dry the well of our brief time together and have gone our ways, but time and experience are relative. What I gained from a closing-time conversation with Jordan and Sally in a small town bar seems out of proportion to our time spent talking.

But I will not forget.

And that is the proof of words.

QUARANTINE

I need more than water
On my brittled roots—
Tendrils in dry sand, waiting
For something—anything
Outside my control
To wash through me,
Around me, acknowledge
This stark predicament—
My slow blundering
Through burdensome time.
Long silences made common
Deadness of thought
Stretched by time,
Looming delay of defeat—
Constant wondering.
Weariness.
I wear myself like a stone
In a slow stream
Shaded by Willows
Hung from muddy banks.
My rough edges,
Barely burnished
In brackish slime,
Wait for some Michelangelo
To pull me from my wedge,
Back to his strewn studio,
And with his mad euphoria
Shape me back into
Who and what
And why
I really am.

300 WORDS

Just do it

*I write because I don't know what I think
until I read what I say.*
~Flannery O'Connor

Assignment: *Spend fifteen minutes writing a 300-word journal entry about, well, anything.*

Sometimes I wonder if Fitz even knows what our lives are like. I mean, he gives us weird writing assignments and leaves out things like, well, details. It's like all he knows how to do is assign work. And oh, of course, writing is the only essential skill we need to learn, even though in the same breath he says things like, "Nobody cares about you... And everyone should learn how to swim..."

That's just mean on every level.

But there he is right now, leaning back in his ratty old chair, pecking away on his computer and checking the "big brother" app on his iPad letting him see if we are "responsibly" using our iPads. Since nobody cares about us, I guess he won't even find the time to care about me, so I will just type away and try to get this stupid assignment finished before the due date—which is on a day we do not even have class!

I'll complain to my advisor about him. That will teach him to think outside the box. Maybe our beloved headmaster will haul him into his stately office and threaten to fire him unless he becomes a better teacher—one that lets us do what we want. (Only kidding!) (Actually, no, not really).

Uh, oh... Fitz just asked me to put my work on the humungo TV in our classroom. How humiliating! He even calls this

"Public Humiliation." Now he is going to point out everything I have done wrong with this assignment.

Here it comes.

He is even standing up.

This is bad...

(Actually, it wasn't so bad. He even said my writing is pretty good. He even had a few good ideas for how to make my journal entry even better.)

Whoa... Look...

I got an A on this!

[*And exactly 300 words*]

THE DOWNSIDE OF DIGITAL

Forget who you were

You can't ride a horse and smell the flowers
~Chinese Proverb

It is oh-so-blithe and oh-so-easy to be carried away by our passions. Our youthful exuberance, once so freighted with joy, desire, and unfettered expression, soon outlives the evolution of who we were and what we now are. Our stream of dumb TikTok videos, immoderate Instagram postings, and impulsive Facebook rantings and revelations rarely age well. We look back at what we wrought in our nonchalant exhortations and casual laments of youth. We shudder at the antiquated visage and insipid montage on the screen. We loathe our leanings with visceral disgust and deepening regret. What god of fate shaped our decisions? Who did we try to impress in that forgettable space of time? What can now be done to scrape the internet clean of our insanities before some boss, school, business, or lover discovers our young and tawdry selves?

The companies and conglomerates controlling the dissemination of our online selves are sociopathic predators and insidious purveyors of our public histories. They are abettors in our indulgent and profligate leanings—and the more tawdry we are, the better for them to shape our profile into an algorithm fit to be monetized and manipulated to satiate their insatiable desires and the torrid appetite of their consumers.

Few of us will admit our addiction to the high of the internet —myself among them. I am somewhat consoled that my daily dallying on the internet is dull to the point of naivety. I have a Facebook account and a Twitter feed—much less the present incarnation of X. I read the BBC for a fact-check on what is happening in the world. I check out new essays in "The Atlantic" and "The Economist." I might post an innocuous picture of some picaresque scene on a hike with Denise, and once a week or so I post about an upcoming concert of mine or share some essay or poem I wrote—but when I *browse* Facebook, the shit hits the fan. I am now locked in. Some ignorant misfit from Maynard leaves an inflammatory post about some town official. I read the competing derogatory and affirming responses (though I am still sane enough to steer clear and add my muck to the maelstrom). I click on Marketplace to see if any new ads for Martin guitars are posted.

I end up messaging some guy in Bucksport Harbor, Maine, about a truck cap:

"Will you take $100.00?"

"Message me if you can."

My Marketplace inquiries inevitably devolve into watching video reels on the side of the page. I'm sure every platform has them now. There is a clip of a sailor rounding Cape Horn, guiding his homebuilt sloop perilously close to some Antarctic peninsula, which leads me to another reel of a family of four sailing for some island near Vanuatu to await the end days. This adventure shifts to some Liberian freighter banged to twists of steel on rocky shoals only God knows where—and then my stream inexplicably shifts to a series of videos about people seemingly killing themselves in varying iterations of tragedy— flying in suits off mountain cliffs, tumbling off mountainside roadways, being killed by roaming bears in Alaska, or being mauled by angry rhinos in Nairobi.

In the end, nothing resembles my passion for sailing. It is death, gore, and idiocy. I despise myself. I question the core of my being. Is this my subliminal desire? Is this where my primordial fantasies live—to watch people die in utterly stupid circumstances? Is this the algorithm of my life? Are these videos the subliminal leanings of my fallible self?

If so, I need a therapist, like yesterday—or sixty years ago.

We internet hogs are complicit in the desiccation and evisceration of our public and private lives. The implacable virus and pertinacity of Facebook are no doubt matched by every other social platform, so much so that I am loathe to think of the dark web and its lurid leanings. I shudder at the sheer possibility of the possibilities. I think of Thoreau arguing against our infatuation with progress: "It is best to avoid the beginnings of evil." But the lure and the oh-so-sweet notes sing Siren's song, luring us into an entrapment. How now will I be known? How will I be heard now? An anonymous poet on a blank page is a haunting horizon. My eviscerated spirit wonders if there is any noble ground betwixt and between.

But there is not.

My cleaver needs be sharp. My amputation needs be clean and final, despite the ironic folly of this errant posting, yet I know I will not plunge the axe upon myself. It will no doubt die a slow, peaceful death within a deepening silence amongst old friends— a soft uncurling of the strands of my past, as if I am a lingering guest telling one more story before I go. Or perhaps many stories, for I have many left to tell.

I fear the reality of being offline. How will I stream my beloved livestream concerts? How will I find elusive parts for my sailboat without the help of my catboat group? How will I stay in touch with old high school friends or know when their children are born, when they marry, or when my old comrades die?

Whose life will be diminished to never see the orange salamander I spotted in a cleft of rock, my morning hike, or hear the echo of my latest song?

I am none the worse for the day I was born. Forgive my new silence, which I pray heralds the dawn of a more invigorated life.

I need to return to a simpler time lest I be ravaged in the looming time. I need to live and breathe what is palpable, real, and ineffably me.

I am yet here, alive and tethered to my native ground.

See me on the street and regale me with your day.

Let me smell your flowers.

WHEN I READ OTHER POETS

I never wonder
What is coming.

I am rarely transfixed
By the silky sinews

Of their clever words.
I wonder more

What burr they found
Clinging to their socks?

Just how did they suckle that seed
In some Styrofoam cup?

What cheater's soil
Did they steal?

Did it grow in natural light
Or beneath some burning bulb?

What potion made it blossom
With untouchable fruit?

I don't read;
I tremble.

What wild tea brews
In its broth of dried leaf?

What fool would ever drink
The bitter hemlock?

What fool would flee
From the seeds of truth?

WHY WORDS MATTER

Write, dammit, write!

But if we fail, then the whole world, including the United States, including all that we have known and cared for, will sink into the abyss of a new dark age made more sinister, and perhaps more protracted, by the lights of perverted science. Let us therefore brace ourselves to our duties, and so bear ourselves, that if the British Empire and its Commonwealth[e] last for a thousand years, men will still say, "This was their finest hour.
~Winston Churchill

No less than the sodden soldiers tasked with storming the beachheads of Normandy in World War II, we are living through an epochal event in human history. Nothing in my sixty-two years of life comes remotely close. The pandemic is not a storm on some other shore; it is not a drought in some arid county or backwater village; it is not a political upheaval in some far-off nation—and it is not a time to put our heads in the sand and our asses to the sky. It is a challenge—a massive challenge—a chilling paradigm effecting and transforming the entire world. It is upending and re-tasking the daily, once-normal lives of billions of people. You are, by dint of fate, simply one of the many, but *no less than the trees and stars; you have a right to be here,* and you have an obligation for your voice to be heard and recorded in the incessant book of time.

In some future time, your own children will invariably ask what your life was like during the "Pandemic of the 2020's" (or whatever term history will use to record this time). Trust me, memory is not as impregnable as one might hope. Time, left to itself, dulls the edges and blurs the margins. It magnifies the trivial and diminishes the meaningful. In the end, memory is a fine and broad canvas but an unwieldy and imprecise tool.

Words, however, are a sculptor's chisel in our hands. They cleave and shape malleable stones into enduring testaments to our betrothed humanity—our common quest to be fully human.

The written word is the holy grail of smoking guns—the nuggets of gold sifted from screeds of ore. We are gifted a mandate to record in words the entirety and enormity of this time in our collective lives. You can show your children—and the countless generations following your children—how *you* definably lived in the light of the morning and how you lived in the dark of the moment; how you spent your days; what you did with your days and nights; what you were thinking about—how your family did things together, managed things together, and managed life apart.

Your children will doubtless be amazed at how seemingly normal and magnanimous your jewel of life played itself out during this time—how you managed to be normal in the midst of abnormality, but also how so many people, including you, responded to persistent challenges in profound and perfect ways.

While many did not.

But you can say, "What I did was to write." You indefatigably plied pen to page. You kept on learning, you kept on reading, and you constantly adapted to new realities. How you did all this will flash as a cherished memory, a source of unmitigated strength, and a heady heirloom for your family—even if right now it seems as dull as a Lifetime movie. In real and palpable ways, what is dull now will one day be the rough, honest, and poignant gems of memory—the first churnings of wisdom.

Let time do the polishing. It always will. Let today be simply words scratched on an empty page.

I write every day. I don't say this proudly or boastfully. I write out of habit—one of the few good habits I have left. Writing is, and has been for the past forty-five years, my way to slay the day. It is a crafty ploy to play a desperate game against life. It is a crapshooter's gamble against the odds. I tackle each day before it crosses the goal line before me. In my way of playing the game, no day gets ahead of me; no reality beats me at my game, and I am never defeated.

I beat each day back into words—muddy, dirty, and tired words, but words nonetheless—and words make stories, and stories create meaning, and meaning gives purpose, and purpose builds grit, and grit builds strength, and our newly found strength empowers us to tackle any challenge.

Everything hard in life is a story of facing challenges—and a story worth telling. Especially now.

There may be no tomorrow.

So write, dammit, write!

THE WAGGING FINGER

I will never give up on you

You can always edit a bad page.
You can't edit a blank page.
~Jodi Picoult

Where does the classroom end? If it ends in school, it dies. If all we learn, practice, and work to do in school fades into some blurry memory of possibilities, we will soon be lost in the irretrievable cloud of ignorance. We will abnegate hope and make little of our lives. We need to live a new paradigm of learning—to extend the classroom and make our lives actual universes of learning deeply—to expand above and beyond murky and distant horizons—to grow when and where and how we grow best, which, I can say with confidence, is rarely accomplished in the confines of the classroom.

I have the luxury of having lived many lives. I do not wake up in the morning and instinctively remember that I am a teacher. I wake up early and remind myself that I am also a poet, a dishwasher, a builder of stone walls, a woodcutter, a sailor, a wrestler, a football player, a fisherman, a junk man, a train-hopping hobo, a folksinger, a dad with seven wild and untamed children, a husband and an average kid growing up in Concord, Massachusetts, and now a loitering townie in Maynard.

Everything I have been, I still am. Aside from teaching comma rules, I do not know what boredom is. I do not remember a day that did not dawn without some sense of the possibilities of any given day, and I am certainly not going to be satisfied that spending my few hours each week blathering to you is enough to change you.

Only you can change you.

I am the wagging finger, a sorry substitute for John the Baptist howling prophecies in the desert. I know, I know. I know... I am just your English teacher. I should know the limits of my reach. I should know your lives are saddled and burdened with cartloads of burdening and consuming weight. I know I am only your teacher, not your master, and I know (really, I do) you are busting your asses to do what needs to be done.

To live is to try. I can still try. I can try to show you that I will never give up on you. I can still try to erect some scaffolding you can cling to as you build the tower of your dreams with whatever planks, beams, and cornerstones you scrounge from the stubborn fields of your lives.

I sense the metaphor within every action in my life. I worked as a gardener for many years. My humble mandate was to show up when someone else had a dream. I would plow and till the clumpy soil of their suburban lawns, churn in piles of compost and manure, lay out beds, and show the timid how to plant and prune grapes, apples, blueberries, and peaches. I would lay out lines for corn and beans and hills for squash and pumpkins. I would build trellises for tomatoes, cucumbers, and peas. But that was it. I never tended the actual gardens. I would tell the new gardener in a curmudgeonly drawl, "I prepared this sprawl of opportunity. The rest is up to you." I was happy enough to leave it be. Their gardens became, for better or worse, their own gardens, free from my meddling hands and fickle expectations.

So it is with your writing and every endeavor in our year together. I will do what I can to help you prepare your garden, but the fruit is up to you. The seeds you sow and the care you put in will be the harvest you reap. When I post an assignment urging you to do this or that or try this or that, I am yet a hired hand fated to help you get going, not a serf to do the work for you. I have no illusions that I will move you, but perhaps I will shift you, ever so slightly, towards the genius of your inclinations. Find some distant moon on your own. Cultivate your garden there. Make something of your life. Make something within another person's life.

Go to bed tired. Wake refreshed. Yawn and move on.

Erase this and write your own.

WHERE FATHERS GO

Walden Pond moans
Like a lost whale,
The thin ice
Bellows behind us,
Cracks and rings,
As if spit from a whip.

The sharp, hard steel
On over-sized skates
Etch unspeakable joy
Into the slate-grey
Reptilian skin—
The cobbled shores,
Hung with leaning firs,
Worn stone and silting sands,
Count down the ticking time
Left to us.

Our mismatched hands
Grip together
In the fading light—
On a January afternoon.
You pull me toward
untouched, darker ice
Where fathers
Should never
Take their sons.
You circle tighter,
Spinning like a bullfighter,
And you let me go—

Splayed across the ice,
Arms outstretched,
Screaming back to you
Out of the black hole
Of memory.

ME & MUSIC

A Folksinger's Manifesto

This machine kills fascists.
~Woody Guthrie

I'm not really sure why I sing what I do. At any given time, I am not sure if I am meant to be an old ballad singer of Celtic music to which I have some historical lineage, or should I follow my original bent of passion for traditional American folk music? Perhaps I'm better as an imitator of old country songs, or even better, the cowboy laments I love for some intrinsic reason I cannot fathom? Maybe I am meant to sing sea shanties and rolling dirges of weathered oceans? How can I deny my love for the classic rock 'n' roll music I imitated and iterated for so many years listening to Dale Dorman radio shows or stealing vinyl from my big sister Patty? Or maybe I am destined to sing the songs I write about living and growing up in New England and all the baggage and possibilities borne from a life lived in small towns in small places.

I really don't know, so I dabble in them all. All I really know is that every evening, and often every morning and afternoon, I set myself down on my couch in the family room and pull one of my battered guitars from its stand and start playing whatever fills my mind in that stolen gift of time—sometimes for a short burst and sometimes for much longer—way longer. I do this every day, as in every day, every night, and most every morning. It is my private addiction. I don't seem to get much better as a guitar player, but whatever reservoir of songs is left in my aging mind is continually refilled by the strains of music I know and love.

I wish I could say I love all music, but I only really know a narrow strand of music in an equally small field of songs. I wish it was different. In some ways, I wish I were different. I wish I embodied the bandwidth to take in, with some semblance of equanimity, the diversity of music obliquely chafing my skin through the passage of time. Some classical pieces move me in ways I can't fully fathom. I wish my arms could span the keyboard like eagles wings and lead some sycophantic orchestra in something resembling greatness. I am jealous of every jazz performer I've ever met, seen, or heard. I imagine myself playing a trombone in some New Orleans parade, blowing a trumpet in a Mardi Gras festival, or in some smoky, cellar speakeasy.

I could play this game with any kind of music. The genre makes no difference. I feel, in some subliminal way, the power of rap—the creative, angry, and inspiring laments and rants giving voice to the voiceless and unearthing the enormity of injustice. I understand and sing along to the syrupy stupidity of show-tunes making joy in the midst of a sorrowful world. I am enraptured by the rhythmic passion of reggae, the insistence on what is real, relevant, and happening, even if it is only a forgettable paean to a small slice of life, such as sipping a cup of coffee, cutting down a mango, or waking up alone.

I realize most punk songs are remarkably like my own, but they grind with crystals of sand in their gears while I pour more soothing oils in my figurative crankcase. I listen to the hip folksters my kids listen to. The songs are gritty, raw, and real, full of wordplay and slices of tradition. My children and their friends remind me that I was once young, and if Fate bodes well, we will all be once young. I listen to the two strings on a Chinese erhu and ride some ancient barge down some flowing river in Guilin some two thousand years ago. I do not know why I can listen to Mississippi John Hurt all day, but I do.

Such is the power. Such is the power. Such is the power!

It is to daub and dabble in the possibilities of difference.

I am a daubing, dabbling songwriter, folksinger, poet, and writer of anonymous essays. My craft is dependent on words. Without words, my songs are iterations—simple and archetypal. My poems are workman-like—palpable as pinecones on a corner shelf. My essays ramble on (like this essay), but some few of my craftings bring words to some higher level. It is the conundrum of hope. I am now old enough to see through myself. I live in the shade of better people, cultivating the palpable out of the ether of thought. I am small beside the ocean of inarguable greatness, and so I nestle myself closest to my enamored few. I am a songwriter who feels like a little kid in a playground shooting hoops next to Larry Bird. I am a poet who wonders where Walt Whitman got his words, how Mary Oliver found the perfect shell, or why Basho laughs at the world—and where Shakespeare defined it. I would wait in an endless line to peer through Wendell Berry's window just to see a real essay unfold. I would rather watch Herman Melville write *Moby Dick* than watch Billy Joel perform at Fenway Park. I would rather parse an interesting phrase than glimpse the Big Bang of the universe.

Words. These damn words... It is always a battle in the trenches against a camouflaged enemy.

I am at war with words because it is always the right words that elude me. This game of hunter and prey is the only game I play and the only game I know, for there is always a better word, a better refrain, a more resounding chorus, and a better line to close the phrase and capture the thought. There is always something—some teetering branch just beyond my grasp—close enough to reach for, yet too far to risk.

I fear I will lose my audience.

Both of them.

I am a small man in a small world. I close my eyes and open them. Nothing much changes. The grass is green, or less green. My car runs or is broken down. I will need to go see Bones, Lenny, or Tom Cummings to fix what I cannot fix, or I might invite Hatrack, who can fix anything—even faith in humanity.

I have a beautiful family, a beautiful wife, and, yes, a beautiful life. I have friends I trust and turn to. I go to work happy, and I come home happy even as I realize how transient happiness really is.

I am never bored—as in never, ever, ever bored. (Except at faculty meetings.) My body is old, but still somewhat rugged. My mind is stubborn, but not yet fixed. My soul weeps, yet my heart sings. My life is an unending paradox—a seething conundrum and a puzzle unsolved.

I have ceased arguing with God, though we still keep in touch.

So I sing.

Music is the only wispy tendril binding us together in our inextricable journey of community, purpose, and destiny. We think we love music because, well, it is good, but really, we love music because it rings some familiar chord in our minds, hearts, souls, and beings. What we anticipate is realized. "Love..." really "is a burning thing." She doesn't just love you; "she loves you, yeah, yeah, yeah." The answer isn't found on Google; it is "Blowing in the wind." This is what music does—it jolts a shot of dopamine into our coursing, oxygenated blood. Music is an unspoken affirmation of our inclinations and a celebration of the tribes we adopt. Where music sings, unity begins. No genre of music is better or worse. If we listen long enough and if we discern the greatness, we discover why music—the massive panoply of music—is mystifying and magical in equal measure.

Or we don't.

But there is always a redemptive moment, and there is always a secret chord to win the day—though folk music usually comes in last.

Music is what makes me ingloriously vain and keeps me infinitely humble. I play in pubs and hallways, not concert halls or festival platforms. I do not regret my relative anonymity, nor am I jealous of anyone; for who else can I be? This. This is the body I wear, though I won't tell you the size. My voice is rough, low, and dutiful. My guitar is like my old F-150 pickup—capable enough to carry my songs where they are meant to go and strong enough to tow the detritus of my songwriting behind it.

It is too late to be someone I am not. The vicissitudes of time have chiseled me into a pile of chips, but what remains is stronger than the edge of any honed and tempered chisel. No blade known to man and no iron created in the forge of Hephaestus can scratch the hard metal of my core. The chips weather into the soil or blow away in the dustbowl of life.

But something always remains.

Thankfully, this is me and, more than likely, you as well. Every life is the diamond left behind after the mortal coil unwinds—if you are stout enough to slough off your old and curmudgeonly skins. Music is a sea of diamonds—the unfettered scattering of perfection and possibility strewn on the fields and fountains of this muddy orb called earth. If you can croak, you must sing. If your fingers move, you must pluck the nearest taut string and discern its subtle, irreducible ring. If you can grasp anything, bang a primitive rhythm on tin cans and stretched skins. If there is breath left within you, blow your conch shell, dance, swirl, and leave a waltz of footprints in the sand. If you can only speak, let your words lilt and ebb and flow and be your song.

We can't avoid music. We must become music in whatever shape or form in the endless and evolving unwinding of our lives.

We are not dust. Our genes stumble forward. Our progeny are the immutable notes we leave behind—that "ripple in still water, where there is no pebble tossed or winds to blow."

I hope my students don't read this essay.

I have broken every rule I taught them.

But so does music.

A HUMAN THING TO DO

When Knowledge Isn't Enough

Men have become the tools of their tools.
~Henry David Thoreau

I have been reading some recent articles about Bing Chat, Chat GBT, and other artificial intelligence interactions with a mix of wonderment tempered by skepticism and alarm softened by wry humor. The whole endeavor seems like an experiment likely to evolve and transform into something unique and astonishing, if it hasn't already! AI represents a quantum leap forward into the realm of interactive conversations, artistic creations, writing in multiple genres, expressing political and philosophical views—and god knows what else. It posits a tipping point in the war (yes, now a war) between artificial intelligence and our mere mortal and limited intellects. The blessing and curse of AI rest in its abilities to winnow the chaff of the internet into a seemingly logical, coherent, and intelligent discourse—something many of us soulful sorts crave on any given day.

We crave knowledge and context. We slaver endlessly for impermeable truths to lighten the load of simply being human day in and day out. For many, AI will be a welcome way to find the best restaurant in Manhattan. For others, AI will appeal to a penchant for arguments with an internet-scouring machine driven by logarithms. I already have plenty of friends who do the same. For lonely sorts, AI offers a voice to share the dark nights of the soul. Hurrah to the machinations of progress, for the list goes on like a fading freight train into the infinite multiplicity of our leanings and dispositions. AI is like the proverbial drunk uncle who shows up for holiday meals. We do not really want him there, but neither can we close the door on him, and come next year, we will welcome him again.

For some, AI will simply make creating tiresome content—an essential job for many—a less painful profession. For teachers and professors, it is a nightmare. Which student, distraught at a looming deadline, will resist the Siren song of temptation? How could or can a hapless teacher discern originality from blatant theft? And is it even theft? Or is it simply using an available resource to help craft a better essay, poem, or short story? In a real and palpable way, AI is simply cheaper than hiring a gifted and pricey tutor to do the heavy lifting for overburdened students and, yes, savvy frauds, so perhaps it is a convenient equalizer as much as it is a pernicious enabler.

In the end, the tree falls in the direction it leans, and where you stand depends on where you sit.

Curiosity did not kill the cat within me. An equally curious student of mine wondered guilelessly if AI could write a poem, and while I could not even fathom the implications, I let him use AI to write a poem, but first he had to write his own poem. I told him it had to be a poem about a trip down the Concord River; it had to incorporate two similes and one metaphor; include parallel structure; explore man's quest for meaning; and it had to be at least 100 words. For fun, I required spelling and punctuation mistakes—the bread and butter of any middle school writing assignment.

Damn me and him, my wily student produced two poems worthy of an amateur poet. I was not as aghast as I hoped I would be. I was just not sure who wrote which poem, who was the real author, or who was the machine. The parameters of the assignment, not much different than my painstakingly crafted rubric for the assignment, were met with an astonishing ease— enough that I am thankful I now loiter in my golden years as a teacher on the cusp of retirement and more noble, less perplexing pursuits. I graded his AI poem as a collaboration and his original poem as a "nice try." I am still not sure who was more clever—the person or the scourer—but at least the universe has two more lofty poems exploring the human quest for a purposeful life.

Danger, changer, tool, and weapon—we can clammer on about the potholes and the traps, but AI is not going away. It is moving forward with an inexorable purpose, force, and fate. AI will not be stopped by naysayers, prophets, and interventionists. The more we interact with AI, the more it will learn about being human and even soulful—at least up to the point where a falling branch or winter nor'easter shutters our internet access.

Who knows how or will ever try to break this bucking bronco of scientific progress? It is chattering force untamed by acquiescence. It is an Amazon package placed by our porch door, and our name is on the box.

Who among us will not open this dicy gift of curiosity?

I can't take a stance. I don't know where to stand.

AI and humanity are like a bad Tinder date. There is no trust, and there is no foundation. There is no clear path forward. Still, we try, and at the end of an awkward dinner in the North End, maybe we can still be friends?

We can use AI or abuse AI, or we can simply turn it off.

Such a human thing to do.

But we won't.

PREPARATIONS

Charlie slurps the sky with his snake tongue
And catches the invisible first flakes
And spins himself wildly through the backyard.
It is the moodiness of New England
Turning winds steadily from the northeast—
The perceptible shift from calm to storm.
A cacophony of maddened grackles
Dart through White pines tilting in stilted dance.
Dell starts his old snowblower one more time,
And then points at me like an old schoolmarm,
Reminding me of the work to be done:
I tighten the flapping tarp on my boat
And oil the boots I should throw away;
I remind the kids to check their cubbies
And to unload the groceries from the van.
Denise begins filling up the crockpot
And sings, "It's a Great Day to Be Alive."
There is a constancy to our motions—
The deer are bedding down in crisp oak leaves;
The town trucks are loaded down with salt;
I hear weather reports from passing cars
And see whole families looking upward.
Leddy wonders who will shovel her walk.
The dogs prepare for a long winter's sleep.
Nana and Papa call from Florida
And tell us of the news' reports from there.
We make vague plans for long weekends this spring.
I know as soon as the snow starts to fall
I'll remember things I forgot to do.

MY DIRTY LITTLE SECRET

Tell. Show. Think.

As the least drop of wine tinges the whole goblet,
so the least particle of truth colors our whole life.
~Henry David Thoreau

Here is my dirty little secret: I hate telling people how to write essays. I hate it. It reeks of intellectual arrogance and personal deceit, like I have somehow cracked the shell and feasted on some nut no one else has tasted—which is the sheer dung of a raging bull. All I have really done is put on the page whatever is in my bloated head at any given point in time—like now.

Despite what the more learned will say, an essay is just a conversation with a perceived reader, and until the day I die, I will always be the first and last reader and the ongoing author, arbiter, and constructor of my conversations. At the same time, I am vain enough to hope I have some palpable and engaged audience to edify, enlighten, and educate—some part and parcel of the universe interested in what I think, what I have done, or what I aspire to be—whole segments of society eagerly awaiting my every word, every thought, and every action.

We all need our dreams to awake unscathed.

In my solipsism of self-revery, I am convinced you need me. I am in a war of words with you—and with other writers—a battle to be remembered or to simply die. But really, I am just a manipulator—a psychopath posing as an empath. I want you to believe me, trust me, and rely on me to give you something you need, want, and treasure. I carve words out of the impossible and the implausible that might somehow wash over you like a cascading waterfall and drop you in a placid, placated pool of newfound understanding. I struggle to wash you clean of your ignorance, misconceptions, and prejudices; otherwise, why write?

If nothing I write changes you, transforms you, or simply pisses you off, I have failed.

I write because I have to write.

Writing consoles the inconsolable part of me. I write because when I speak, I invariably sense a diminished and insecure me. I need the balm of time and space to refresh and invigorate my thoughts into some testament, powering through the vicissitudes, ravages, and vagaries of this mystery of existence. I cannot write to those who are not curious about the truth. I will not dissipate my energies on quaint observations or polemic screeds.

Here I am now past the cusp of sixty-five years—a full forty-five years of scratching words on pages—and I have yet to lose my sense of wonder or feel I have shucked a full oyster. My sentences today are not bending towards a conclusion; they are simply an evolving part of my Sisyphean labor to keep the boulder of truth before me—even as it threatens to crush me under the power of mortal gravity.

My long coil is not fully coiled, nor do I fear a looming sleep.

Aye. "That's the rub. To die, to sleep, to wake no more..."

That's not in me.

Sorry, Willie. Do the assignment.

It is due tomorrow.

A SIMPLER TIME

When words are no longer mine

Simplicity, simplicity, simplicity! I say, let your affairs be as two or three, and not a hundred or a thousand; instead of a million count half a dozen, and keep your accounts on your thumb nail.
~Henry David Thoreau, *Walden*

implicity. Simplicity. Simplicity. Good words to ponder, though I am sure Thoreau's pithy phrasing was no great insight on Henry's part, but just a fresh minting of an age-old wisdom. It does, however, capture the urgency and essential message of *Walden*, a book I teach in my freshman English class, to slow down and pare down the extraneous clutter embroiling our lives. It is hard to argue against simplicity, but it is lugging a pile of bricks up a rickety ladder to put the sophistry into practice. We shudder with every step. We lose something on every rung and end up hobbled and empty-handed, with little left to cap the chimney. We rarely find the fortitude and the wherewithal to "let our affairs be as two or three, and not a hundred or a thousand, instead of a million."

This is especially true in our burgeoning pedagogies and curricula as teachers.

As an old and, some would say, lame hand at teaching, I wonder if our stunning array of initiatives, practices, admonitions, and obligations is the proverbial hand trying to clear a muddy puddle, for no matter how diligently and purposefully we try to clear the waters, we ultimately fail in our defiance of physics. More just doesn't equate with better. More, in fact and practice, makes less—though it may sound better, especially when paired with a well-intentioned, albeit righteous, signaling of virtue. It may proclaim our sense of justice, equity, inclusion, sustainability, and enlightenment, but it also burdens teachers, students, parents, and administrators with a dizzying array of demands that are as impossible to meet as they are to implement in schools tasked with educating the inevitable future of society.

As the tail wags the dog, we risk making droning sycophants of students and automatons of teachers. Our students crave a mix of understanding, affirmation, and accomplishment, yet they will say, do, or write anything to raise their plaque of excellence above the moiling fray. They need, want, and pray to position themselves in the top tier of the dutiful and diligent—or at least above the bottom sludge of the indifferent.

The grades we dole define, delineate, and calibrate success and failure like a brand of fiery iron, or they soothe like a healing balm—or cut down like a sniper's bullet. The best plan of battle —and the easiest and most expedient tactic—is to rote and reiterate whatever elusive enlightenment is expected of our students and proffered to them. Our quixotic quest to be correct (and to not be corrected by overseers) puts the horse before the cart, and, as unwieldy as it seems—and if a higher grade is the loftiest goal—this absurdity remains the wisest conveyance of choice. That this is an equal burden on their moiling, duty-bound teachers is a conundrum not bound in the convoluted equation. We teach our students to gorge on whatever wormy bait we dangle on barbed hooks. We wrangle them to shore and drop them in our creels; however, at the end of the day, it is the dead fingerlings we celebrate. The ones who get away are deemed the recalcitrant rebels and ne'r-do-well's.

But, as teachers, we have done our duty and showcased our diligence. We follow the scribed line and are duly praised for furthering the murky, increasingly ponderous mission of our school—but it is not as much enlightenment as it is entrapment. We are mere machines spitting out algorithms rewarding conformity and consensus, not the pliable, wondering, and inspired prophets we were hired to be. We may strive, but we simply cannot count *half a dozen and keep [our] accounts on [our] thumb nail.*" Our hands are too busy, and our palms are too full. The informing and invigorating air of the iconoclast is bred out of our students—and ourselves. "*Freedom*" becomes, in the words of a familiar song, *"just nothing left to lose,"* and only the wayward, stubborn, misbegotten, or irretrievably lost go down that road. We are judged mutineers on The Bounty if we set our ship against the Captain Bligh's of newly enlightened education. Our own homebred captains, blessed with a crew of us salty, experienced sailors, are tasked to scrub the decks, coil the lines, wind the marlin, hoist the sails, and peel the potatoes—all while manning some lofty masthead squinting and seeking some distant shore. *"Thar she blows"* we cry from our tenuous perch, yet we live in a beggars banquet where the conscience of the majority is sublimated to the edicts of a few, and we beggar teachers lose our raspy voices in the maelstrom and bellowing chanting of a more powerful sea seething in a current of change and transformation and the droning incantations from both the left and the right— all of them hellbent on getting us crotchety codgers to see their light as the only true insight.

Perhaps our captains are more wise than us sailors. Perhaps our captains have stood on the masthead and seen with clearer eyes where the ship must go. If we do not bow to their wisdom and experience, and if we do not hop-to when we need to hop-to, our journey is a forgettable trip hauling trivial cargo to some familiar anchor in some placid bay—not an odyssey and adventure to find some paradisal island blooming with succulent fruit and untold riches. If their lofty vision truly is paradise, how can we not sign up?

But we have signed up.

Our names are inked on a papyrus manifest. We are together on this Flying Cloud of education. The ship goes nowhere without its crew. So inspire us, ye' captains! Give us purpose beyond the litany of creeds and duties. Show us the promise of our destination. We will do whatever needs to be done to see the journey through, but do not conscript us onto your brig of conformity; do not waste our genius on pedantry; and do not confine us to the scuttlebutt where our gossiping, seething, and reckless banter rules the day and sullies our spirit.

I will proctor any study hall, coach any team, sit at any lunch table, write any report, meet with any parent, console any student, or grade any sheave of papers late into the night if only

I can palpably sense my classroom is mine—all and forever mine —so whatever gaggle of children I am charged to unerringly teach can and may experience the true breadth and depth of my mind, heart, soul, and being.

My ship is not only my school (and truly my only and beloved school), but perhaps also every school. I trust the inclinations, but not the leanings. I sense the fishtailing swerve of competing hands at the wheel. We pitch from port to starboard. The ballast shifts. The compass loses its bearings. We sail one tack, then haul-to on another tack. We go windward. We go leeward. We invariably get stuck in irons and drift slowly and aimlessly at the beck and whim of a malevolent tide nudged by an implacable god. There is no polestar for a waypoint, no moon to light the night, no beacon to mark the rocky shoal, and no clear voice to bark clear, consistent orders into the vaporous, thudding wind and air. In the fray of circumstance and destiny, we do what good sailors do. We survive. We save the ship from itself. We steady the helm. We trim the sails and shift the ballast. The winds abate, a new course is set, and the journey goes on.

Then we go back to our classrooms and teach what we know is best.

Or at least we try to.

No one can argue in any articulate or compelling way against the unequivocal justice of equity, inclusion, and diversity. Only an ignorant miscreant loathes furthering a sustainable planet, and it is a dreary, cynical dolt who beats a drum seeking to marginalize, disenfranchise, or diminish any student or hobbles their stumbling path to progressive enlightenment. At the same time, is it an anathema to question the careening path laid for us to follow? Is academic and intellectual freedom a dream deferred? Is it a fool's errand to insist on the mastery of craft over the molding of disposition? I am not arguing the validity, necessity, and need for an enlightened, inclusive, and forward-thinking curriculum. My unease, angst, and anger are more an unsettled parlay against myself, a warning shot fired by myself against myself across the bow of my own clumsy ship. I rattle my chains only because I feel the burden dragging me down into a sea of conformity and milky consistency, and while the fire rages within, my defeat seems inevitable. I shed my warrior skin and consigned my vision to the unfolding of Fate and the shifting sands of circumstance.

For the first time in my decades of teaching, I question my calling.

In our evolving lexicon and practice, a teacher is increasingly a tool to cut the line drawn by a social engineer—a committee of a few, an adjunct department, or sometimes a hired, tiresome polemicist tasked with bringing a more relevant, enlightened, and purposeful pedagogy to our table. As teachers, we are, by and large, dutiful, magnanimous, and spirited. In the same breath, we are tired, overburdened, and dispirited by the stunning array of expectations, admonitions, and edicts laid out to better us, yet we are rarely overcome. Our rooms fill as the bell chimes, and for some small chunk of time, we become the arbiters of a malleable, manifest destiny. We believe in ourselves until we sense the elephant lurking in the corner. We know we have missed something. The elephant rears in agitated circles, reminding us to tick the boxes on the checklist prepared for us and to do what we need to do—but do not forget this or that or that and this.

So we do this, and we do that, and, no doubt, we do more than we are expected to do. What was once our simple and sublime lesson evolves into a troupe of monkeys leaping from branch to branch, chanting competing mantras of idolatry. Students gasp for limited air. We console ourselves that somehow our lesson on conjugating verbs is intuitively related to global warming. The box is checked. Our peer review will be flawless. Maybe tomorrow we will actually teach how to conjugate verbs —just verbs—stupid, simple verbs—not, despite this screed, transient, benumbing verbiage.

I know too well how my words peppered on a page come back to haunt me, yet I am strangely calm and detached. These words are no longer mine. They are embedded in a small wave curling upon some nameless shore. They will not betray my recalcitrance or strain the shape of any beach I walk. My words will not wear down any ancient, rocky outcropping. I will roll gently against the shore and just as gently slip, unnoticed, back into the sea. I live on a stage in a classroom, but I crave my anonymity as much as I crave my freedom.

Just give my slice of freedom back to me.

It was mine before it was yours.

Maybe the only real gift I give to my students is my freedom, and the more simple our lives, the greater our freedom, and the greater our freedom, the less we will need to recalibrate the intricate workings of our conscience.

Maybe someday, on a sultry day, some old student of mine will sigh and remember a small strand of seaweed wrapped around their ankles. Might it bring back some memory of a simpler time, and *"Simplicity. Simplicity. Simplicity"* won't sound so stupid anymore.

And might they smile… f

For time remembered is the only real time.

EVERY POET NEEDS A FIELD LIKE THIS

Unalterably their own,
Gifted with recognizable patterns,
If only to see the power of change—
The inexorable sublimity
Of juxtaposed images upon time,
The crows and swallows captured in the snare
Of a poets strange and vengeful vocation.

Every poet needs a chair like this,
One that welcomes devolution of thought,
Insists on a fleeting perfection,
And precludes the protocol of other duties—
Who cherishes anonymous silence
And waits out the passing of summer storms,
The torpid heat and long, lingering droughts.

Every poet just needs to get a life.
Just do it and be done.
Poets can only throw boulders so far—
And even then, it's not that impressive.

Poets are ornery and stubborn
And drawn to pensive, melancholy nights.
Poets mutter, "bullshit" when they see it.
Poets hate tired webs of frivolity;
They know there are better ways
To make a living.

But if you still want to be a poet,
Just accept that no one cares about you
Or your obtuse ways of seeing the world.

There is not a polite way to say this:
"If you really want to be a poet,
Live like one."

TRUE ASSESSMENT

Your grade is not always you

Your old grade book is a waste of space and time.
Don't hesitate; just throw it out.
~Starr Sackstein

Assessment is just a softer term for the harsh reality of grading—a slightly more terrifying word, but if we do not assess everything we do, we become the proverbial bearers of repeated mistakes, miscues, and misunderstandings. Few things annoy students more than a grade pulled from thin air and riddled with inconsistencies—a critique more punitive than enlightening.

But grade we must. It is the Sisyphean chore and duty of every teacher.

But does it have to be?

Should teachers be the final arbiters of Fate? Is there enough room in the grading salon to allow students a shoulder to lean on in the barter house of grading? Should our students live like criminals, turning themselves over to the authorities for every malfeasance and misdemeanor in their academic lives? Short of perfection, this evolves into the lot of a student's life, but if we do not let them join in the assessment party and if we insist on being their judge, jury, and overseer, we have squandered the greatest skill they need to master—to deconstruct and rebuild their efforts with clear eyes, moral candor, and infinite hope of betterment. Our teaching ought to teach how to self-assess. Invite students in. Let them share, dialogue, and assess with us and with each other.

Research shows we retain little of what we *hear* in the classroom. The odds increase (though not dramatically) when we also *read* what we are supposed to learn; however, learning increases dramatically when we *present* what we learn—and even more so when asked to *teach* what we know.

My students see me as a bit of a pious bear when it comes to learning punctuation. As I stand behind my metaphorical lectern and begin pontificating on the efficacy of punctuation, the room fills with what I call "grammar gas," which always—as in always—works its way into the darkened souls of my captives until even the most focused, grade-grubbing scholar fades from view into solipsistic reveries—and who sometimes simply slip into a hypnotic trance, a stasis that actually mimics paying attention.

But (the proverbial "but"), if I free them from myself to "practice" punctuation by watching videos or laboring through interactive self-grading quizzes and worksheets, they will work endlessly until every single answer is correct. They will strut around the classroom, proud as peacocks, flashing a new fan of tawdry feathers, pronouncing victory over the larger foe. The magic is that they see what they need to do and how to do it, and although they will never use the word "assess," they live the experience of assessment—they control their respective destinies. They intuitively understand where, when, and how they are screwing up and what needs to be done to rectify the screw-ups. Putting these newfound skills into future writing pieces is another ballgame, but when the red pen of discernment circles the comma splice, they are the ones to take the blame. They look deeper into themselves for a solution instead of lamenting my grading the nits and twits of some archaic punctuation rule—a rule I barely taught them and one they can barely grasp in their desperate claws.

As teachers, we must assess their own misdeeds and malapropisms. During exam weeks, I am amused by teachers who proudly proclaim that not one student in their class got higher than a C on their exam, as if it is solely the fault of lazy students unprepared for the exam. I bite my tongue and never actually say what I really think. These arbiters of Fate had all year to teach what was to be on the exam. It was their battle plan that failed, not the soldiers incompetence on the warring plain.

Who really deserves the blame?

I shudder to think if my back surgeon needed to cram before boring into my spine with a pricey drill. I wonder how much another teacher knows—or what I even really know. All I know is that knowledge needs to be organic. It needs to grow in a well-tended garden fertilized by constant attention to what makes the flowers blossom and the fruits grow—but instead of relishing a rich and fertile garden, too many students finish the year trying to make sense of a weed patch of information until they hardly know the weed from the crop. We move through our curriculums as if driven by a dark, fated force, knowing no other way. We teach. We assign. And we grade. The ongoing, vicious cycle of grading leaves little room for true and effective mastery. We give what we think is helpful feedback and helpful criticism, but more often than not, it is a barb of degrading commentary—even when we assume we are being kind, helpful, and supportive. It diminishes more than it develops, and it traps our weary students within an enveloping catatonia.

Give up on the harsh commentary. It doesn't work. It really does not work. If I give a student an A on a paper, they will read every comment I write; if I give a B, they may read most of the comments, but if I give a C or below, they won't read a parcel of my criticisms on their damned essay. Who willingly walks into a room to get their head batted around with a sledgehammer or fettered with an annoying feathercock? None of us needs to be assessed more than we—students and teachers alike—need to assess ourselves. We are the creators of our work. We need to assess what works and what falls short using helpful, hopeful, effective, sustainable, and practical tools and techniques.

I get how overbearing I sound. I am better at pontificating than problem-solving, and I am loathe to invite anyone to come into "my space" and tell me what I should and should not do in my classroom. None of us do, because all of us are doing our damnest to be good teachers. I am amazed every day by the sheer dedication I see in my colleagues as they prepare their weighty curriculums, grade voluminous sheaves of papers, meet with lost and wayward students, and ease the minds of overly anxious parents. We are prey to our own inertia in all endeavors of life, and we will sail our ship off the edge of our flat world before admitting we are misguided and misdirected. We need to pull up our socks, put on our brave faces, and rethink and retool the grading paradigm. We need to channel our limited energies and diminishing time to teach students how to assess themselves and how they might move forward after dissecting and parsing their respective efforts.

The phoenix rising in the corner of every classroom is the beast of time. No sooner has one task been completed than another rises from the ashes. The lesson planner becomes the tail wagging the dog, and, to paraphrase Thoreau, "We do not ride the railroad as much as the railroad rides upon us." Our destination is distant, and our direction is fixed. The very notion of giving time to students to assess and reflect upon their work is a path fraught with peril and ambiguities, and so even the most well-intentioned and experienced educator is caught in the tangled juxtaposition of duty, obligation, and tradition—and, ultimately, the energy for transformative change remains more a dream than a reality.

But you can't jump a canyon in two jumps. We need to make the decision to change the way we grade, and our students need to learn to assess their own work in practical, pedagogically sound, and sustainable ways—and we need to make the leap, or at least some of us have to, if only to tinker with what is possible.

I am wary of my propensity for pontification. All I know is that a good portion of my life is spent reading, marking up, and grading essays and other assignments. In the crunch times of the year, this amounts to several hours at night—time when I should be watching NCIS with my kids or walking around the neighborhood with my wife, chatting idly with the Jones's and Smith's of the world.

It is crazy because we grade as if we are the ones being graded—and we are! These marked-up essays and assignments make their way into the critical banter in the hallways. They fall into the hands of parents who eviscerate and parse our responses more ardently than their own children's work. We become the fodder of disdainful gossip and rumormongering. My soft, imperfect way of grading "usually" works. I receive relatively few complaints and more than a share of praise for the efforts I put in, but I no longer think I am doing the right thing. I need to focus on teaching—actually teaching what I know backwards and forwards and up and down—not some grumpy millworker separating and dividing the wheat from the chaff with a baseball bat. A teacher should not assume the role of sole assessor and arbiter of right from wrong. Life itself is pretty good at that.

My own evolution as a teacher has played itself out in stuttering stops and starts. I worked for many years as "the woodshop teacher," a moniker still befitting. I remember those days with healthy dollops of nostalgia—times when my most anxious moment at night was to remember to pick up ten 2×4's at the lumberyard on the way to school. But maybe the approach in the woodshop is a better way. When I worked in the shop, I never graded the students' projects; I would grade the process of the creation, which certainly leveled the playing field. Each student knew what the final product was supposed to look like. My busy carpenters worked from drawings, plans, and blueprints. There was a logic, structure, and sequence to the workflow, and they could palpably "see" when something was or might go awry. These bumps in the road never birthed a time for criticism—and the student willingly and eagerly sought the help they needed—and most of the time they wanted to do it on their own and, in so doing, "owned their mistakes." Self-assessment is the time given to "figure out" what is going wrong and how to fix it. They did not take the project home to work on the mistakes; they came to the next class ready to work through and overcome the setback. It is a lesson in teaching that is buildable and doable in any academic classroom.

The lightbulb for me is to process and do the heavy work in the classroom where the teacher has oversight of the process and approach—be it writing an essay, completing a lab report, compiling a presentation—or most anything. Homework (if needed at all) requires a discerning focus on what can realistically be completed at home in a *brief chunk of time*—not some back-handed convolution to extend the classroom into the bedroom. Homework needs to be specific to the needs of the work being done in the classroom—not some well-intentioned, untested artifact best left to tomorrow.

With seven kids of my own, I see firsthand, time and time again, homework demanding gobs of processing time and not enough practice time. Students are not equal robots on common assembly lines. There is no reason homework should be a source of anxiety, failure, and trepidation—homework must be doable and calculated to take a certain amount of time, not a list that will take some students ten minutes and others thirty minutes. When I assign thirty minutes of reading for homework, I make sure it is thirty minutes. I provide, whenever possible, audio that is thirty minutes long. If it is an essay or writing piece of any sort, I provide a detailed writing plan—a blueprint for them to follow where I only expect a certain *type* of content, not *quality* of content. If it is something I want them to learn and practice by rote, I make sure it is measurable and limited using self-graded flashcard programs and interactive presentations and quizzes. If I grade any one piece of an assignment, it is the writing of a metacognition, which is a brief reflection of a student's experience of their experience and the process of completing their work. The refining of the content is always done in the shop —meaning the class itself.

My epiphany is no great thrust of genius. It has been the common practice of many teachers for years. It is a cornerstone of the flipped classroom, but it is not an approach welcomed or practiced by the majority of teachers, who stubbornly cling to their own incantations of the tried and true, some who sincerely disagree with me, and some who are too strapped for time to realistically rethink and retool what they already know and do. The downside of my approach is the time and effort it takes to front-load the classwork and unerringly balance the homework. The resulting upside is a more empowered, confident, and engaged student. Administrators would be wise to spend less time meeting with teachers and more time leading workshops to empower teachers with the tools and time to develop and sustain this approach.

By engaging the down and dirty work in the classroom, assessment evolves into a natural, engaged, and continual action. Each student processes their work in an empowering, non-punitive way. Teachers need to see how and where a student struggles with clear eyes, an open mind, and a malleable heart. We must help our charges when needed, but free them to figure it out when and if it is appropriate and sustainable, which can only be done in the heady and invigorating dynamic of the classroom —the sacred hall where teachers have deliberate control of a collective destiny and where expectations can be carried out with some semblance of clarity and purpose. As teachers, we cannot, and never will, control the dynamic of the home environment.

Ever. Ever. Ever...

As always, I drone on, and, no doubt, I make leaps before contemplating the dangers of what I preach. I am a kid in a candy store, alive in a wondrous moment. I am alive and free, plotting, pondering, and planning how to teach in more profound and enduring ways than my current ways. I am not totally ignorant of my biases. I am yet part and parcel of the problem, and changing my ways (stubborn as I am) is a long leap across a wide canyon, but I sense the horizon and imagine the view from the other side. It is a panorama of purpose, potential, and possibility.

We are undaunted seers seeking a solution to an enigma.

We can figure it out together if we assess it together.

But only if we try.

DIVERSITY DAY

Life in a court of pedagogy

*But he hasn't got anything on!" the whole town cried out at last
The Emperor shivered, for he suspected they were right. But he thought,
"This procession has got to go on." So he walked more proudly than
ever, as his noblemen held high the train that wasn't there at all.*
**~Hans Christian Anderson, *The Emperor's New
Clothes***

It is kind of weird—and more than a bit arrogant—but I have
this separate part of my journal where I hide my entries
reflecting some primitive incarnations of thoughtfulness and
balance—scrabbling's that represent and resemble honest and
real wisdom. These are the essays best left unpublished, if only to
conceal my entrenched views and candid ignorance from my
professional peers. I came here to this "journal" today after
receiving a school email noting I am "required" to attend the
diversity sessions during our winter professional day—as if the
magnitude of the command will somehow inspire me to embrace
the possibility to improve my moral character and my
pedagogical practices.

But it does not inspire me. It enervates me more than it
energizes me.

I am hoping if I craft a response in my "Wisdom Journal,"
some kind of nuanced and balanced thought will come out of it
—some elixir to make compromise palatable—but I doubt it.
Wisdom is a hard stone to cull from frozen ground. My stubborn
nature will emerge. I will refuse to see the other side; but then
again, the other side will refuse to see mine. I am left to dig my
muddy, yankee soles into the slippery ground of this new,
emerging spring and brave the elements in another senseless
battle of wit, wisdom, and prophecy.

My required attendance is my intellectual dilemma: I am simply not interested in someone I did not choose to promulgate their passion and profession and willfully parse my understanding of diversity. I am in no way, shape, or fashion disinterested in the subject—nor is it off the radar of my life and how I deliberately live. I object to being forced to listen to a certain person or persons with whom I have no relationship or affinity at all, or, even worse, I know them and have no interest in their point of view, their personal perspectives, or their politicized point of view. I am a dull New England Yankee at heart. I distrust any self-proclaimed captain barking orders to go hard a'lee and sail unopposed against my will and wisdom onto a rocky shoal of a sultry, emerging paradigm. If there is no Ethos in the Logos, how will I experience the Pathos—the richness of heartfelt depth—within the heady rhetoric?

I am chained in fetters against my raging, stubborn will to spend a dulled day of my life immersed in a senseless sea of doggerel purveyed as sacred truth. If I show reluctance, I will be vilified and labeled a bigoted perpetuator of myopic thought and white privilege; however, if I acquiesce and if I sow seeds of change, I will be lauded and praised as a newly enlightened and benighted teacher—hence the paradox of my predicament. My relatively benign job to teach 8th and 9th grade English seems dependent on my agreeing to whatever is on the agenda of a middle school professional day, empowered by a lofty edict to embrace some bandwagon thinking of superior virtue, needed change, and noble action.

Where is Socrates when you really need him? Where are the sultry colleagues who might agree with me? Who framed the scaffolding for this now urgent priority? What, really, is the point? Has my life been so unexamined as to willfully discard my past speculations about right and wrong? Is there some flaw in my life un-mended? What have I done to deserve this magnanimous flogging? What seer sees so clearly into my soul, my motives, my ruminating, and my urgency to curve the bent of my elusive genius and disrupt the path of my hard-wrought, existential angst?

I hear the refrain, "It is only one day," a day I am paid well to endure. It is a day rich in possibilities to hear new voices, new ideas, and new ways of understanding. If this is the case, how different is it from any other day? I am no dolt to conformity. I do not live to reassure my comfortable self. I box my own ears in a continual search for what is ineffably me, for what is definably right from wrong, and for what actions I need to take to smother and silence the incessant bantering of the anti-woke—a misanthropic gang of misfit sycophants politicized by dangerous demagogues. The notion I need more hands to bandy me about is an insult to affront. I am the proverbial horse being dragged to water, yet I am not so thirsty as to drink the potion prepared for me. Find other mares and stallions to follow your shimmering mirage.

But, dammit, not me. Give me back the day. My soil is ill-suited to your seed. Send me off to ponder and leave me alone. See clearly and put clothes on your vain and egregious emperor.

At the end of the day, let us compare our respective fruits.

We will see more clearly whose basket is full.

AD POETICUS

I hear the great expressions
of surprise when the lights go out:
the rustling of drawers fumbling
for candles, and children's joy
breaking in squeals, bouncing
on strangers' beds, clutching
small fists—blind now
to stern and judging eyes.

The walls of this hotel
are thin plaster,
and the rooms full.
Most all of us are travelers
tired by long train rides
in hot bunks
stirring lukewarm cabbage.

Still, I sense a greater continuance—
more cynical belching of soft coal smoke
pouring from insatiated bellies,
from wheezing brickstacks of old power plants—
undisturbed by problems in distant lines,
and down whose gullet is forced the dark fuel
torn in gashes from quiet emptied earth

quiet emptied earth

(I shake my head slowly:
sounding, quacking, calling
from cattail blinds,
drawing stray fowl,
warbling a strange prolegomena
towards a tentative coherence.)

In what is otherwise darkness
I can see the sparking wires
dancing like maddened snakes,

lighting only the smallness
of a rounded hilltop
trimmed bare—
neither rhythm or convulsion.

I am drawn that way
until my heart pounds out of me,
gushing whale's blood on pitching decks,
sensing the idiocy of approach,
knowing no other way.

~The Lihua Hotel, Beijing, 1989

A TEACHER'S ENIGMA

Listen first to the farmer

*Tradition is not the worship of ashes,
but the preservation of fire.*
~**Gustav Mahler**

Are tradition and progress an incongruous pair? You might think so given the cacophony of competing sects in most any educational community who struggle with competing paradigms pitting the Ethos of tradition against the Pathos of progress in a quixotic quest for Logos that might bring sense to argument. Diametrically opposed canons of thought lock in a literary civil war mimicking the political gulfs tearing at our communal seams—as if tradition cannot coexist with progress. A tree falls in the direction it leans; hence, the gravity of our hobbling prejudices and politicized souls creates an impassable morass of tangled undergrowth, but sadly, especially for me and my ilk, the honed ax of tradition is no match for the chainsaws of progress.

It seems the new literati has won. I am left standing with the remains of the day, my muted voice gurgling a final dirge. The victors console me: "It is all for the best, Fitz. You fought a good fight."

But all is not lost.

I still have some fight left in me; there is still time to rage against the dying of the light. Neither am I alone. There are still some unmuted voices singing ageless songs. Connor Soukup, a ninth grade student of mine, wrote in his most recent essay: "Tradition is the vine upon which all change grows." He argues that the best fruit is ultimately rooted in the soil of tradition. His wise and unaffected words grant me pause for thought—and hope.

Do we really nurture the soil as much as we pluck the heartiest-seeming fruit? Do we forget how everything we teach springs from desperate, plying tendrils we never see or feel but simply trust? Is this trust misplaced? Only a fool would erect a treehouse on a sapling, and only a greater fool would make a walking stick with a sprig from a thorn bush.

But we do it all the time. We teach students *what to think* more ardently than *how to think*. We give them fine homes instead of lumber to build their own. We celebrate conformity and call it diversity. We condemn questioning as ignorance and bolster the egos of budding sycophants. We make Bibles out of drivel and praise the progress of the meek as they fall in line with precious visions of progressive thought. We are a culture with a lover's passion and impetuous infatuation for the new. We buy our fruits fresh and pile them in neat bins and handy satchels. We want the succulence of juices perfectly ripened. We want the sweetest nectar imbued to our charges—and ourselves. We are swayed by vendors and fishmongers but seldom taught by farmers or fishermen.

The night should never present to me the challenge of an open and empty page to fill with my oily viscera and unfettered thoughts—so I apologize for my extended ramblings and vague metaphors, but I am not a teacher by trade nor a writer by vocation. I remember so little of what I was taught. Even these words come surprisingly slowly as I pry stubborn, crumbling stones from shallow postholes. What I was is who I am and will always be. My tarnished soul, however, is yet unsold. I can only yawp the enigma of my life into the gaping maw of creation.

I am an old gardener out in the sun too long, weeding long lines of turnips and cabbage, beans and gourds, strawberries, and corn. The fields of Concord were once my labor, not a serene vista or sculpted subdivision. I trusted the wisdom of age as much as I trusted myself. I listened more than I spoke, and I lived more than I ever planned.

An old hand from Pine Tree Farm came to my house one day to help me plant a garden. He looked at my neat and symmetrical lines staked in a weedy corner of the yard and said in his wizened Italian slang, "This year you growa' the dirt. Next year, we'll make a' the crop."

He said, "We." And that made all the difference.

I am a carpenter with hands and limbs brittled by youthful exuberance and leavened by cantankerous bosses. I am a boatbuilder whose seams leaked in placid seas; I am the housebuilder whose doors were never trimmed and the woodcarver whose birds never flew. I am because I was. I live because I breathed the primordial air of tradition and drank the dark wine of ancient vineyards. I grew in the stolid ground below me and in the airy heavens above me.

I am yet battered and bruised, but equally intact and not wholly ignorant.

In spite of it all—and through it all—and because of it all, I read deeply and wrote wildly. I rambled and searched. I fed my soul with the bewildering and astonishing detritus of literary tradition. Even now, I go back as readily as I go forward. My roots are in the soil of the past, and I cannot unshackle myself from the mother of my fading intellect. I am not here to validate you, much less embrace your vision.

Nor am I here to stand in your way.

It is your perfect garden, not mine, that needs tending.

After your fingers are caked with toil and your head sullied in epiphany, bring me your fruits; show me your vine; let me chew on the bitter roots; and then perhaps I will borrow your seed or splice your rootstock alongside my own.

By dint of circumstance and inclination, I am a teacher—an unkempt gargoyle whose clothes are frayed, who can never find his glasses, whose gait is hobbled and betrayed, who locks the doors of his precious classroom and fears the next person to pick the lock will ply him with ways to do him better—someone who somehow can't accept the coiling, ignorant leper locked in his cell of tradition—the village idiot at peace with his misconstrued vision and motley crew of students—teenage boys nipping and gnawing at each other's heels, sprawled in piles on couches and chairs and spinning off stools around a large cherry table—mocking, taunting, and laughing with each other.

I am a wary guardian. I protect my brood with a beastly, primordial menace until I am sure the woods are safe, the danger is past, and their nascent wits are still about them. I see in them the promise I never had in my halcyon days of youth. I see in them inextricable patterns of continuity, arcing back and jumping forth like monkeys leaping from branch to branch. I can only hope they trust that I am waiting below to catch them if they fall.

And fall they do.

And rise they must.

I am not like my students, except in memory, nor do I want them to be like me. I want their realness to distill and catalyze a reverence for their own lives and evolve into whatever they wish their lives to become. By and large, they simply want to do well and harvest some semblance of freedom amidst scatter-bound lives—lives incessantly subjugated to competing demands and duties. I tell more stories than I teach. I tell them I was raised and set free as a feral ADD whizkid and classroom dolt who followed a thousand bents of genius and can't let go of my inner scaffolds. I am the flawed Odysseus of my life—hero and anti-hero, fool and king of my own journey. The impulsivity of irreverent, reckless travel shaped, taught, and guided my wary wiles of instinct, yet despite the odds, I somehow made my way into the greatest of traditions within the hallowed and harassed walls of a hollow classroom, and woe or wow, they are stuck with me for the year.

Experience and memory teach quickly. No one needs to tell my students the world is equally cold as it is warm, so I kindle fires with shreds of bark and dry twigs. I stoke the fire with bolts of split oak and spitting pine. I watch and let go of these wild, playful pups to tend the flames of their intrinsic soul and passion. I tell them to figure it out and give a damn. I tell them the only way out is through. I call them out and let them slide. Their lives are inexorably built upon the granite slabs of their own traditions.

I trust they will survive, yet I know the odds too well. Only life can really teach them. Or maybe *The Odyssey, Moby Dick,* or *Walden...* Is it tradition or progress—or both? I really don't know.

I mostly feel.

Teach the books you love, and I will teach mine. I am the blind bard speaking the truths, valid or not, that I unearthed on meandering paths and silent coves. The sea is wide, and the journey is long. Find your own port of call and live your life wisely.

I mean no harm. I am a teacher, and I am almost done.

Please leave me alone.

I have a word left uncovered.

DEATH

The only way out is through

The darker the night, the brighter the stars,
The deeper the grief, the closer is God!
~Fyodor Dostoevsky

Sometimes I don't know where to begin. Though we all went about our lives this past week in somewhat normal ways, I am sure, as with me, we all lived and contemplated the horror and tragedy of Nathan's death and the equally untimely death of Edoardo's dad. There is no rulebook to help us know what to do, feel, think, or say. All we can really do is move forward, for the only way out is through.

Today is my 61st birthday, and as happy and glorious as today is for me, it still gives me pause; it impels me to think back on my life and the long, winding, and often rugged roads I have traveled in the many years coiled behind me—and hopefully still before me. I have been a partner and companion in unmitigated joy and in numbing sorrow. I've lost too many friends too quickly and too unexpectedly. I carry too many words within me that I never spoke but wish I had. I turned away from the too many opportunities unfolding before me—lost chances from grappling paws I will never regain. Each day begins anew. The morning sun is an expectation of dawn and a reminder to lace up my old boots and map out a new destiny for a solitary day.

One boot-step. One day at a time.

In this cool, dark night, I make silent vows to become as new as the coming day. I search for the strength to wake with both joy and sadness, to find my commonality with humanity. I am not alone, nor will I ever be alone—even when burdened with a crushing weight. I read and heard Edoardo's words in a recent journal entry and podcast reflecting on the recent death of his dad:

It didn't matter that I've shed thousands and thousands of tears; It didn't matter that life was giving me so much heartbreak, for it only matters that I smile through this storm called life. Life to me, is a river with twists and turns, and at times it seems impossible to navigate through; however, it is your choice to let this monster called life knock you down—so get up and set your own course.

These are the times when the teacher becomes the student. I am as equal a partner in your life as you are in mine. I am incredibly thankful. As much as you sometimes drive me crazy, you are also a wondrous gift, and I will never ever forget you. I can't and never will. I hope and trust you realize I really don't care if you master the rules of common usage, if you italicize book titles, if you forget to do your homework, or if you visit me weekly for recess recall. I hope you know I know you do give a damn, and you are trying to figure out this thing called life—even when there is no clear answer or any palpable sign of a path through a dark wood.

Sometimes I don't know where to begin—Tyler died. Luke died. DA died. Nick died. Spenser died. Nathan died. Mike died. Will died.

All young. All hearty. All soulful.

All real as memory.

My fingers fumble on the laces of my boots. My words are trapped in guttural silence. I do not know where it will end. I fear I straggle behind, so I turn to you and hope you will turn to me, and we can begin the new day with each other, beside each other, and for each other.

It is our only way through this thing called death.

And life.

WHAT PUMPKINS ARE FOR

As much as I swat I love
This bothering incessance
Of mosquitos in still air
After warm rain.

Standing in the throaty exhaust
Of the old Farmall
I urge the dogs
To make the trip with me,
Down to the community plots
Where I've planted nothing
But brag patch pumpkins
And a string of river bass,
If only to sit
On their immensity
In the moon cool nights
Of hoarish fall.

Skip died this past spring
Shoveling out winter's heavy manure,
So I plant her garden
With talk of August tables:
Tomatoes, corn, beets, cabbage—
Ostensible things
I'm sure she'd agree with;
Though planted, I figure,
Somehow not quite right.

It is just weird to think
She finally can't
Do anything about it.

But that is what pumpkins are for.

A BETTER TOMORROW

Explore, Assess, Reflect & Rethink

Our first crash course in remote learning is done. The wise work now is to separate the wheat from the chaff and assess what worked and still works and what should be cast aside as detritus from a noble effort. I have always required my students to write a "metacognition" after each assignment as a way to *explore, assess, reflect, & rethink* their unique experiences of common assignments and assessments. These dreary, one-more-thing-they-have-to-do drudgeries evolve over the course of the year from stuttering incantations of frustration into honest and compelling reflective exercises mirroring the "meta" of "cognition" in rich and nuanced narrative voices.

As educators, we would be wise to do the same while the bloom still clings to the vine and the muddy dew is still fresh on our hands. No doubt, it seems remote learning is not going away. The likelihood of the coronavirus magically slipping into mere memory diminishes with each passing week, so yes, we need to prepare—but no, we do not need to make rushed and hurried decisions and leap into "professional development" until we are sure what needs to be and can be developed over the course of the summer before the looming reality of the Fall semester. My cantankerous self already fears the looming slew of opportunities hell-bent on doing me good. I am an old and hardened soldier, leery of being pushed into the mud before I dance to the old songs I know.

It would be handy and convenient to simply accept, "We'll listen to the experts," but who is to say with clarity who these experts are? As a teacher, I would answer, "We are—each and every damned one of us!" We have all had our flashes of innate brilliance, and we have all had our share of fizzled duds, but we are, by and large, willing to transform what we know into what we need to do. To administrators, I say, "Give us the tools and let us build our own castles on the foundation of our unique school communities." If we are unwilling or incapable, then by all means dictate and proscribe what you will in dollops of ladled wisdom and stubborn persistence. To students, I say, "Be the kid who figures it out, not the lazy slouch who figures a way out. This is your new and inescapable garden in which to wither or bloom." To parents and guardians, I say, "Embrace the beast and do your best to tame the wild urge to let the beast run wild. You are no less a part of your child's education than any teacher or school. You are the model of your child's future. Be strong, wise, and demanding—not fearful, fickle, and floundering."

Oh, to be a fly on the wall and hear the chats of our students, the mumbles of our colleagues, and the scrambling of administrators trying to put this whole ecosystem together, mixed with the exasperation of our bewildered and befogged parents as educating our students morphed from walking in to logging on; from engaging in the sensate repartee of the classroom and the bustling of a school community to shifting on the fly into the hard screen of Zooms and uploads, halting connections and distracted, unkempt students still deep in the torpor of sleep.

Even as summer begins, most of us are tired and weary. We live in a world cobbled together with loose stones and thin mortar. It is easy to lose faith and fear what lies ahead on the looming horizon. For the past three months, school was not what it was, and in many cases, not what it should be, yet somehow much of it worked—often to astonishing degrees. On successive days, we have been the hero, and we have been the fool. In spite of any and all frustrations, our own experiences must now shape a new paradigm that can—and must—work.

Our lives and our experiences must become parables to guide our future. We should start by imagining or reliving those babbling and disjointed conversations about what was good and what was bad, who was right and who was wrong, what worked and what didn't work. We need to focus on our individual successes as teachers, our efforts as students, our thoughtfulness as administrators, and our undeniable rights and roles as protectors of our progeny. We must explore, assess, reflect, rethink, and separate the bruised fruit from the perfect fruit. This cannot begin and will not commence until there is an acceptance that education is a three-legged stool. There needs to be true and searching reflection on the part of educators, students, and guardians, for we all play an equal role in our classrooms, offices, and homes. We must shape together the dynamic that determines the success or failure of the second iteration of Remote Learning 2.0.

It is a new day and a time for new ideas.

The bell tolls for you.

And me.

And us.

THE BOAT MYSTERY

*If one does not know to which port one is sailing,
no wind is favorable.*

~Seneca

Wooden boats have always cast a spell on me, but like a distractible child, I can't cast this sorcery away. I can't tuck the lure of a ribbed and planked hull into some sensible and well-ordered tackle box. It is even more true when these boats are old, worn, and rich in brine, rot, and history. The bulging seams and weathered mast hoops bring out the irrationality in me. They make me forget I am trapped in a time of gigabytes and reality sitcoms. They make me forget about my students waiting for assignments. They make me forget the oil bills, car loans, mortgages, and 401 K's. I forget town meetings and piano lessons. I forget I ever tried to paint my lawn green with bags of Ace Hardware fertilizer. I exist in a cloud of unknowing. My thinking is a fog of dreams rolling under a full moon. I forget, and they become me, and I become them. Still, despite the raging voices of common sense, I forge on with my lifelong madness. I chart a course over familiar shoals and note my log at every changing of the tides. My eyes scan for a lost shoreline. Sometimes I can't turn away. And so it is with this old catboat I've been eyeing—a forty-year-old, 25-foot Wittholz catboat owned by The East End Classic Boat Society—offered to me for $6000.00, payable in two installments. It almost seems doable, but ultimately, after the reality check, it is not.

I live with a dream within a dream deferred—a dream pulling our dory alongside a bigger boat—a dream passing the kids up to Denise and steadying the tender as she hauls them, failing like dolphins over the taffrail. It is a day spent fishing and jumping from the bowsprit. It is sunrise sailing on a morning tide to some other harbor or cove. It is a burning sun setting across

Penobscot Bay. It is the smell of coal burning down below—wet wool, coffee, tea, and biscuits.

We have a boat—a smaller, 17-foot Wittholz catboat named Lolo, which is solid, tough, and pretty as all hell. I wonder why she is not enough. Why can't I be happy just daysailing around the coves and beaches of Cape Cod? The kids love it. Denise loves it. Her Uncle B built Lolo in his barn in New Hampshire. He used it for a few years and later gifted it to us as a wedding present. We took our honeymoon on Lolo, sailing from the Cape to the Vineyard and, with sturdier sea legs, back to Boston. Why want a bigger boat with bigger headaches and expenses? Why be willing to live so close to the bone just to get closer to the water?

My life remains full of the flotsam of sailing, a patchwork of memories stitched together by a common yarn. I worked for a spell as the deckhand on Violet, a Scots Zulu, sailing out of Martha's Vineyard—fifty tons of Scottish larch, white oak, pounded hemp, and pine tar. She plowed through the maddened waves of the sound like a bull, splitting walls of water and upending unwitting passengers, wine coolers, and bottles of sunscreen in a torrent of foaming water and seaweed. I was the trusted firstmate and the lowliest deckhand. Whenever the captain said, 'do,' I did.

My only escape was a hearty climb up the rigging to engage in some perceived task or chore, but mainly to get off the deck and into free air. I clung to the topmast with one arm. With the other arm, I would free jammed blocks, slap tar, and unfurl the ship's pennant—or I would rest in that holy place like an incarnation of Ishmael, far above everything I ever was before—always looking eastward, my heart always pounding. On the deck, I coiled lines, made beckets, spliced wire, and wound marlin—and all the while the brilliant, ornery Captain Maynard barked incessantly to hop-to, bitter to the cud to sail rich folks around Buzzards Bay, while he struggled to realize his own dream of sailing once more around the world—a dream I hear has him now with his wife and two boys sailing somewhere in the South Pacific. I owe Captain Maynard more than he ever paid me.

I've sailed since I could wonder. As a kid, I sailed on White's Pond in Concord, making tack after tack in the homemade plywood sailfish my father built in our garage. I would sail all day, every summer day, whenever the day allowed. I had no life jacket, no teacher, no soccer practices—nothing but childhood and a lawn to mow later. I was eight years old and leaping to the sails as my tender ship invariably flipped in whatever gusts came our way. I later mastered a dry scramble over the windward rail and onto the daggerboard, posting triumphant salutes to my father, who watched, amazingly unconcerned, from shore.

Later, as a seasoned middle school sailor, I would sail the bigger waters of Stinson Lake in New Hampshire. I sailed our Sunfish imitation until I recognized the ominous signs of every different squall line boiling in from every direction over the White Mountains. I traced broad runs across Stinson to Clem's cabin. As I sailed coolly by Megan Tassini's dock, I tilted my head even more coolly in her direction. I ghosted in the calms and surfed the gales on a broad reach. When there was wind, I fished for bass and trout, dangling crayfish I captured in the shallows by the dam. I imagined myself going over that dam and down Stinson Brook and into the sandy Baker and through the roaring Pemigewasset, and then into the moody Merrimac and, finally, into the unforgiving Atlantic, and thence to anywhere.

Age never tempered my infatuation. When I finished my staggered attempts in college, and when I got out of debt and onto the water, I bought a 1929 Anderson catboat in New York and sailed her to Cape Cod with an arrogant crew—me and Tommy Bilodeau, Dickie Kerr, and Jim McClellan—all of us (except Jim) ignorant as all get-out, punching our way through a raging Nor'easter, laughing, singing, and praying—pretty sure we knew where we were, though oblivious to our idiocy. Our unrecorded journey was an adventure in learning. This first boat, which I could call my own, sank the next day in the harbor near Monument Beach on Cape Cod. A small stub of mast pointing to the sky marked her grave. Somehow, cheap boxes of macaroni fell into the water leaking through the hull, where they swelled in the bilge pump until Fate took over. She sank alone in the night while I was off watching Jimmy Buffet in Boston and singing drunkenly along to "A Pirate Looks at Forty." That trip was my first, though not my last, maritime disaster. The next morning, I stood alone on a pier while a gaggle of tourists gathered on the beach to see my misfortune. They gawked and were aghast and amused at my novice ways. An old salt made his way to me and simply said, "You must have known she was a leaker."

'All life is a trip on a leaking ship,' I wish I had replied.

But I did not give up my dream.

A few years later, I bought a brand-new boat—a thirty-foot plywood sharpie ketch—which Hurricane Bob promptly battered and beached two weeks after launching. I rebuilt her at a greater cost than I paid for her. I never even gave her a name, just MS 5782. I sailed her up Maine and back to the Vineyard. I almost lost her—and myself—in a fifty-knot squall while cutting across the Gulf of Maine. Even now, years later, I am amazed at my equanimity, shrugging my shoulders at the whim of my dalliance with death, facing what I stoically accepted as my last moments of a shortened life.

It still was not enough. I bought another catboat, tired in the stem, tired in the keel, and tired in the ribs. I proposed to Denise in the cockpit as she sat high and dry in my front yard. I never did get that boat back in the water—or the next boat after that. We later sailed on Lolo. She was a good boat. We kept her on a friend's mooring in the water off the beach in Eastham. We had many good sails, never more than a half an hour from shore. We played in the mudflats until the tide came in and floated Lolo, and then Denise and I would drag all seven kids in a line out to the boat, kicking and splashing in their Scooby-Doo life jackets.

They thought they were swimming in heaven.

They probably were.

You'd think that was enough. But the dream soon engulfed me once more. Shaking out a reef off Lieutenant's Island, I'd make a sight towards Stellwagen and imagine us in a small schooner, some ship I didn't have to take back to shore—a ship we could call home. I imagined a quieter time with just us and the kids sailing on a boat for the whole summer, maybe a scow sloop, a small schooner, or a bigger, beamier catboat. Sometimes

I'd get practical (to my eye) and plot ways to get my captain's license and sail rich folks around, but never be as bitter as my old boss. I imagined reading the literature of the sea with anyone willing to share and keep logs of our adventures. I dreamed of diving, fishing, and swimming in the cold waters. I planned to live on clams, scallops, and Pringles. I even got so far as figuring out what it would take to make it a reality.

But money. It always boils down to money. It still does. My head is always calculating for when another boat comes along.

And then this damn old catboat. I never should have let it root in my heart. I never should have made the call or listened to the man describe her—like a child or a grandfather remembered. It is something words cannot explain. My words are only the finger pointing at the moon, never the moon itself—and that moon is arcing over a looming horizon. It is not a desire to get away. It is a need to get on; to get on the water and listen for the selkie; to know the tides and learn from the stream flowing through me; and, when I have learned, to teach others whatever I learned from my mixed education; to teach my kids; to shout like a man overboard lost in muffled darkness; or, at the very least, to speak from my experience, though it is experience I lack.

Everything I've done on boats is a transient memory, a fleeting glimpse into what can only be my soul. In the greater scheme of seafaring, I am still a greenhorn. The winds and the tides fill me with fear, but the dream lives on.

I keep making my way down to the water.

I stand on the shore in awe of the mystery.

THE DISARRAY IS INEVITABLE

As I lay the tools out
On the broad workbench, forcing
Form and symmetry
On my basement workshop.

One man should not need
Such a pile of screwdrivers,
Pliers, sockets, wrenches,
Hammers, drills, saws;
Clamps, files, squares,
A long row of coffee cans
Filled with screws:
Flatheads, phillip heads,
Torque heads, alan heads;
Ring nails, roofing nails, finish nails,
6d, 8d, 10d, 16d, 20d;
Lag bolts, machine bolts, ring bolts;
Flat planes, jack planes, rabbet planes…

I work slowly—
A curious zookeeper
Filling cages with disparate beasts,
Each bleating, howling,
Whimpering for attention
And relevance.

Tools I will never use again
Are tossed in an old apple crate.

It fills slowly.

I am part
Of an ages-old meditation
Carried through time—
The culling of the herd.
The field left fallow.
The awkward branch pruned—

A ship's hold filled, ballasted
With a galleon's gold.

I hold each tool like a poet
Palming words before
My harsh and critical eye,
Wondering if this one
Or that one,

Or maybe even this one,
Is worth saving.

LOGOS, PATHOS & ETHOS

The Uses and Abuses of Rhetoric

Three things can not hide for long:
the Moon, the Sun and the Truth.
~Gautama Buddha

Nobody likes to be wrong, but it sure makes living easy when convinced we are right. Few of us walk around writing, saying, or thinking, "Boy, my opinions and views are certainly shallow, uninformed, and alarmingly trivial—but here is what I think..." We need to be assured that what we know and feel is valid, real, and informed, for there is a serenity in knowing we know—or we have at least reached a level of knowingness somewhere near to certainty. I admit a certain jealousy sweeps over me when I hear or read someone say exactly what I already think and feel (and thought I knew), but I just never found the words or the way to say it with equal eloquence and clarity. Or I am at a party and two prodigious minds are arguing a topic, and I find myself swinging dizzily from one side to the other: "He's right. No, she's right. But he made a good point. Now her rebuttal is better."

It is even worse when I butt into lofty conversations with my limited skills and sketchy half-ass information. I slink away with my tail between my legs like a proud, yet sheepish, cur—and hope they don't notice. I am their prey and victim lost in my trepidation, stymied by vacillating thoughts and ultimately defeated by the majestic and compelling use of rhetorical language—which is simply effective and persuasive speaking or writing. But do not fear or accept your awkward stuttering labor to be heard. Becoming a more adept rhetorical speaker and writer is a skill we can learn and practice in every facet of our academic, social, and intellectual interactions.

The first skill is to stop. Think. Then think some more. Then only speak after the thought has ripened into a virtue worth proclaiming. Lao Tzu had it right almost three thousand years ago when he wrote,

> *Knowing you do not understand is a virtue;*
> *not knowing you do not understand is a defect.*

Lao Tzu was doubtless annoyed by vain sycophants obsessed with being right but not equally obsessed with knowing what they should know before opening their opinionated mouths or wetting ink on papyrus. The wisest and most enduring advice is to stay the hell out of conversations you have no right or aptitude to be in, and to wade, not leap, into truth.

Sadly, Lao Tzu's wisdom is lost on most people, for our lives are full of moments where we are carried away by the ephemeral sound of our own voices and not by the content and wisdom of our arguments. We only need to read or hear the endless screed of online postings, political rantings, and absurd comments pouring driveling inanities into the cups of our everyday lives to know the malevolent dissonance of our leanings. We live in opinion-full, yet shallow, times. I am just as guilty as any of you. Regrettably, it is often impossible to undo what we say, write, or post. The only practical and wise thing we can do is to start fresh, choose our arguments more carefully, think more deeply, and know when, where, and how to say or write what we want to say or write. Only then will our rhetoric rise to a sublime level. Hopefully, this set of criteria for speech-giving will not banish us to a collective vow of silence, for there is much each of us knows, perhaps more than any other person on the planet.

The second skill is to understand why a gaggle of thoughts and opinions cannot be dumped on the page like an elaborate jigsaw puzzle. We must complete the picture for our listeners and readers. We must let our listeners and readers feel like a part of the building process, for without a sympathetic audience, our words are but emptiness in a vacuum, and our rhetoric devolves into a self-aggrandizing show-boating of superior and subtle thoughts. We will not convince anybody of anything.

A good rhetorician understands their audience as fully as the subject matter, and they are willing and happy to meet their audience on a common field of play with a common set of rules for the game at hand. I worked for many years as an apprenticing boatbuilder—a woodshop teacher living out a youthful dream. My monotone mantra for building a sturdy boat adhered to the old maxim: "Form follows function." It is much the same with rhetoric. How we build our arguments and state our cases must be crafted with the same adherence to sound and effective principles of construction as a craftsman building their boat. No doubt, there are new and radical boats launched every day, but each one of them must float. Every dory must move through the water in some semblance of the way the builder hopes their dory will row or sail; otherwise, it is a failure—an interesting design, perhaps, but still a failure.

Some stout-hearted people have mastered the art and craft of rhetoric through experience, reading, practice, common sense, and uncommon intuition; most of the rest of us are best served listening, watching, reading, parsing, and perfecting the time-worn, time-tested formulas and spontaneous oratories of the truly gifted—those wise sages who drew sap from a telephone pole, fed a galleon with a loaf of bread, sipped dew from a blade of grass, or simply made sense from insensate sound.

The final skill (which I need to practice right now) is appreciating the power of brevity and discerning the limits of what you know well enough to speak or write sensibly about. At the very least (and before your next argument), remember what Mark Twain wrote: "If you don't lie, you'll never have to remember anything."

So this is where I leave you off because I am pretty sure I have reached the limit of my erudition on rhetoric—though not my interest in the subject. I ought to be satisfied at this point to be, as Buddha once said, "the finger pointing at the moon."

If you really want to master the art of rhetoric—if truth is mightier than the sword of your opinions—you'll figure it out.

Aristotle will be really pissed off if you don't.

THE SILVER APPLES
OF THE MOON

Pluck until time is done

Stories are a communal currency of humanity.
~Tahir Shah, *In Arabian Nights*

The most powerful and enduring connection we share as a human race is our desire to hear and our need to share stories. We engage in the art of storytelling more than we realize. We describe our kids' soccer games; we critique the latest HBO series; we tell ribald jokes or remember a long-lost friend, event, memory, book, or experience. We listen to stories in songs, in long-winded meetings, in late-night BBC broadcasts or during smug and slanted talk radio, on long car rides, and in intimate conversations with friends and lovers. We tell stories for reasons deeply embedded in our psyche, unfolding in our common chemistry. Storytelling is a natural and intuitive response to every situation—and a lifeline to reality.

Sometimes, when stuck with a rather boorish person, we wonder why-the-sam-hill this purveyor of pedantry insists on repeating insipid stories, yet most of the time we listen politely, reflect, and respond—usually with stories of our own. Out of this verbal give and take—our personal and cultural oral tradition— we reflect, grow, and expand the range of our limitations. It is our way to "shuffle off our mortal coil" while still alive. Through stories, we live outside and beyond the confines of our short sojourn on earth, but while we are here and struggling through the soft gum of everyday life, stories feed our roots and spread our canopy in tropism towards an infinite sky.

Stories worth telling once are worth retelling again and again. Out of this stream of unconscious revision, a story is perfected until it becomes part and parcel of our personal, interconnected, and communal eternity. The best stories survive the ravages of time. We know and sense with an almost mystic unknowingness how a particular story is too good or too important to forget. These stories become the iconic canons of our universal literature.

Go back to those stories, like spawning salmon to the streams of their birth. Know the source. The best and most enduring stories lead us there, even against the tides, currents, dams, and shoals barring the way. Tell, retell, hear, and read the stories carrying us to these places. Banish the trivial and search for and embrace the profound stories that weather the ravages of time. Ask why you read what you read, listen to what you choose to listen to, and tell what you feel needs to be told. Do not accept the debased and vapid simply because it is there, easy at hand, and glorified, extolled, sold, and commercialized in driveling abundance.

Seek the higher fruit:

...walk among the dappled grass
and pluck until time and time is done,
the silver apples of the moon
and the golden apples of the sun.

Today is as good a day as any to look back and begin moving forward. Keep plucking until time is done. Shut something off. Turn something else on. There is something else on your shelf. Something else churns in your mind.

There is a story in your range. It lies within your crosshairs, waiting for you to unleash the bow and open the page.

Or simply listen.

Therein lies the gate to wonder.

BIKES FOR SALE: $2.00

The boys sit and count their money
Long before it comes.
They spend the morning
Untangling piles of old bikes
From summer weeds
Grown through rusted spokes
Wrapped around stuck gears
Hobbling stubborn brake cables.

They spray locked chains
With bursts of WD 40
And remember different wipeouts
On rides around Tobin Drive
Or off makeshift jumps
Built out of two by fours
And sheets of scavenged plywood,
As if every tumble
And every skinned knee
Wrapped in bandaids
Adds another dollar of value.

They scrawl signs
With crayons and markers:

Bikes for Sale: $2.00

I listen, watch, and smile
And wonder if they know
How every bike and every story
Is a purse of gold
Pulled from the pocket
Of this almost mythical
Childhood.

THE FREIGHT TRAIN

My apologies for a teacher's rant

If there is no anger, there is no fire. If there is no fire, there is no warmth. If there is no warmth what can save us from our argument with each other.
~Fitz

The value of an ingot of lead is not measured in size, shape, or words, but by the heft of the content. The inane drivel of political polemic, subtly cast as affirmations of our intrinsic goodness, touted as cultural competency, beggars the imagination and is, sadly, light as a feather, wispy as vaporous winds, and as vacuous as a lifetime movie. I intrinsically get what you—the plural you—are attempting to do in your condescending and intellectually trite email. You do get a little pissy if the insubordinate soldiers among us question the motives you crafted with meticulous adhesion to the norms of your empire. You bask in intractable glory as crowned anointer of righteousness, while we poor fools are just errant migratory fowl fleeing a dissolute history bent on disappearing.

We matter. But only because we exist. Which is lucky for you.

I wonder sometimes how dull and senseless your life would be if we did not have to breathe the same fetid air in the same moldy hallways. Honestly, without me, you do not, will not, and cannot exist. My recalcitrance makes you possible. Without you, tuition would be cheaper; free lunch might actually mean "free lunch." Maybe kids who need tutors but can't afford them can get them. Perhaps institutional everything would ameliorate like a dying vocabulary word—some word like peregrination—for we are, all of us, engaged and committed to our distinctive journey's.

Really, look deeper...

Do you really want a world without me? My pain in the ass and sultry admonitions must mean something. I can't be so completely lost as to lose all sense of redemption; plus, I make your job possible, and it could well be that you make more money than me—so I am your bank, your retirement, and the key to your modus operandi. You need *me* so you can draw the distinctions between *us*. We are an ecosystem that is dependent on each other. My life is your life. Your life is mine. Together we arc to the nooshphere promulgated by Pierre Teilhard de Chardin—a web of shared and common understanding—the Omega Point, where we all actually and fully understand each other, despite time, place, and distance. We are the opposite poles of polarity, the balance of Yin and Yang, and equal heirs to rebuttal.

But we are too shallow to go there. It is easier when I suck and you don't. You need me to paraphrase you. We redefine irony. You want me to change, but if I do, you are out of a job—back to some dive bar in Key West. Back to coaching JV soccer to rich white kids on fall afternoons.

Here is my advice: You, too, must change. Start with your emails. Your emails read like they were spit out of an algorithm. It is literally a chore to read them. Also, you and your carry are dull—dull in the sense of dull because we know what any of you are going to say before any of you say it. To bow to the collective you is to bow to a machine. I don't yet sense that any of you are real. There is no Pathos in your Logos, and God only knows if you have an actual Ethos to make me at least consider what you say to be real and true and forged in the belly of an actual mind, heart, soul, and being.

Just stop being a predictable machine. I should do the same. I am equally predictable. You know this already, so why imitate my insanity?

I feel like a psychopath actor in a cheap Netflix series trying to convince myself I am real and not an actor. I actually like my job, and I want to keep it. But, old as I am, I get the feeling you want me to change into you—to garble your new lexicon into the capacious gullet of my throat, out of which every word of my life has been breathed, uttered, borne, and clasped into the chains of my understanding, not your canned screed lisped as gospel.

You just came back from a four-day conference, and now you are "humbly striving" to be an ally, as if you now embody the epiphany of what being an ally represents. Allies die for kindred spirits on the battlefields of life. They will actually, physically, die for you. As in die. Dead. Lifeless. No more. Caput—all because of you, for you, and in spite of you. But I doubt you are willing to die yet, at least not for me. You are an ally to ambition—a noble ambition, perhaps, but still just verbal nuancing bathed in false modesty and beguiling insouciance.

You are actually quite a woose.

I would never hire you as a bodyguard. I doubt you know how to change a tire or replace an electrical outlet—not that tire changing or electrical outlet installation defines anything. It is just a lame metaphor for someone who is somewhat useless to the actual world. In all other regards, you are quite impressive—self-possessed, gregarious, witty, and destined for power. You proudly believe your all-school email loathing your white privilege and lamenting the impossibility of your ever being a true ally is taken as a self-deprecating truth and might somehow inspire the ignorant masses wandering the hallways and morph us cantankerous misanthropes incarcerated in our dank cells of ignorant inertia into someone like you.

Maybe you actually believe in your Martin Luther-Kingish dream. At least in the moment. At least in the one millisecond of eternity you spent writing your email—but not living it or even fully understanding it. You are, however, keeping your job. In the meantime, "ally" seems like a good thing for you to be. It sounds better than pretentious—or false, gratuitous, or stupid—and all the other monikers you really are.

It is not totally unlikely that you may someday be my boss.

In the end, I wonder who is more full of fallacies—me or you? I really don't know the answer.

You might.

But I don't.

GOSSAMER THREADS

Don't walk in front of me... I may not follow
Don't walk behind me... I may not lead
Walk beside me... just be my friend
~Albert Camus

Know what you are as fully as who you are. I will never be what I aspire to be. I am too malleable for true knowingness. I am a sixty-something white suburban man, educated and ignorated in a single iambic breath. I am a big, broad, encompassing family; I am a captain and crew on a barquentine of crazy and diverse friends; I am the invigorated pension for idiosyncrasies and passions betraying my foibles, follies, delusions, and epiphanies, and who has—and probably always will—dabble on the sidelines of society, dance in the aisles of delusion, and gorge on the possibilities of any given day, all the while enmeshed in the pettiness, prejudices, and bigotries of my upbringing, leanings, pursuits, and dissonance.

I am wise, but only in a fleeting way. I know this. And then I don't. I think. And then I forget. My wisdoms contradict and indict each other in an evolution of convictions weaving, darting, and disappearing. I stutter for normality and hunker in the trenches. I drape my words in camouflage. I smile when smitten. I shrink when solaced. I am an enigma within a conundrum settled on a foundation of dust.

Yet, here I am—perhaps the happiest man alive.

What gives this gift—this pompous proclamation of what every person aspires to proclaim? Somebody has to be the happiest man alive. Why not me? This aging poet hobbled by insufficiencies in a gimpy, fraying body prone to bitching and bemoaning the proclivities of my mortal coil—our mortal coils—and who is somehow still here tying the ether of words to the chains of life?

Why? Because my chains are not normal chains. They are gossamer threads spun in myriad splays of entropy from the center of a universe fastened to the infinite edges of wonder—a wonder inimitably and intractably my own.

I feel the touch of humanity blessing my humanity. I feel the soft wool of love in a distant echo, repeating my name into the dark night of my soul. I taste the sweet pith in the tartness of the seed. I smell my skin burning away my idiosyncrasies. I see my soul pinpricked in the Pleiades.

I hear a distant bell calling me to prayer.

I am not alone, nor can I or will I ever entertain the thought. I am infinite song looped in every key, measured in every beat, strummed in chordal rhythm, harmonized by the enchanting choral of love echoing in the diminishing reverb of time.

I am.

I am.

I am.

METAMORPHOSES

It's something I've hardly ever thought of—
This simple and rattling old diesel
Always got me here or there and then some.
At first I think this engine cough and wheeze
Is just some clog and easily explained—
Some bad fuel, maybe, from the new Exxon,
Or just shortsightedness on maintenance.
I've always driven in the red before,
And these have all been straight highway miles.

*(Except for that short trip out to Zoar Gap
to catch the last of the late season trout,
surprised to find them still rising, sipping
my high hackled Humpy's and Coachman's
from dark pools in glazed and shimmered twilight.)*

But that was nothing and of no account.
I drove Tuesday down to the town meeting
And argued about the new town landfill,
And proposed cutbacks in school athletics,
And then to Sears for a fifteen amp fuse.

At any rate there is no way around it.
I smile sheepishly, curiously
Glad I'm really not in any hurry.

Still, I feel like a fool out flagging trucks,
Gesturing for help I can't give myself,
Hoping my dry lines don't need to be bled,
And I would have to spend that time thinking
Of some way to explain this empty tank
To someone who probably knows better.

You know, I always thought that maybe
Something like this could happen to me—
But not now,
Not yet.

YANKEE CANNONBALL

The rails of a writer

You gain strength, courage, and confidence by every experience in which you really stop to look fear in the face. You are able to say to yourself, 'I lived through this horror. I can take the next thing that comes along.'
~Eleanor Roosevelt

I stood in a long line, waiting with Pipo for his first ride on a roller coaster. Things moving in strange ways are a big deal to him. When he first came from Haiti to live with us, he was eight years old and had never even been in a two-story house. On his second day here, we took him to Floating Hospital in Boston and strode into the elevator with an insouciance, which, in retrospect, reflected my utter lack of cultural awareness for a young boy in a strange land. The door shut, the elevator moved, and Pipo clutched me, screaming.

Now, eighteen months later, he stands wringing his hands, intermittently laughing and grimacing at the thought of "The Yankee Cannonball," the last rickety wooden rollercoaster in New England.

"Will it be scary?"

"Yes"

"Will I scream?"

"Probably."

"Will I throw up?"

"I don't know. I might."

"You better not!"

"We really don't have to go."

"Yeah, we do."

I can see his head racing a hundred miles an hour. I distract him by yelling at some high school kids swearing at each other. "Don't do that," he said, aghast I would dare parent a gang of total strangers.

"Why? They shouldn't be swearing."

"What if they beat you up?"

"I'll hide behind you."

"Mama will beat them up if they beat you up."

"She better. Comb up your hair so you're forty-eight inches tall."

"Oh, man!"

Leaning on his toes, he was just the right height. We squeezed into the car. The single safety bar held me in a crushing gut wrench while leaving Pipo astonishingly free to squiggle and squirm. "Do people ever fall out?"

"Rarely."

"What does 'rarely' mean?"

"It means that only kids who ask a million questions fall out."

"Whoo hooo."

"Oh, yeah…"

The car slid toward the first hill. The chain grabbed our car and hoisted us up towards the highest peak of the Yankee Cannonball. Pipo held the hand grip, smiled and raised his eyebrows in mock fear. "There's the bus! I wish I was on the bus. I like the bus."

"I like the bus, too."

"I know."

The first hill caught us both by surprise. "Oh, man."

"Oh, Jesus, Mary and Joseph."

I couldn't stop laughing. Pipo squinted his eyes and held the bar in front of him. I think he held his breath for the full ninety seconds of roller-coaster riding. The girls behind us used every form of the F-word ever created. "Was it fun?"

"No."

"Want to go again?"

"No. Never again."

After the ordeal, we found the rest of the family in the water park. Dripping and shivering, they ran up to Pipo and asked if he really went on the Yankee Cannonball. "Yup, but never again. No way, Jose. Who wants to go on the bumper cars?"

Denise looked at me like I was a misfit father forcing his son to be a man. "He wanted to go."

"Yeah, right. Was he even tall enough?"

"With a micron to spare. It was another one of those things he just had to do."

Denise and I understand this heroic side of Pipo. When he decides to do something, he'll do it, no matter how much angst it causes him—or us. He is not as interested in overcoming fear as he is in facing fear. He embraces fear as an experience and not merely as an emotion. It is a lesson in courage from which we can all draw inspiration.

The Yankee Cannonball is also a perfect metaphor for the written word. The empty page looms in front of us like a rickety roller coaster. We can't call ourselves writers if we refuse to get in the car and go. We can't call ourselves writers if we do not tell the whole story, replete with every dip and turn recreating our inner and outer experience. We can't give in to the temptation to leap from the car at the first sign of trepidation, nor can we tell the story from a distance.

But this is exactly what so many writers do. They mistakenly believe the cold reality of their detached assumption is more important than the multi-dimensional dynamic of experience. It is much safer to have opinions than to question assumptions. We want facts, and we want a sense of assuredness we are making wise decisions in our lives, but are we always willing to take the ride with Pipo through the hairpin turns of experience? Are we willing to distill our facts through the directness of experience?

Without the parable, there can be no sermon.

Our lives are full of these parables, through which we can contribute an enduring legacy to the world. These legacies are the journal entries, poems, songs, stories, novels, and essays whittled and shaped to capture a reader's imagination, fire their passions or simply stir the embers of a world in need of pondering.

I have no problem with the well-wrought essay presenting an impeccable line of reasoning and logical argument, but if I sense a fallacy, a hypocrisy, or a lack of magnanimity, I quickly create a distance between myself and any writer hell-bent to set me straight.

Seek out writers who know what they say, and you will be rewarded with a truth you can cherish and turn in your mind for years to come. To become a powerful writer, you must return to the source of your own wisdom and chip away at the stone of memory until it takes shape—the infinite and varied shapes of literature and writing held in our eyes and opened in our hearts, smelting the iron core of our innards into hard, ringing words of hardened steel.

For years, I have had an idea for a novel, but I never actually sat down to begin writing it. The idea was too complicated, the characters too diffuse, and the length too daunting in the face of a busy lifestyle, but I thought of Pipo getting on the Yankee Cannonball in spite of every rational fear he had of rollercoasters.

So I set myself down to take an hour or so out of every day and began writing my book. My car caught the clicking chain and took me to the point where gravity took over. I am barely down the first hill, but the ride is exhilarating and real. I see the track laid out before me, and, like Pipo, I'm not sure what every turn and twist will bring, but I do know there is an end to the ride. It is at that distant point that I draw my strength.

Maybe I will walk away woozy and say, "Never again."

But at least I will know.

Think of what you really want to write.

And start writing.

A WRITER'S PARADIGM

Let the chips fall where they will...

*We must be willing to let go of the life we planned
so as to have the life that is waiting for us.*
~Joseph Campbell

My entire adult life has been spent writing personal essays. In fact, whenever I write anything else—a song, a poem, or a story—I can trace its birth to some essay I have previously written. Personal essays are how I figure out who I am, what I live for, and what I aspire to be or become. My essays are me. I write from my head and heart, using as many time-tested tips, tricks and techniques of the writer's craft to say what I want to say as clearly and powerfully as I possibly can.

I want and need you to do the same. You are a perfect and poignant person. Your voice is as valid and real as any other voice in the universe, so everything you do not write or try to say is deducted from the potential beauty of the universe. You do not feel, think or believe any less than me or any other person. What you might not believe or realize is that essay writing, aside from getting a good grade or getting into some ritzy school, is an intellectual empowerment of your life. Crafting a well-wrought essay keeps your brain alive and your blood pulsing. An essay plants a pattern of your inimitable footprints. An essay defines the trail of your earthly sojourn.

All I can do is give you the tools to build an essay. You, however, are the materials you use to build the essay. I can't make you swing the hammer, cut the boards and build the house of your dreams. The crafting is up to you. If you are not willing, you are resigned to mediocrity. My class is useless to you.

But if you are willing, if you blow the sparks of your life into flame, then the fire of possibility will be lit, and your life will shine like a beacon in the night. You will inspire, comfort and console those lucky enough to read, hear, and cherish your words.

The four main pillars of this class are *Read, Write, Create, and Share*. The first three are the hardest because they require real work, effort, and often drudgery in the midst of your taxing and stressful life. But to share... To share is as simple and hard as finding the courage to press a button and release your words to a wider world, and, as sung by Guy Clark, "Let the chips fall where they will/I got boats to build."

In the simple song of Guy Clark, he does not imply he merely wants to build a boat—he wants to rebuild himself! He is "tired of the same old same." He is tired of the "same old songs with the same old lines/ the same old words with the same old rhymes." Clark wants his words to take him to new places in a brave and enduring way.

He built his boat. It is time for him, for all of us—and yes, me—to "sail into a brand new day."

Get off your ass.

Build your boat.

MORNING COFFEE

Tommy or Charlie or Emma
Must have been here before me.
There are plastic dinosaurs
Positioned on my chair
In various poses of intimidation
And courtship.

The Brontosaurus,
Who somehow made it
To the top headrest,
Rears on hind legs
And tries to reach
The spider plants
Growing in styrofoam cups
On the crowded piano.

The lazy Triceratops,
Trapped on an unsure leather arm,
Circles and stares warily
Across at T-Rex
Who roars and roars and roars
In magnificent moodiness
And waves his absurdly tiny arms
In the primal morning mist.

Before I sit,
I lift Barbie gently
From her soft, safe canyon
Between a quilted pillow
And a knitted cap.

I am surprised by her serenity
In such a difficult time.

Ken is nowhere to be found—
Joe is disconcerted
By the lack of order

And discipline.

A stuffed bear is still asleep
And knows nothing.

I settle myself delicately
Into this meticulous playground
And make an offering of myself.

What more can I do
To perfect this perfect moment?

I sip my coffee slowly
And bask in silence
And wonder—

Do I dare disturb the universe
With something
As impalpable
As a poem?

XENIA

If a man is cruel by nature, cruel in action,
the mortal world will call down curses on his head
while he is alive,
and all will mock his memory after death.
But then if a man is kind by nature, kind in action,
his guests will carry his fame across the earth
and people all will praise him from the heart.
~Homer, The Odyssey

Beyond Marcio and Andre's plot, walled unceremoniously in orange highway fencing, I hear Marcio weed-whacking around the cracked and leaning stones of an old New Hampshire graveyard set some two hundred years ago on a hill outside the edge of the camp. Andre is gently brushing the grass clippings from the ancient etchings on the stones. There is no mandate from any governing body to take on this unmarked task. I am sure it is just something Marcio and Andre do as a sacred duty—it is there and it needs to be done. Perhaps this work brings Marcio back to his wife and children in Honduras and the passing of many generations before him in his native land. Perhaps Andre, young, brash, and joyous, is simply remembering a young love he has promised to return to in faithfulness. Andre and Marcio, in their giving of egoless and uncharted magnanimity—this anonymous gift—make this place, Windsor Mountain, a better place to be. Be faithful to any place you are, for this binding simplicity sets the cornerstone of any community. At the same time, it tempers and tames the often reckless flame of personal desire in the interplay of freedom and responsibility.

We have a duty to where we are. My life is a small but jagged coastline cut into safe and welcome harbors. These are the places that in some way, shape, or form I can call home—and "home," as Robert Frost writes, "is the place where, when you get there, they have to let you in." I can't quite figure if it is just happenstance, weakness, or some unconscious deliberation of a higher faculty I don't know I have, but at every final tack I enter into unspoken contracts with a stunning subterfuge of different communities—communities hammered out of malleable and enduring gold, gifted by the continuity of time and visitation, pouring out of a mystic, tidal mingling of giving and receiving— called *Xenia* by the ancient Greeks.

If you have the means, make one place your true home, for there will always be those who, cast adrift by time and fate, will need to call your place their home. None of us can start to live fully without a place to set out from and a place to return to. Like a sail without a ship, we soon drift and sink in a tangle of sodden rags lost in a sea of unknowing. The plastic boundary of Marcio and Andre's garden is not there to wall away a wandering and malicious herd. It is there to preserve a future bounty to share with a broader community. Today, I thank them for lifting the blinders I might otherwise comfortably wear. They remind me to live fully wherever I am and to leave my door unlocked, for at any hour of the day or night, some part or parcel of community returns to me.

It is my duty and responsibility to welcome them home.

The wayward and wandering reflect the majestic mosaic of the world and leave us clothed in a richer garment when they— these noble vagabonds—leave. They remind us we have unfinished business. They remind us to rein in the harness of solipsism and strain the shackles of practiced routines and easy assumptions. They remind us at any time and any place to build ships in line with our dreams and embrace the crew who share our visions, for the boatsmith who builds his own boat seldom ventures far from shore. To those who measure breadth before depth, my own journeys might seem narrow and mundane, but, against a rhumb line through a sea of stars, all voyages and adventures pale in comparison and are, in truth, infinitesimally small and parochial.

I know I will never still the restlessness inside of me, but I also know that at any given time I am, at best, an imperfect captain on an impatient and unpredictable sea, but there is always a brine-worn and willing crew to point out the polestar and guide me to a perfect shore—perfect, because it is where I need to go and where I need to be.

Right now, this place, Windsor Mountain, this jewel in a tangled canopy of New Hampshire, is perfect. It is where I want and need to be. It is where my family wants and needs to be. These words are only a finger pointing at a moon, tethered to the gravity of hospitality, arcing around a world trying nobly to do what is right. We are only trapped by selfish ignorance and misanthropic righteousness. No place is so base that it cannot be made better by giving ourselves—and our homes—to a broader community.

Above the oscillating hum of a weed-whacker, a car is crunching its way up the rutted gravel road leading into the camp. I know that whoever they are, they will be welcomed like a gift from some ancient god. If they are tired, they will find a bed; if they are lonely, we will sit beside them; if they are hungry, they will be fed, and by filling them, we too will be filled. If I want to share in this meal, and if I want to share in a more glorious life, I have to lift myself out of this chair and make my way to them.

In the end, we are only free when we care enough to give a damn about who, where, and why we are. A community is only made real when it becomes an action.

Live beyond yourself, and do what you need to do.

Do what we need to do...

TEACHING

Pruning weeds and flowers

My teachers could have ridden with Jesse James
for all the time they stole from me.
~Richard Brautigan,
Trout Fishing in America

This is the Sunday morning when I wake up and think it is still summer—but it's not. The bulge in my briefcase is the pile of exams begging to be graded by tomorrow—and there are the advisor letters to be written, the academic comments to write, and an ever-burgeoning list of details and tasks defining the end of the school year—the coda to a year of teaching when teachers morph into bureaucrats. But everything will get done—and done in less than two weeks. In every profession, there is a push season—a heavier time when we struggle alongside Sisyphus to push the boulders of demands and expectations to a lofty summit. When the ball keeps rolling back down to our side of the mountain, the internal struggle begins, and we ask ourselves if this is—or should be—our fated slot in life.

Last weekend, I sat by the blaze of our backyard campfire talking with Jerry Moss, a good friend of mine and a long-time teacher at a local high school. A young teacher from my school joined us, and he asked Jerry what words of advice he would give to a new teacher. Jerry laughed his inimitable hearty laugh and said, "You can't just like teaching. You have to love teaching, and when you start to dial it in, it is time to get out." I've thought about the pithy implications of his words all week. I ruminated through my frustrations and struggles of the past year, and I do have to say, even with all the balls still in the air, I really do love teaching.

I love teaching because whenever a pack of kids come through my door, I still feel a surge of duty to "improve the nick of time." Every class is born as an opportunity to reflect the joy and miracle of life through the simplicity and sincerity of our actions. Together, we take away the sifted ore of education that alchemy has magically transformed into an enduring hope of possibility and advancement. The kids remember what we do, and we remember what the kids did. These are more than just vain thoughts; they are as real and inexorable as the morning and evening tides.

Like a lone sailor on an empty sea, no teacher can outrun the storms of progress, though valiantly we try. In the next few days, I have to submit my curriculum documentation—a fairly dry affair of the texts and techniques I use during the course of the year in 8th grade English, which, in theory, should reflect why I do what I do in the classroom. My juror will tell me that it will help me grow as a teacher to document and reflect upon my curriculum—as if they know how much or how little I have already reflected.

The wise and practical part of me implores me to just do it and be done, while the fire of the poet and the call of the iconoclast in me rattle the chains of obligation if only to embolden and express the wild left in me. The documentation is one of my Sisyphean boulders because I can't say what I really want to say. I am forced to use a lexicon created for me, not through me—an academic style describing much yet revealing little—and that is read by remarkably few. There is no place to say what I really want to say. There is no part of the rubric seeking out my soul. There is no place for me to say that I simply try to encourage my students to stand at the abyss of knowledge and leap, or that I urge them to take the rough stones of words and build a wall to shore up the sands of time, or to weave with the skill and guile of Penelope gossamer threads out of the maelstrom of changes in their inner and outer lives, a ratty shawl standing as their unique testament and tapestry to eternity—even though this is exactly what I try to do.

If what I teach does not add to my students' sense of wonderment, I have failed as a teacher. If I can't prove to them that making their subject agree with their verb is an essential skill of life, I have failed as a teacher, and so I agree we need to know why we teach what we teach, but our curriculum must explode out of the depth of a real life, lived fully and competently, not simply culled from a tome of expectations crafted by a distant board of overseers. I won't put in my curriculum documentation how often I stand in front of my students with no clue what I will say next. I do not brag about how often I rely on the hard, unfailing wisdom of experience to put the right words in my mouth.

I worry we hire teachers based on their degree of education and not on the degree to which they have lived. There was very little in my resume to recommend me as a teacher when our headmaster hired me. He took a leap (very much unlike him) based on his gut intuition. Shackleton rarely spent more than a few minutes interviewing the men with whom he embarked on his epic journey. He sought a crew that he knew would stand heel to toe with him in difficult and evolving situations—stout souls who redeem the possibilities of every moment and keep the adventure—and the community—alive. In the same spirit, our students need to sense our wonder and our faith in the shared mission of the school; otherwise, there is no soil and no food for their own wonder and their own faith.

The teacher who loves to teach knows teaching is a desperate and forgiving affair—desperate because we pack the bags of our students as if they are never coming back, and we are convinced each of them is embarking—at that very moment—on a difficult and trying journey; forgiving because there is a certainty they will return tomorrow, and we will have to accept them back into our fold with all of their innocence and arrogance yet intact.

This is the reality of my life, born every day in the classroom, as I try to teach, guide, mentor, enable, and enlist the wide-ranging panoply of students who care—and who do not care—with equal enthusiasm. Jerry's wise words, "You can't just like teaching; you have to love teaching," are not just a vague guide. They are boulders in a wall of common sense—a foundation that has stood and will stand the test of time. We read books, stories, and poetry not because I feel it is good for my students, but because those books are still energizing and good for me and have stood my test of time. I do not teach them how to write—with unvarnished honesty, I show them how I write, how I wrote, why I read, and what I read.

Each day is an essay come to life on the windy plains of Troy. We are all children and soldiers. None of us are ever fully prepared for the battles or tranquility of the classroom (much less life), so we hone our wits and open our arms. We accept with equanimity the evolving and revolving reality of what is real and enduring, but not fiery admonitions forced or proscribed by a distant oracle. I love to teach, and I know I can't get the boulder of Sisyphus over the hill unless I continue to grow and learn and accept and defy. I need to grow in experience, to learn with humility, to accept with humor, to defy with understanding, and, above all else, to live in the center of possibility.

Weeds grow tangled among the roses. Every child, every action, and every memory becomes a paradigm of possibility.

Suckle the rose of expectation.

You will be filled.

IT MUST BE A FINE LINE

Between a published poet
And some dabbler like me
Who cannot dare to say
"Oh, why I am a poet—and you?"
Whom I would assume
Is not a poet.
(People rarely are.)

We presume poets
Are not things like plumbers,
Engineers, or accountants—
Adjunct professors, maybe,
Or bored intellectuals
With rich spouses.

Really,
Who has time in the day
To play words into
An actual poem—one
That means something,
Does something
And not so incredibly
Gratuitous and self-aggrandizing
As to draw attention
To itself using
Clever tricks
And bookish craft?

As a poet (I mean
If I were actually a poet)
[I am embarrassed
I wrote that]
I would certainly
Never write something
This inane. This stupid—
Unless there were no other words
Left to play with.

GIVE A DAMN REVISITED

A graduation speech yet delivered

Man is nothing else but what he makes of himself.
~Jean-Paul Sartre

I was not born to be a motivational speaker. I was born to figure out the pieces of a puzzle called life. To me, life has never been clear. I have never been sure about who I am or what I am meant to be. Hell, I am at the age when many of my friends are retiring. They are buying condos in Florida and golf clubs at Dick's Sporting Goods. They are settling in while I am still trying to "figure it all out." It is like pieces of a puzzle—I get the edges all lined up and a bunch of almost sections in the middle, but I still haven't finished this damn puzzle, even after all of these years.

I am a middle school and high school English teacher and a wrestling coach in a fairly well-to-do school in a fairly well-to-do town—an ignorant squatter in one of the most educated regions in the world. Needless to say, I am not at the pinnacle of my profession. I do not have a single teaching award on my walls. I've never been the head of a committee. I've never been consulted to figure out a vexing educational conundrum. No one calls me boss, and no one asks me to make the rules.

I come to work—just like, well, probably you.

I am a teacher. I teach my classes; I advise my homeroom; I coach my teams; I grade assignments; and I post my grades. It is a pretty simple life. Sometimes, it is boring. More often than not, it is a weird sort of amazing.

You are students. You come to school. You go to your classes. You play your sport. You learn. You try. You succeed. You rarely fail. But sometimes you do. You make friends. You lose friends. You feel isolated. You feel loved. You get hair in your armpits— or you don't. You are big, and you are small. You get good grades, and you do not get good grades. Yesterday was great. Today sucks bitter lollipops. You hate B Day more than C Day. Sometimes you think more about the chicken nuggets for lunch than if A equals B, then what the Sam Hill adds up to C, or if your essay has a unified theme, or if your declensions are correct —or if your hypothesis is as bad as your lab partner.

Yeah, I know, Mr. Whoever hates you. Ms. Somebody never helps you, and Mrs. Meany always gets your grade wrong and even had the malevolent gall to keep your grade at an 89.99999 and not the A- you deserve. But, you know what? Mr. Whoever probably loves you. Mrs. Somebody will, no doubt, help you, and Mrs. Meany is the only one who knows your real grade is probably closer to an 81.333, for the reality is we create our own realities, and in the next breath we deconstruct those realities. We —including me, you, and everybody else—shape and create our lives to be whatever they become. We are the shapers and arbiters of our own destinies. The hands that shape you are not the hands that make you. I am not as old as I think I am, and you are not as young as you believe. A few short centuries ago, most of you would be paired with a partner and destined to plow rocky ground until the day you could no longer plow your muddy, bouldered, desperate fields.

So quit feeling sorry for yourself.

All of us have some control over what we *can* become. We create what we *will* become. So ask yourself: What stories do you want to pass on to your children? What footprint do you want to impress on this delicate and pliant earth? What rock unturned could lead you, me, or us to a greater and more fulfilling life? Will you make the changes you need, want, or hope to make today? Tomorrow? Next week? Next year? Or years from now?

Or ever?

I am not here blabbering untruths. I am celebrating what is as real as acorns strewn beside an aged oak. I am just a sightseer at a sunset, but you—you, the indefatigable you—you are the commander of your starship. Only you can power the journey to your well-lit moon, arcing some ellipses around an equally wet and puddled imitation of earth.

Only you can give a damn and do what you want to do. Only you can give a damn and become who or what you want to be—and it starts now. Not tomorrow, after recess, or after you buy two bags of Doritos from the school store, or Sunday night when the assignment is due on Monday.

Don't squander the chance that now—right now—gives you. Don't be nice later. Don't choose when to respect what needs respect. Don't forget who needs remembering. Do not be a lesser you.

Be who you dream you are, will, can, and might become.

Give a damn about everything that needs a good giving a damn about, and everything—as in everything—will fall into its rightful place. Give a damn, and doors will open. Keep giving a damn, and your world will mold itself to the depths of your soul, the boundaries of your potential, the limits of your intellect, and the untouchable ceiling of your spirit.

You will be remembered. Songs will be sung about you. You will never die. Your mark on the world is indelible ink on a massive overlay of parchment.

Give a damn and figure it out.

Fill your page with you.

THE ART OF THE ESSAY

At play in the field of words

The only good is knowledge
and the only evil is ignorance
~**Socrates**

I sing a codger's lament to the only tune I know. It is an old song irretrievably trapped by the confines of solipsy. I have been teaching essay writing for twenty years, and I have been writing essays for many more years than that. Now, damn, suddenly I feel like a fawn in a new field distanced from her mother. After years of breaking down the craft of writing essays, I am befoggled by a gnawing uncertainty, even amidst a whispering of success. Here in this night, under the glow of a summer moon in the woods of New Hampshire, I need to extricate myself from the gnarled roots binding my molding trunk of towering tree and twisted, malshapened branches to the loose and rocky soil. I am a hoarder of ideas stacked in cluttered hallways in need of some reality TV show to rescue me from my compulsive urges—to force me back to the simple and ineffable joy of putting words to thought, an urgency to ideas, and sense to the mimicry of sound.

I need to become once more the mendicant pedlar begging for truth within the confines of an empty canvas. I do not need to reinvent myself, but only to reimagine my ponderous pedagogy— to style a new paradigm cobbled coarsely out of the stones of my meandering mesh of experience. It is not a proclamation of "out with the old and in with the new." It is an honest assessment, borne from reflection, urging me to mentor more than teach, goading me to guide more than impulsively lead, and reminding me to accept more often than I reject.

Some of you who have been my students might disagree. You will kindly assure me I do and have done this—and for a few of you, I may have led to clear and embracing waters. And, yes, I am vainglorious enough to bask in this translucent glow as I mold, shape, and give faith to the receding shadows of solace.

I am a codgery old man with a limp in my step and a hill yet to climb, but I'll be damned if I'll let the creak in my bones keep me from my trail. I need the summit to see what I have left below, and I need, paradoxically, to bushwhack back home and journey forward within a koan of my own making. If the nut remains uncracked, I can steal a line from Ken Kesey and say, "At least I tried, Goddamnit; at least I tried."

My limited humanity—my common humanness—is my foil and my foe. I survive on the fodder of others. Without them (and without you), I am nothing. My thoughts are just ether in the wind unless and until I bind them into palpable form. I need you more than you need me. Like a bawling child on a long car ride, I beg to know what is in it for me. The answer is deceptively simple.

What is in it for me is in it for you.

Intentionally or not, all writers write for an audience. They might try and focus on a broad swath; they might try to lead some small sect down a narrow passageway to some hidden chamber; or they might try to use words to ring a cocky gong in the echoing hall of a single, reasoning, and reflective mind. In every case, unless you are a speechwriter or propagandist for a demagogue, a true essay seeks to convey and create a palpable, enduring truth for the whole of humanity. If, when all is said and writ, the essay cannot convince the roaming diaspora of difference (and often indifference), the essay itself is a failure—a noble exercise maybe, but nonetheless, a self-flagellating failure. What remains is a lonely and inexplicable truth tethered to an unmet possibility. That and a frustrated writer—and a lost, confounded, and bewildered audience.

The writer must be the first audience. All creation flows from there. Every essay must navigate rocky shoals, step gingerly through thickets and thorns, and find paths through dust-blown deserts, all the while uniting a timid, fickle crew to believe in the power of the journey and the promise of the destination. You, as the writer, must be a prophet, seer, and disciple. You must know, feel, and believe that what you write is necessary and needed—and you need more than a dreamy will. You need the skills to capture the imagination, craft the intellect, and ignite the desire in words. Words must dance, weave, and flow as if uttered for the first time in the mingling broth of existence. A single crystal of creation beckons the birth of an essay. The timeless, polished gem hung on the pendant of a page announces the essay itself—a gift to an anonymous world arcing through the foreboding vacuum of the universe.

We are inextricably entwined. There cannot be a disconnect between you and me, for what is in it for you is what is in it for me. If what you write rings with resonance for you, your clanging gong will ring for others, and, more than likely, for me as well. I will wake from my torpor. My senses will bristle with a lover's passion; my prejudices will shatter, and my ignorance will be cast aside like a ratty shawl because I have been led by you to you—the eternal and indefatigable you. Your parting gift, your hard-wrought essay, is my beginning—my chance to reinvent myself with sturdier skins of truth layering themselves upon me in a viscous resin of welcomed wisdom.

My newly hardened skin will finally face the vagaries and vicissitudes of life with newfound strength. My intellect is deepened, my soul is magnified, and my life is richened. I become a new person in the democracy of a transformed and evolving world. I feel the heartbeat of promise in the joy of significance. I am humbled yet empowered; enlightened yet curious; timid, yes, but brave enough now to cull the detritus of my mind. I can craft thoughts of my own into the narrow confines of aching prose—I can let myself go and be at play in the field of words. To be a writer is to inhabit another body and somehow make it your own. It is a tricky affair to intrude your clumsy, balky self into the fleshy viscera of someone who is not, nor would ever aspire to be, you.

But there is no other way.

I am who I am—a stretch of stars in a dark sky, wave-worn shells on a curling beach, a frail man in a sturdy body gathering trinkets and treasures from winding roads, celebrating in words whatever is within reach of my grasping labors. I am a word-slinging, song-singing, ballad-mongering teacher, poet, husband, father, friend, and occasional foe.

I have not set out to be who I am.

I simply find myself here.

I am amazed and humbled in equal measure. I pinch my weathered skin and creak my balky bones to convince myself that my blessings are real. The mill of time has never crushed the seed of my being. I grow in dry soil or wet loam. I produce more weed than intentional flower. I am as limited as I am expansive, but I am all I need to be.

I do not need to dream, nor am I a conjurer of fate. I wake each morning beside the woman I love. My children, now all grown, still float like butterflies in every cluttered room and fill every empty space. Friends do not knock on our door. They walk in unannounced, leaving gifts, joy, solace, and community.

Each day layers upon itself. In this garden, I am free, real, and eternal.

I do not need a future heaven.

I am already there.

RACCOON

I've stopped the chinks
with newspaper and rags
wedged tightly
against the wind—blowing
cold three days now.
I feed the fire and curse
its hissing and steaming
mixing green oak
with sticks of dried pine
calling myself
Raccoon
grown fat in the suburbs
sleeping in hollowed elms
waiting for the lights
to go out.

A PLOWMAN'S THANKS

For a time I rest in the grace of the world,
and am free.
~Wendell Berry

It's Wednesday night, and I'm sitting in Josh LoPresti's plow truck downtown, in front of the Colonial Inn, sipping Cumberland Farm coffee and killing time. I drove to the DPW lot and logged in at 8:00. It is now almost 10:00, and the first flakes are dropping lazily. Soon enough, the lazy snow will morph into the expected blizzard. I'll get a call from Tim Jones telling me it's time to head out and start plowing clean the roads of Concord, the roads I know so well. I'll hit all the side roads while he scrapes the mains. It's a dance we've done together many times—and Tim many more times than me.

We will, no doubt, plow all night. And probably all the next day, too.

The downtown is eerily quiet. Occasionally, a car drives around the disappearing green. The inn, still locked in the pandemic, is stoic, still and silent, save for a few dimly lit windows and a sign banging and blowing in the increasing wind. There is no music there tonight. There has not been music since I last sang there in mid-March. *'A few weeks'* I thought back then, but here we are, some thirty-six weeks later, with no end in sight. I had been singing at this inn every Thursday night since a March night in 1983. A good place, I thought, to start my life as a folksinger—a stepping stone to lead me to a greater stage.

That greater stage has not come to pass. Instead, singing in this old New England inn is my stage and, it seems, my only stage. It is the only stage I need. My crowds are small; my dreams are tame, but my joy is immeasurable and immutable. I don't need anything more. I have what few can ever have or hope for —a place that is uniquely my own, a place that consoles and energizes me with equal portions of grace and magnanimity. It lives with me and has grown with me from my restless and often reckless youth; it has blessed, widened and humbled me; it has been a second home to me, Denise and our seven kids; and it gives me infinite hope in a future not diminished, cheapened or forgetful.

This, too, shall pass. The livestreams Denise and I started so many months ago have filled the gaping hole of the empty inn. I can't really find words to measure my thankfulness to all the folks who have stuck with me, an aging, unapologetic folksinger, and for Denise, my perfect, beautiful and energized wife who manages, leads and makes the connections in this brave new world of internet concerts. This diaspora of an audience from around the world lifts our souls as they listen, watch and cavort with us throughout this monstrous *thing* that has hobbled our collective normality but has not defeated our collective community.

Tomorrow night, I will be a tired, unkempt mess of sorts. I will, no doubt, forget the words to familiar songs and laugh off the physical weariness in the joy of the moment. I will be attached to the kinship of the tangible, the ephemeral and the eternal. I will be singing to the distant and familiar you. I am nothing without "you."

As if preordained, the snow starts swirling in a chaos of white. It is time to drop the plow and strip-clean the waiting streets of Concord. My coffee shakes in the cup. The hydraulics whine in obedience. The truck rumbles and bellows like Old-Man Kenney's draft horses, who plowed the sidewalks when I was a kid.

This is my town, and every street tells me some old story of everyone I ever knew and all I've ever been.

It is time to start remembering...

WHAT NOW?

Amor Fati – "*Love Your Fate*",
which is in fact your life.
~Friedrich Nietzsche

My books, after endless editing, formatting and revising again and again, are now out in the wild. My feral birds have flown; my leaky boat has left the harbor on a windward tack. I am now bushwhacking an unmarked trail in an unfamiliar forest.

I feel strangely alone.

My books are like kids who have all left home and have lives of their own. I know, after my winnowing of words, that these sheaves of parchment are above the ordinary; by how much, I have no clue, aside from kind words from friends and whatever gut instinct roils my belly after thirty years of teaching writing. It is like I woke up in some episode of "Survivor," and I have a task, a few tools and several friends to get me started—sell as many books as you can in as short a window as possible.

Winner takes all.

Whatever all is…

Now, I simply wait with the patience of Santiago for the silent Marlin to snag my hook and tow me where Fate tows the fated. Even then, the sharks may circle my dory and devour the flesh from the carcass of my words. I will be left with the bleached bones of a fleeting triumph, disappearing in the silting of an ebb tide. Some torn pages blow scattered among driftwood. Some beachcombers are scavenging for polished words. A diaspora of ink spreads among rivulets in the sand.

The Yankee candor that rules my inner voice urges me to smile and move slowly in motions oiled by forethought, patience and laconic wit. It is a soothing, low-bellied toll of admonition to accept who I am and what I parcel out to humanity.

I am not proud or boastful.

Neither am I timid or shy.

I did what writers set out to do. I wrote out the rhumb line of my existence. I shipped my wares in a packet to a distant warehouse, and now, stuffed in satchels, I pawn them door to door. I hope one of those doors is your door—some portal to your mind, heart, soul and being. And then, stealing words from Black Elk, "My heart will soar like an eagle."

And I will go back to my desk and start writing again.

PRUNING

These trees have driven so many friends batty,
Wedged in unstable crotches, embracing
Hollow, heart-rotted limbs, reaching tentatively,
Maddened with indecision.
From a distance your gestures
Are very lobster-like—
Waving a last embattled claw,
As if dueling some carnivorous kin
Backed into a battle you cannot avoid.

You are disposed towards duality.
I regret what I told you earlier.
I should have taught you to attack the orchard
In a swath-like way,—eliminate extremes,
Root clean at the base suckers growing
Straight up or down or in or across —
The disarray of strewn limbs
And slender, whippish sprouts
Will prove your labor
Is at least partly glory.

The kids could follow you
With feigned workishness,
Filling the truck they love to drive,
Heaping tangled piles down below—
Piles we'll burn on an eager Sunday,
Lighting tinder-dry Christmas trees,
Lobbing gasoline bombs
Heavied with chainsaw oil,
Ducking behind flanneled arms,
Turning your back to the flames.

We talked earlier of a nebulousness
And then defined ourselves in that direction.
It was you who wanted this job,
Eager to join the winter pruning
And prove your mettle.

You were attracted by talk
Of using nothingness,
Of anticipating space—
Being at the point of decision,
Parsing the moment,
Bridging innumerable futures.

I laugh to see you now
Apoplexed by the tangible,
Contorted by inexperience,
Frustrated by the tangled gnarl
You are caged in.

The hardest part is always
The leaving out—
Begrudging mediocrity,
Leaving what should be.

AFTERWORD

I've always made my way down to The Three Rivers. Even now, as I sit on my back porch, I hear the rush of the Assabet a half-mile to the north, already filled with an early and surprising winter melt. Any leaf of me could fall and be carried back to the fork of the Sudbury and Concord Rivers, where the three rivers meet at Egg Rock. My entire life is a continual returning to these rivers and the confluence of my common ground—the water, fields, woods, and village of Concord, and now, just to the west, the small mill town of Maynard.

More and more I remember less and less, but there are still granite walls defying change for another thousand years and still a few hills to defy development; still a few farm stands with the same trucks and tractors parked by weathered sheds; and still a few cantankerous old souls hiding their smiles behind seventy or eighty New England winters. I wonder if they remember the kid who worked for them so long ago. I wonder what they remember. I wonder what they wish they had kept.

This diaspora of ramblings, reflections, stories, poems, and essays is my way of keeping what I remember—or at least what I need to remember. Musketaquid is the native name for the Concord River. Someone once told me the name meant "slow-moving river." It seemed like a fine and apt name to me, so much so that it didn't bother me to discover the actual translation is "grass-grown river."

The fields are now all wooded over—a bramble of hawthorne and Swamp maple hiding almost every view—but it is still a slow-moving river—and always will be. Even the Nipmuck and Pennacook would agree with that.

These words are what I add to the rivers. They are the rivulets and streams of my experience that become a smaller part of the Musketaquid flowing into the Merrimac, and thence to some greater sea of understanding and insight. They are the good, the bad, and the ugly drafts of my life, scattered with the randomness of the winds and tides driving me and carrying me to so many shores. Fate always brought me home—home to these rivers—these stoic, plodding rivers coursing through my life.

Thanks for reading.

~Fitz

BIBLIOGRAPHY

Poetry

RACCOON

THE CABIN YEARS

THANKSGIVING

BIKES FOR SALE: $2.00

CROWS & SWALLOWS

A SUMMER'S JOURNEY

THREE RIVERS ANTHOLOGY

COLLECTED POEMS

Writings

REMEMBER THE TIME

SELECTED ESSAYS

A TEACHER'S JOURNAL

GIVE A DAMN & FIGURE IT OUT

Music

BALLADMONGER

ORIGINAL SONGS & BALLADS

FIRES IN THE BELLY

OUT OF THE FORGE

CAMPFIRE

THE GREATEST CAMP SONGS OF ALL TIME

DAWG HOUSE

A SALTY DAWGS' HOOTENANNY

THE PLOWMAN'S ROAD

THE EYE OF THE BEHOLDER

CONTACT

For readings, book-signings, workshops, tutoring, presentations or proofreading and copy editing—or just to support my writing, please contact:

John Fitzsimmons
15 Marlboro St.
Maynard, MA
01754

Email: fitz@johnfitz.com
Tel. 978-793-1553
JohnFitz.com
TheCraftedWord.org

Venmo @johnfitzmusic
PayPal @johnfitzmusic

Much appreciated—and thanks again for reading.

Fitz

November 11, 2023